THE CRIMINAL WORLD OF SHERLOCK HOLMES

*The Crimes & Criminal World
Of The Great Detective,
Sherlock Holmes;
With Insights
Into the Criminology
of Arthur Conan Doyle*

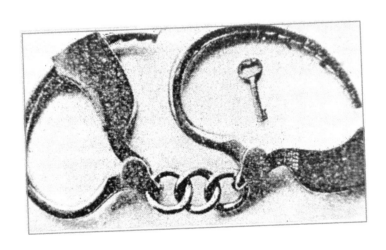

Kelvin I. Jones

The Criminal World of Sherlock Holmes, Volume One

Hardcover ISBN 978-1-78705-864-4
Paperback ISBN 978-1-78705-865-1
ePub ISBN 978-1-78705-866-8
PDF ISBN 978-1-78705-867-5

Published by MX Publishing
335 Princess Park Manor, Royal Drive,
London, N11 3GX
www.mxpublishing.co.uk

Cover design by Brian Belanger

ACKNOWLEDGEMENTS & DEDICATION

The author would like to offer his sincere thanks to the following people, all of whom have been instrumental to this project: Firstly, to John Bennett Shaw, who told me if I ever wrote such a book, he'd buy it; secondly, to Sam Gringas, who thought I should write much more than I had, regarding the subject of Holmes and the criminal world, in which he figured, thirdly, to Dame Jean Conan Doyle, Doyle's youngest daughter, who told me about Sir Arthur's connections with Blackheath, and lastly, to Barry Hoad, who showed me where 'The Cedars' was, when we were both at the tender age of fourteen, and we then visited it. Thank you all.. This book is dedicated to my dear wife, Debbie J. Jones. 'Forever we.'

THE CRIMINAL WORLD OF SHERLOCK HOLMES

A Guide to The Criminal World of Sherlock Holmes, Crime, Forensic Science Techniques & Criminal Investigations

VOLUME ONE:

THE CRIMINALS AND THEIR CRIMES

Illustration shows a burglar's smelting chemical laboratory, once in the Black Museum, thought to have belonged to the master burglar Charlie Peace, at what was then known as 'New Scotland Yard.'

New Scotland Yard, circa 1890, home
to detectives Lestrade and Gregson, in
the days when Holmes also would have
known it. From Arthur Griffiths'
'Mysteries of Police & Crime'.

PREFACE TO VOLUME ONE OF
THE CRIMINAL WORLD OF SHERLOCK HOLMES

By Mark Albertstaff, Editor,
Canadian Holmes.

'The Criminal World of Sherlock Holmes' is a straight-forward title for a book with hidden depth. In this first of three planned volumes, British Holmesian, Doylean, and all-round relentless researcher and writer, Kelvin Jones takes the reader into Victorian England, walking side by side with the great detective. As the long-time co-editor of *Canadian Holmes*, I have had the pleasure of featuring a few of Kelvin's articles in our journal. These articles bring to light new ideas, new research and are always popular with readers.

In 2017 Kelvin won the Derrick Murdoch Award for the best article of the year in *Canadian Holmes* for his work 'Sherlock Holmes and the Cromer Connection,' which was the basis of his 2018 book *Sherlock Holmes And The Cromer Hound*. Kelvin's articles have certainly not been confined to Canada or Canadian journals. His articles have been found, read and enjoyed around the world.

Kelvin's writing output is impressive. His list of books on Amazon is as deep as an ancient tin mine in Dartmoor. The works include Sherlockian pastiches, myths and legends centred around his beloved Cornwall, and of course, books exploring Conan Doyle and all aspects of the Sherlock Holmes Canon.

Kelvin's knowledge and previous writings fold nicely into creating this present book. Parts of those other books have been drawn on or expanded upon for this volume but the approach is all new, and distinctly Kelvin.

The genesis of this new series goes back more than four decades to the 1980s when VCRs were new, Thatcherism ruled England and Jeremy Brett was top of the mind for Sherlock Holmes fans, as the networks began broadcasting Granada Television's 'The Adventures of Sherlock Holmes'.

In those days before social media and even wide use of email, fans of Sherlock Holmes either met at the occasional conference or local meetings or corresponded through the post.

This volume kicks off with a general history of Sherlock Holmes and his French contemporary Alphonse Bertillon, whom Dr James Mortimer in 'Hound of the Baskervilles' regarded as one notch above Holmes as a detective. We also learn of the likely friendship between Holmes' and that other famous French criminologist, Francois Le Villard.

The next chapter is based around poisons in the Sherlock Holmes stories and nicely weaves in a history of poisons and those most often found during Victorian times. This chapter discusses a variety of poisons, including those which were plant-based and ones that Holmes may have investigated while he had access to the laboratory at St. Barts Hospital, where he first met Dr. Watson. Kelvin neatly brings in the use of opium during the era but also Holmes's use of the drug, De Quincey, author of the famous Confessions of an English Opium-Eater, as well as the anonymous article 'A Night in an Opium Den' which appeared in The Strand Magazine just seven months before the Holmes tale 'The Man with the Twisted Lip' featuring the Bar of Gold opium Den.

The next section has got to be a unique one in Sherlockian books. This extensive part of the book lists all murdered, murderers and murder attempts found in the Sherlockian Canon. From Abergavenny, a case mentioned in passing in 'The Adventure of the Priory School,' to Cadogan West from 'The Bruce -Partington Plans.' With all this between the covers, there is something for all Sherlockians in this book and the next two volumes will, I am sure, fall into the same category. Readers of this book are sure to gain a better appreciation of Kelvin's knowledge, passion and long devotion of all things Sherlockian.

Mark Alberstaat, Editor of 'Canadian Holmes.

Holmes, master of forensics, but also master of disguises, seen here as a plumber' with rising prospects' in 'Charles Augustus Milverton.' Drawing by Frederic Dorr Steele, in Harper's Magazine, 1904.

Students at St, Bartholomew's Hospital, London, where Holmes conducted many of his early forensic studies, like the beating of corpses to determine the nature of bruising, post mortem. This has always been a subject of speculation among scholars and doctors alike. Sir Robert Christosin, who gained a reputation as a forensic toxicologist during the period just prior to Holmes' career, believed it might be possible to determine whether it was discernible by beating corpses of both pigs and humans. His results were indeterminate, which he must have found annoying. since he had hoped to determine by it, the culpability or innocence of Edmund Burke, the body snatcher.. One wonders if Holmes' results were similarly vague. Note here the cigarette at the lips of the seated student, a practice which certainly would not now be tolerated.

THE CRIMINAL WORLD OF SHERLOCK HOLMES: ONE

CONTENTS

MAIN TEXT ILLUSTRATIONS.
The Ubiquitous Jack The Ripper. Part the First.

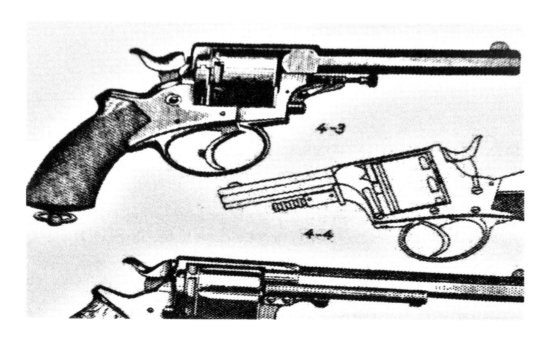

A selection of popular Webley revolvers. Sherlock Holmes would most likely have used
the ex Irish police Webley, a heavy affair, at the top of the illustration.

Conan Doyle in later life, on board a ship, sailing on the Adriatic Sea, on one of his many spiritualist tours. Although he was, at times, ready to get rid of Sherlock Holmes, he never lost his profound interest in the subject of criminology and, by the time of his death, had acquired a library of historical books on the subject of criminology, which he evidently had studied in great detail, well before he wrote the Sherlock Holmes stories. Sadly, the collection did not survive, its contents being sold off at auction by one of his his sons.,. Photo, c. Brian Pugh.

Two Italian female prostitutes, interviewed by the criminologist, Caesar Lombroso. Lombroso believed that most criminals were born with an inherited predisposition to turn to crime, and that women were no exception to the rule. The women pictured above, are from the discreetly bowdlerized English translation of his book, 'The Criminal Woman,' and examples of women he describes as 'perpetual offenders'.

Below: A Victorian pornographer's view of a desirable female in this non - accredited 'artistic creation' from Leonard Smithers, the much maligned but supportive publisher to the 'Decadents,' shows a very different view of womanhood.

PRELUDE: HOLMES ON CRIME AND CRIMINALS.

"I propose to devote my declining years to the composition of a textbook which shall focus the whole art of detection into one volume."

— The Abbey Grange.

"It is a capital mistake to theorise before one has data. Insensibly, one begins to twist facts to suit theories," – A Scandal in Bohemia.

"How often have I said to you that, when you have eliminated the impossible, whatever remains, however improbable, must be the truth?" – The Sign of Four.

"Like all other arts, the Science of Deduction and Analysis is one which can only be acquired by long and patient study, nor is life long enough to allow any mortal to attain the highest possible perfection in it." – The Sign of Four.

"It is a capital mistake to theorise before you have all the evidence." – A Study in Scarlet.

"The world is full of obvious things which nobody by any chance ever observes." – The Hound of the Baskervilles.

Holmes meets his nemesis, criminal mastermind, Moriarty.

THE ART OF DETECTION

Sherlock Holmes once said of himself: "Art in the blood is liable to take the strangest of forms." Holmes admitted that he was descended indirectly from the French painter Vernet, and that he had a decidedly artistic streak in him. Curiously, for the most part in Watson's many chronicles, Holmes otherwise kept an almost unbroken silence on the subject of his ancestry. On one particular occasion, however, he broke the pattern. He and Watson had been discussing the question of heredity when suddenly he volunteered:[1]

"My ancestors were country squires, who appear to have led much the same life as is natural to their class. But none the least, my turn that way is in my veins, and may have come with my grandmother who was the sister of Vernet, the French artist. Art in the blood is liable to take the strangest forms.

When it came to his own science of deduction and criminological analysis, however, he was the supreme scientist, the reasoning machine, the rational and utterly determined cerebral observer of phenomena. At a scene of crime, nothing escaped his attention or scrutiny. And for the period this was unusual.

Holmes was a man of his word, and was not only "well up" in all the latest developments of crime investigation, but he was also an innovator when it came to blood tests and ballistics. Holmes was investigating murder long before the high powered electronic microscope had been developed and before fingerprinting had been advanced to the status of "an exact science," following the innovations adopted by Scotland Yard, mainly encouraged and suggested by Galton, although not actually initiated by the British police force until very late in 1901, by which time India and the USA were already using their own systems with undoubted success. Holmes' understanding of the effects of various poisons on the human body.

Holmes published many monographs sporadically during the course of his long career, and over a number of decades, towards the end of the 19th Century.

---

[1] Holmes had demonstrated his astounding and innate powers of inferential ability to his friends at university, as related to Watson in both 'The Gloria Scott' and 'The Musgrave Ritual.' In both narratives we see clear evidence of what Edgar Allan Poe described in his Dupin stories, as the principle of 'ratiocination,' a method of perception and reasoning which Holmes had perfected.

At the time of Holmes' excursion to the land of his forefathers, the English police force had not yet realised the considerable advantages to be offered by forensic science. [2] Indeed, the successes it enjoyed in the area of criminal investigation depended greatly on the existence of a body of informers who provided inside information on the deals of the current underworld.

Holmes looked to the continent for inspiration. He was aware of the limitations of the Detective Department of the Metropolitan Police Force who had not yet grasped the nettle and whose methods of investigation were, on the whole, woefully inadequate.

The Frenchman, Alphonse Bertillon (1853-1914), was already highly regarded at this time as a pioneer among criminologists. He began his career as a junior clerk in the Paris Prefecture and was a self-made man lacking a formal education. Although it was not until 1879 that he made his system of 'Bertillonage' available to the world at large, by 1877 his 'anthropometric method' was already formulated. Up until this time the classification of criminals' records had been an absolute nightmare of disorganisation so that it was almost impossible to collate data and achieve swift results when an investigation was under way. Bertillon devised a series of anthropometric measurements of the body (especially of the bones), and he was able to classify this data so that the trade mark of a criminal in seemingly diverse crimes could be instantly recognised. He worked from three basic premises; a) that there is practically no change in the dimensions of the osseous framework of the body after the twentieth year, b) that because the relation in size of different parts of the skeleton to one another varies greatly in different individuals, it would be virtually impossible for two individuals to exist in whom the bones measured by his system would be of exactly the

---

[2] It is quite fair to say the British police exhibited a distinct reluctance to adopt the undeniably effective method of tracking criminals by means of fingerprinting them.. The great pioneer of the fingerprint classification and recording of fingerprints, Sir Francis Galton, published his book, "Finger Prints" in 1892, establishing the individuality and permanence of fingerprints. The book included the first published classification system for fingerprints. In 1893, Galton also published a second book "Decipherment of Blurred Finger Prints," and then in 1895, the book "Fingerprint Directories." He was well advanced for the period and his books were both thorough and highly systematic, but the Yard remained tentative. One suspects Holmes was well aware of their overcautious approach and lamentable lack of imagination.

same dimensions end c) that these dimensions could be accurately measured by means of a lens and callipers.

Bertillon's unorthodox system revolutionised the French detective department almost overnight and it was not long before he achieved international recognition. Indeed, by 1888, when he was at the height of his fame, mention is made of him by Dr Mortimer, ('The Hound of the Baskervilles').

"I came to you, Mr. Holmes, because ... I am suddenly confronted with a most serious and extraordinary problem. Recognizing, as I do, that you are the second highest expert in Europe -"

"Indeed, sir! May I inquire who has the honour to be the first?" asked Holmes, with some asperity.

"To the man of precisely scientific mind the work of Monsieur Bertillon must always appeal strongly."

"Then had you not better consult him?"

"I said sir, to the precisely scientific mind. But as a practical man of affairs it is acknowledged that you stand alone. I trust, sir, that I have not inadvertently -"

"Just a little," said Holmes.

Why was Holmes so piqued by Dr Mortimer? Clearly his implication that Holmes did not possess a "precisely scientific mind" aroused his anger and especially so since by that time the Bertillon method was already attracting a fair amount of justified criticism.

One of the problems with the anthropometric system was its sheer clumsiness. So many measurements had to be taken that the operator was liable to a considerable margin of error - something that the later system of fingerprinting avoided. Because so much data needed to be stored, the business of collation was also not easy and this slowed down the possible apprehension of a criminal.

It seems highly likely that Holmes met Bertillon and discussed the system in detail with him. To his observant eyes the flaws in the system would have been glaringly obvious-and I have no doubt that with his usual outspokenness he would have made its shortcomings obvious to M. Bertillon. Certainly, his apparent attitude shown in conversation with Dr

Mortimer points to some kind of rebuff or disagreement and Bertillon was not a man who took criticism in his stride.

By the turn of the century, the growing wave of criticism of the Bertillon method reached its peak with the case of the two William Wests.

In 1903 an American called William West was committed to the U.S. Penitentiary at Leavenworth, Kansas, where he was measured by the Bertillon method. The clerk there was reminded of another William West who had been similarly measured and committed in 1901. He compared the two sets of measurements and discovered that they were almost identical. The two men's prints were then taken and compared. They were of course completely different. From that time onwards the Bertillon system lost all credibility.

"My measurements are surer than any fingerprint system," Bertillon boasted, but the development of fingerprint methods in the 1870's proved him to be over confident. There is little doubt that since Holmes held Bertillon's system in such low esteem, he would have sided with the advocates of the new system then gaining prominence among European criminologists.

If France was the home of one of the pioneers of criminological method, it was also the birthplace of graphology. Even by the time of the first chronicled case, Holmes displayed an understanding of the importance of this relatively new branch of scientific investigation. Soon after setting up house with Dr Watson we see him examining the handwriting of one William Whyte.

"This is a queer old book I picked up at a stall yesterday - De Jure Inter Gentes - published in Latin at Liege in the Lowlands, in 1642 ..."

"Who is the printer?"

"Philippe de Croy, whoever he may have been. On the flyleaf in very faded ink is written "Ex Libris Gulielim Whyte." I wonder who William Whyte was. Some pragmatical seventeenth century lawyer, I suppose. His writing has a legal twist about it." [3]

---

[3] "De Jure inter Gentes" translates literally into "Of the Law between/among Peoples", and would refer to International Law (although Jus inter Gentes has a fractionally different meaning). As Donald Redmond demonstrated in his masterly book on names in the Holmes canon, 'A Study in Sources,' the owner of the old brown book was William White (1604 - 1678), the Master of Magdalen College, who was ejected by his parliamentarian colleagues in 1648.

The late Victorians tended to regard graphology as an eccentric subdivision of the occult along with telepathy and table tapping. However, in France, things were decidedly different. The pioneers of handwriting analysis as a scientific method were the Abbe Flandrin and his pupil, the Abbe Michon. [3] These two ecclesiastics developed a system of fixed signs which enabled the investigator to draw certain tentative conclusions. However, their system was altogether too rigid and primitive to be of much use.

The one man to revolutionise the study of graphology, Crepieux-Jamin, emerged from obscurity at precisely the time that Holmes visited France. His unique contribution consisted of a series of inferences regarding the variability of handwriting styles. Handwriting, he observed, was primarily an expression of character and it expressed not only the fluctuating states of the mind but also the subject's emotional attitude and bodily health.

So successful was Crepieux-Jamin's theory that the study of graphology acquired considerable status among the police laboratories of Western Europe.

Among the leading figures of the French criminologists Holmes contacted was Francois Le Villard of the French detective service. We know from Watson's account in 'The Sign of Four' (a later case, 1888) that Holmes' reputation had "spread to the Continent:"

"(Holmes) tossed over, as he spoke, a crumpled sheet of foreign note-paper. I glanced my eyes down it, catching a profusion of notes of admiration with stray "magnifiques", "coup-de-maîtres" and "tours-de-force", all testifying to the ardent admiration of the Frenchman."

All the indications here are that the two men had already struck up an acquaintanceship years before and were exchanging professional tips. Perhaps here we have an echo of the prior relationship between an experienced detective and a young aspirant.

From France, the young, would-be consulting detective gravitated to the Teutonic countries. Among others he must have consulted was the renowned Austrian criminologist and judge, Hans Gross. Gross, a leading light among German criminologists, had already established something of a reputation among criminologists for his painstaking and highly systematic

[3] Jean-Hippolyte Michon (born on November 21 , 18061 in Laroche-près-Feyt in Corrèze , died on May 8 , 1881in Baignes en Charente), was a French Catholic priest , archaeologist and pioneer of graphology. .

methods and attention to scenes-of-crime detail, a procedure for which Holmes endorsed, bewailing the British detectives' lack of comprehension regarding this vital aspect of forensic procedure. The lack of this later led to falure after failure, as Scotland Yard detectives working on the Ripper atrocities appeared mystifyingly incapable of correctly tracing the murderer. Another twenty years were to elapse before Hans Gross' classic 'Criminal Investigation' was published in an English translation (1906), a fact which in no way exonerated the British detectives, hidebound as they were by a series of polce commissioners who were clearly out of touch with the scenes of crime imperative, regarding preservation of vital evidence. One commissioner even went so far as to instruct an officer to wash away writing on a blackboard, which had been scrawled there by the murderer.

Gross' thorough and painstaking survey of the whole field of detection shows a remarkable resemblance to the methods demonstrated by Holmes throughout his professional career. According to Gross, the investigator had to be prepared to solve "problems relating to every conceivable branch of human knowledge; he ought to be acquainted with languages; he should know what the medical man can tell him and what he should ask the medical man," as well as possessing "robust health and extensive acquaintance with all branches of the law."

This eclectic view of the investigator precisely corresponds to the picture we receive of Holmes from Dr Watson's accounts. The scientist of today is a specialist and his knowledge exists within set parameters. In Gross's day, however, this approach would have been quite limiting, especially since forensic science was still in a state of infancy. The 'unsystematic' approach indicated by Watson's famous 'Sherlock Holmes - his limits,' marked the only possible path to progress for the aspiring detective for he was able to draw upon data from the allied sciences, much as today's pathologist does with reference to toxicology, for example, an area with which Sherlock Holmes was well informed. Gross, like Holmes, regarded the science of chemistry as 'unique in its wide range and its many points of contact with ether sciences,' a predictive statement if ever there was one, and we can be reasonably certain that the two men had much to discuss in the area of organic traces. Holmes' indebtedness to Gross was demonstrated many years later (in October 1900) when he had occasion to investigate the supposed murder of Maria Pinto at Thor Place. Although the family governess, Grace Dunbar, was suspected of shooting her mistress, the case turned out to be one of planned suicide. Maria had attached her revolver to one end of a piece of string and a heavy stone at the other. Having shot herself through the head, the revolver was then wrenched from her grasp and disappeared into the waters below the bridge on which she stood. In Gross's *'System der Kriminalistik'*, a case exactly parallel to this related, so that Holmes was at once able to bring his investigation of the Pinto death to a speedy close.

However, it was not merely in the area of the sciences that Sherlock Holmes excelled as a detective. He was also a man whose artistic streak, probably inherited from the French side of the family, enabled him not only to tread the boards as a protean actor, in America, but also to develop his mastery of the art of disguise, We know, for example, from only a brief examination of the Canon, that he was utterly convincing when adopting a disguise.

Watson recorded that Holmes had at least five small hidden places in different parts of London in which he was able to change personality ('The Adventure Of Black Peter'). During the course of many cases that are recorded, he assumed the disguise of a "common loafer" ('The Adventure Of The Beryl Coronet'), an East End man known as Captain Basil ('The Adventure Of Black Peter'), an aged and deformed bibliophile in 'The Adventure Of The Empty House', a respected Italian priest in 'The Adventure Of the Final Problem', a workman looking for a job who was also described as an 'old sporting man' '(The Adventure Of The Mazarin Stone') a drunken looking groom in 'A Scandal In Bohemia'; also in the same case, a "amiable and simple-minded clergyman," a sailor and an asthmatic old master mariner in 'The Sign of Four', a doddering opium smoker in 'The Man with the Twisted Lip' and lastly, an Irish-American Spy Called Altamont in 'His Last Bow'. In 'The Hound of the Baskervilles,' he also remarks that "it is the first quality of a criminal investigator that he should see through a disguise."

His powers of close scrutiny and observation were of great use to Holmes in this art. The detective Athelney Jones told Sherlock Holmes ('The Sign of Four'), "The stage lost a fine actor" when Holmes became a specialist in crime. His colleague and friend, Watson agreed. "Holmes' very soul seemed to vary with every fresh part that he assumed". ('A Scandal In Bohemia'). Homes tells us that "old Baron Dowson said the night before he was hanged, that in my case, what the law had gained, the stage had lost." (The Adventure Of The Mazarin Stone).

Watson also observed that "his very soul seemed to vary with every fresh part that he assumed" ('A Scandal In Bohemia') and Holmes boasted to Watson that he had "the thoroughness of the true artist" ('The Adventure of The Dying Detective').

It should come to us as no surprise, therefore, to learn of Hans Gross' views on disguise; and there is surely no doubt that his observations on criminals' use of disguise and deception would have provided the endlessly resourceful Holmes with a great deal of useful advice about his adversaries. In the underworld of London, where criminal intelligence reigned supreme, he could, in disguise, spend long hours melting into invisibility in the crowds of onlookers at a scene of crime, or perhaps spending days on the race courses with felons, with no notion that they were being observed.

The list of types of criminals who practised the art of 'fakery' was impressively long and also provided the social commentator, Henry Mayhew, with a rich tapestry of the criminal intelligence of Victorian London.

An artist's impression from Punch Magazine of the brain of Charlie Peace, the cunning and infamous burglar, showing his exploits. The cartoon plays with the theory of phrenology, whereby a man's personality could be determined by the shape of his skull, a theory which fascinated Conan Doyle, and also a theory espoused by Dr Mortimer in 'The Hound of the Baskervilles.'

STUDIES IN SCARLET

How long Holmes may have spent in Germany and Austria studying police methods it is difficult to say, but we may might also assume that he might have next made his way down into Italy to consult with the internationally famous iconoclast and atavism expert, Cesare Lombroso.[4] Interestingly, later on in his career as an evangelistic Spiritualist, Conan Doyle would sing

---

[4] Lombroso was founder of the School of Positivist Criminology, and often referred to as 'the father of criminology'. He rejected the established classical school, which held that crime was a trait of human nature.

Lombroso's praises as a psychic investigator and from several references to Lomroso's theories we find in the Sherlockian saga, Holmes retained a conviction about the criminologist's theories.[5]

The summer of 1876 marked a golden year in the life of this ageing scientist for he had just published his definitive study of criminal psychology, 'L'Uomo Delinquente'. Lombroso might have taught the young detective a great deal about the inductive methods which could be applied to the study of the human animal. While he was not the first writer to search for the causes of deviant behaviour in the physiological and mental characteristics of the criminal type, no one before had attempted to develop this into a scientific method.

Lombroso's picture of the criminal was of a type who reproduced the characteristics of an earlier phase of humanity. He called his theory 'atavism'. It was a controversial theory which, in the years that followed his publication, caused a veritable storm of protest. To Holmes, however, it was a fascinating idea to which he would return on numerous occasions. In describing Sebastian Moran's character, for instance, he refers to "the person as the epitome of the history of his own family", in 'The Hound of the Baskervilles' he remarks that "a study of family portraits is enough to convert a man to the doctrine of reincarnation," whilst 'The Greek Interpreter' opens with a discussion between Holmes and Watson on "the question of atavism and hereditary aptitudes."

There is no doubt that Holmes would have been aware of the contentious nature of the Lombroso theories, regarding crime, criminal type and criminal behaviour. For the idea that, from a statistical analysis plus actual examination of the osseous structure of criminals' bodies, evidence could be suggested of a continuity of tradition that was tantamount to a genetic link between one generation and the next, of criminals, must have seemed to him an attractive one. In 'The Empty House,' for example, after the arrest of Colonel Sebastian Moran in Camden House, Baker Street, and when reflecting on the career and subsequent fate of Colonel Sebastian Moran, who has just attempted to kill him, Holmes remarks:

'There are some trees, Watson, that have grown to a certain height and then suddenly develop some unsightly eccentricity. You will see it often in humans. I have a theory that the individual represents in his development the whole procession of his ancestors and that such a sudden turn to good or evil stands for some strong influence that came into the line of his pedigree.'

This idea of the seemingly unaltered destiny of criminal behaviour was an important part of the atavism principle. Lombroso, for instance, was at the heart of the work that he and his apprentices conducted among the many criminals who they talked to, those people that he measured and those who he took samples from. And he was not alone in in his development of the theory that, for the criminal. the past was a living continuity and a living presence. The criminal was by no means bound by class or the curse of penury or rendered unable to resist full satisfaction for the urge to commit crime. Neither was he a mere creature of circumstances. On the contrary, when Moran raised that silent air rifle, and he looked along the barrel, he was suddenly but irrevocably governed and engulfed by the shadow of his criminal past.

Within Europe, Sherlock Holmes would have been aware of the work on criminal types by criminologists and neurologists like Mingazzini, in his valuable study. Cervello (1895). who came to the conclusion, as the result of the examination of a considerable number of brains of criminals, that there was no special criminal type of brain, adding, that there is not even a normal type of brain, as for a long time in his career, Lombrosos had once believed.[5] He discovered that the anastomatic bridges from one fissure to another were less frequent than in normal brains, and that there was, therefore, more reason to accept a type of confluent convolution pattern, than a type of pattern of confluent fissures.

Mingazzini thus concluded that the surface of the brain in criminals and in normal persons was fairly similar, the only decided difference being, that in the brains of nearly all those he dissected, criminals' brains showed unusual arrangements which were much more common than in so-called normal brains, Mingazzini also stated that his investigations led him to agree with Lombroso. that there were no definitive or marked differences between not only the skulls of criminals, but also their brain functions, that might inevitably lead them to committing acts of crime.

Another significant study of the brains of criminals, carried on during ten years, and published at intervals between 1885 and 1895,when Holmes was busy pursuing for himself a career in Baker Street, and a book which undoubtedly would have enjoyed its pride of place on the bookshelves of Conan Doyle, if not those of his great detective, would have been Professor Tenchini's 'Cervelli di

---

[5] Thus, Lombroso was forced to revise his view.

Delinquend'. Although Tenchini investigated the brains only 130 criminals, not nearly as high as the dissection rate of Lombroso, he considered that his observations were 'not yet sufficiently numerous to permit of definite conclusions'. He did discover, however, that variations in both convolutions and fissures were so numerous in the brains of the criminals he dissected, that it was possible to regard an atypical condition as entirely characteristic of the anatomy of the criminal brain.

By today's more tolerant, and, so we like to think, more liberal standards, Lombroso's theories seem to be quite extreme and racist, if we look at his comments, for example, about female criminals who were tattooed. He explains in his book 'The Female Offender' [6] that atavism helps explain the rarity of the criminal type in women, saying that 'in the case of prostitutes, the precocity which increases their apparent beauty is primarily attributable to atavism, 'for what we look for most in the female is femininity, and when we find the opposite in her. we conclude that there must be some anomaly.' He concludes that the criminal, 'being only a reversion to the primitive type of the species', the female criminal possesses the two most salient characteristics of primordial woman: precocity to a minor degree, and differentiation from the male in the stature and muscular strength which she possesses to a degree, far in advance of the modern female. Lombroso also believed that 'the excessive obesity of many prostitutes is of atavistic origin.'

This innate tendency to generalise on the attributes of women as a distinctive gender, possessing predictable types of 'feminine' behaviour and an anatomy of a certain type which was thought 'desirable' by largely, though not entirely, middle class men, I believe, influenced the young

---

[6] ''La Donna Delinquente,' was the title of what criminal theorists in Europe came to regard as Lombroso's *magnum opus*. Its full title was originally *'La Donna Delinquente: La prostituta e la donna normale'* when published in Italy in 1893 (and it was co-authored with Lombroso's son-in-law Guglielmo Ferrero) but, when rendered into English, the title had been mistranslated in less explicit terms, as 'The Female Offender.' Not only this, but also, (one can only assume), to spare the blushes of his late Victorian female readers, the publisher decided not to include the most significant part of the work -- a partial translation which left out the entire section on the normal woman and which, in a typically Victorian way, sanitised and reduced the direct, explicit and empirically - based style of Lombroso's language.

Sherlock Holmes, to a noticeable degree, a point which his chronicler, Dr Watson, himself a man with experience of women from 'three continents,' was not slow in observing.

Holmes has these observations to offer his colleague about women, for example:

'Women are naturally secretive and they like to do their own secreting' (SCAN)' 'I have seen too much not to know that the impression of a woman may be more valuable than the conclusion of an analytical reasoner'; 'the motives of women are so inscrutable. You remember the woman at Margate whom I suspected for the same reason? No powder on her nose - that proved to be the correct solution. How can you build on such a quicksand? Their most trivial action may mean volumes or their most extraordinary conduct may depend upon a hair pin or a curling - tong,'(SECO). 'Woman's heart and mind are insoluble puzzles to the male. Murder might be condoned or explained, and yet some smaller offence might rankle.' (ILLU). 'Women have seldom been an attraction to me for my brain has always governed my heart' (LION); 'Women are never to be entirely trusted, not the best of them,'(SIGN), and finally. 'I assure you that the most winning woman I ever knew was hanged for poisoning three little children for their insurance money,' (SIGN). [6]

What becomes clear when comparing the views of Lombroso and Holmes, is that they each possess, with an almost uncanny accuracy and similarity, a generalised view of womanhood that is based on *assumption* rather than from completely empirical experience, and this is mixed with what I can only describe, as a perceived fear of women based supposedly on their assumed 'irrationality,' or tendency to act upon instinct rather than strict rationality.

Of course, it is possible to argue that, since these statements are taken at

---

[6] It is quite possible that here Holmes was referring to the celebrated poisoner, Mary Anne Cotton, a girl from County Durham, who would have been of contemporary interest to him. In this late Victorian case, .May had three husbands and 10 children who appeared to have died as a result of unexplained gastric illnesses between 1852 and 1872. Three of her four husbands survived from similar illnesses, and her 13th and last child was born as she was actually on trial. There were also several stepchildren who died. She first came to the notice of the police in 1872, when she predicted the death of her stepson, young Charles Edward Cotton to an official. When Cotton died suddenly a few days later, Cotton collected on his life insurance and when asked for a death certificate, she asked the child's doctor, but he refused to sign one until a formal inquest had taken place. An examination of the body by a doctor then found evidence of arsenic. Two other bodies from the family were then exhumed and these were also found to contain arsenic. Mary Cotton was found guilty of the death of her stepson and was promptly hanged.

random from the accounts of Holmes and his various utterings to Watson, they do not represent a fair regard of how Holmes really felt towards the fair sex. His reactions to distressed females, throughout the narratives, would suggest that he was not immune to their plight when threatened by predatory males (as, for example, in the case of 'The Speckled Band' where his rapid perception of his client's rough and, it seems probable, sadistic treatment, is not only quickly deduced, but also dealt with in a kindly manner. Elsewhere in the chronicles we find Holmes clearly still infatuated with the American high society harlot and adventuress, Irene Adler).

That Holmes found women to be an utter enigma to him is quite evident in many of the accounts. But we should also bear in mind that what he regarded as Watson's 'romanticised' accounts of their adventures together in the world of criminality, were just as he defined them. They are indeed romanticised accounts of their deeds, and Holmes was correct to describe them in this way, depending, as they do, upon invented dialogue, imaginative descriptive passages, and often atmospherically conveyed but forensically irrelevant descriptions of climatic conditions (see 'The Hound of the Baskervilles,' for instance. where the impenetrable Gothic gloominess of the narrative greatly impedes the plot).

We also know that not only are these accounts penned by a fairly average, full - blooded, Victorian male, a man rather like Conan Doyle himself; a man who had an experience of women stretching over three continents, who clearly believed, unlike his flatmate, in the principles of chivalric love (e.g. his amorous perceptions regarding Mary Morstan, in SIGN), but in point of fact, really knew very little about the sexuality of his Baker Street colleague. If Holmes did have homosexual leanings, as some of his later chroniclers and film makers clearly wished he had, he wasn't telling Watson about it, and Watson himself would have been highly unlikely to have even hinted at this possibility, in view of the taboo regarding that subject, as well evidenced in the public clamour and consequent witch-hunt that ensued, following the arrest, trial and prison sentence meted out, for example to Oscar Wilde, his contemporary,

His "grand tour' of Europe, a journey that included contacts with so many of the leading intellectuals of the day, must have provided young Sherlock Holmes with a fine insight into the scientific methods he was later to bring to fruition. But the period that followed may well have been something of an anti-climax for him. In 'The Musgrave Ritual' he records:

"Even when you knew me first, at the time of the affair which you have commemorated in A Study in Scarlet, I had already established a considerable, though not a very lucrative connection. You can hardly realise, then, how difficult I found it at first, and how long I had to wait before I succeeded in making any headway.

"When I first came up to London, I had rooms in Montague Street, just round the corner from the British Museum, and there I waited, filling in my too abundant leisure time by studying all those branches of science which might make me more efficient."

Here is a clear indication of the limited means of the young detective. There followed a period of relative austerity for which his prosperous background had ill-prepared him. Nevertheless, it was also a time of continued experimentation and consolidation.

In his fascinating study, 'The World of Sherlock Holmes', Michael Harrison shed new light on this period of Holmes' life. In the London Post Office Directory for 1878 the tenant of No. 26 Montague Street, Russell Square, is listed as a Mrs Holmes. Since, as Mr. Harrison observes, 'Mrs. Holmes would have been asked to provide satisfactory social, banking and commercial references before a lease could have been drawn up,' she must have been a person of 'respectability,' i.e. a member of the middle classes.

Mr. Harrison agrees that this was not Sherlock's mother, since Holmes would surely have mentioned the fact that he was lodging with her in Montague Street. Therefore, this points either to some irregularity in their relationship, or to the fact that Holmes had married and taken rooms with his new bride.

As regards Lombroso and the popularity of this post-Darwinian school of criminologists, even re - reading Lombroso's book on female offenders today, after a gap of nearly forty years, I find myself being quite astounded by the degree of the work's chauvinism and the lengths Lombroso goes to, to justify his views, based on what appears to be a theory often based on quite selective evidence.[7] Neither of these alternatives seems particularly

---

[7] Like some of the, neurologists and doctors I've met, I remain convinced they can be as misguided or zealously fixated as someone like Lombroso, regarding the conclusions about a topic under investigation - a tendency which has escalated in our own age, when there's been an explosion of pharmaceutical treatments offered to patients suffering neurological conditions, like epilepsy, or in my case, Parkinson's disease. So regular has this practice become that often it can lead to alarming consequences. In my case,. I was offered

convincing and I incline to the view that Mrs. Holmes, the tenant of No. 26, was a relation of Holmes' father, perhaps an aunt. Whoever she was, it is certain that Holmes had come to some form of domestic arrangement, which allowed him to survive the day-to-day expenses of a London existence. The British Museum reading room offered a quiet retreat from his rooms in Montague Street. There the combination of his Continental meetings and long hours of study bore fruit in a series of short monographs. "Upon the Dating of Documents" came first (September 1877), a scholarly treatise dealing with the problems of handwriting identification. Then there was "Upon Tattoo Marks", an offshoot of certain studies conducted among the denizens of the London docks. Finally, there was his tour de force: "Upon the Tracing of Footsteps", a short, detailed examination of footprints with 'some remarks upon the uses of Plaster of Paris' as a preserver of impressions.

For almost a year the pattern of study continued uninterrupted. Then, in June 1878, Holmes was asked to investigate a scandal at the British Rifle Association "concerning alleged cheating by collusion between shooters and scorers during the course of rifle matches," a case which involved undercover work for the young detective (a method which had been recommended to him by Francois Le Villard). Such was the skill he brought to the case that the details were never made public.

---

apomorphine as an alternative to madopar, since it didn't unduly raise the patient's libido and acted quickly than other comparable drugs. Much like Holmes' daily dose of morphine, it could be administered intravenously. When finally given it, I experienced distressing 'psychotropic' effects. Other, alarming symptoms comprised: blurred vision, breathlessness, immobility, headaches lasting two days, confusion, disorientation,, inability to use a keyboard, loss of appetite and self confidence. Having returned home, wheelchair bound, my narrative concluded, my wife asked if the Parkinson's nurse commented about the event. 'No,' I replied, 'other than saying an adverse reaction to the drug, they believe, is quite rare. But then,' I added, reflectively, 'just try telling that to Dr Jekyll.'

ENTER MR. SHERLOCK HOLMES

'No man lives or has ever lived who has brought the same amount of study and of natural talent to the detection of crime which I have done.'

— *Sherlock Holmes, STUD.*

The most famous detective of all time, Sherlock Holmes, made his first public appearance in the December issue of Beeton's Christmas Annual for 1887. The story, 'A Study in Scarlet,' by A. Conan Doyle, was not an immediate success when it was reprinted by Ward Lock & Co. in the following year. That was unsurprising, however, for in August of that year the first of Jack the Ripper's many victims was added to the already high crime statistics of London.

The appetite of the Victorian reading public enjoyed a full enough saturation of bloody murder and mayhem from the popular press of the day and from the highly and often gruesomely illustrated 'Police Gazette'. But perhaps there was another reason for the story's distinct lack of success. The detective within its pages was unlike any other. Arrogant, haughty, contemptuous of the official police-force but equipped with a rapier — like intelligence and all the resources of modern science, Sherlock Holmes reached his results by an apparently magical process.

To today's audience, the facts of forensic science are commonplace. But who, in 1888, had heard of fingerprinting? Certainly the London police did not accept it as a practical science. If they had done so, the mystery of Jack the Ripper would certainly not have remained an entire enigma.

Handwriting identification was also in its infancy. As we have noted in Chapter One, an Austrian judge, Hans Gross, had realised its tremendous potential, but clearly the C.I.D. (set up in 1877) did not think to analyse the three grim letters sent by the Ripper to the news agencies.

In those days, there was a distinct lack of co-operation in some areas, between the medical profession and the police. All but one of the Ripper's victims were removed from the scene of the crime, their bodies stripped and washed ready for the mortuary, thus destroying highly valuable forensic evidence.

This predicament is well reflected in 'A Study in Scarlet,' when, faced with the pathway outside No. 3 Lauriston Gardens, Brixton, Holmes remarks, 'If a herd of buffaloes had passed along there could not be a greater mess.'

Yet, for all their forensic shortcomings, there can be no doubt that the Metropolitan police force, with which Holmes most usually found himself dealing with, had, by the time of the detective's most notable successes, started to make considerable inroads into crime and its detection. Major Arthur Griffiths observed, in Volume One of his crime survey of 1899, ('Mysteries of Police and Crime'):

An 1880s style London policeman.
Note the discreetly concealed
truncheon. My father's, an antique
relic, from the 1840's, was ebony.

'It is beyond the limits of this work to give a detailed account of the growth and gradual perfecting of the Metropolitan Police, from this first germ into the splendid force that watches over every section of the great city to-day. The total strength now, according to the last official returns, is 15,326 of all ranks, so that it has about quintupled since its first creation in 1829. The population of London at that date was just one million and a half; the area controlled by the new police not half the present size. Now 6,000,000 souls are included within the London bills of mortality, and the area supervised by our present Metropolitan force is 688 square miles of territory, or some thirty miles across from any point of the circumference of a circle whose centre is at Charing Cross. How rapidly and enormously London has grown will be best seen from a few figures. Between 1849 and 1896, 615,086 new houses have been built, making 12,279 streets and 104 squares, with a total length of 2,099 miles.

'Throughout the whole of this vast area, which constitutes the greatest human ant-heap the world has ever known, absolutely alive, too, and ever growing, the blue-coated guardian of the peace is incessantly on patrol, the total length of police beats reaching to 830 miles.

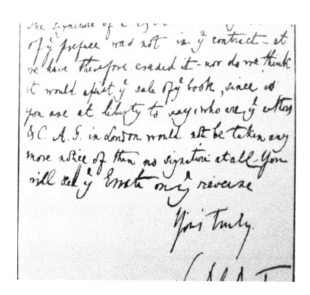

The Victorian reading public were fascinated by the art of reading handwriting. Above: handwriting of Dickens, in one of several occasional articles about the subject in 'The Strand Magazine' during the 1880s and the 1890s.

'He is unceasingly engaged in duties both various and comprehensive on behalf of his fellow-citizens. By his active and intelligent watchfulness he checks and prevents the commission of crime and if his vigilance is unhappily sometimes eluded he is no less eager to pursue and capture offenders. He is exposed to peculiar dangers in protecting the public, but accepts them unhesitatingly, risking his life gladly, and facing brutal and often murderous violence as bravely as any soldier in the breach. In the Whitechapel division, where roughs abound, a fifth of the police contingent in that quarter are injured annually on duty; 9 per cent of the whole force goes on the sick list during the year from the result of savage assaults.

'The last published return (1890) of officers injured shows a total of 3,112 cases, and these include 2,717 assaults when making arrests, 89 injuries in stopping runaway horses, 158 bites from dogs, 4 bites by horses, and many injured in disorderly crowds or when assisting to extinguish fires.'

The date of Holmes' debut (1881) is an important one to the student of criminology. Only a year before, as we have seen, a young assistant in the Paris Prefecture of Police, Alphonse Bertillon, had laid the cornerstone of modern criminology with his development of the 'bertillonage' system of measurements for criminals. And a year before that, in the pages of a magazine called Nature, a Scottish physician named Henry Faulds, made a number of observations about the 'skin-furrows in human fingers (which) ... may lead to the scientific identification of criminals.'

But in Victorian England it was not until 1871 that Parliament finally passed a bill providing for the registration of habitual criminals, complete with photographs and personal dossiers, whilst the system of finger printing did not gain official recognition until as late as 1895.

Sherlock Holmes represented a revolutionary trend, therefore, in the investigation of crime. The public of the time certainly shared his contempt for the official detective force but they were also understandably puzzled by his approach.

This was really because Holmes was first and foremost a pioneer of some of the new techniques which very soon would change the face of Scotland Yard. And Conan Doyle was well trained in many of these techniques.

In this study, the authentic and realistic nature of these methods will be examined, but not simply in isolation. Important too with this legendary and memorable detective was the emerging tradition of European criminology. An awareness of this tradition and of the condition of the criminal classes, plus the remembered and indeed, forgotten murder cases of England in the 1880's, which will be our focus in this book, can only serve to enrich our understanding of the world's most remarkable private consulting detective.

Above: 1880s magnifying lens, made with oak handle, made by my wife's grandfather. The term 'magnifying glass' was then rarely applied, as we see in the Holmes Stories, since a 'lens' was a scientific instrument, as Holmes intended it to be. In this example, the handle is of oak and the ferule, brass.

THE FORENSIC INNOVATOR

"I might not have gone but for you, (Doctor), and so have missed the finest study I ever came across; a study in scarlet, eh? Why shouldn't we use a little art jargon? There's the scarlet thread of murder running through the colourless skein of life, and our duty is to unravel it, and isolate it, and expose every inch of it." - Sherlock Holmes, 'A Study in Scarlet.'

Although he was, as yet, fairly unknown to the general public, by the January of 1881 Sherlock Holmes had already proved his remarkable powers in a number of uncelebrated cases. London, with its colossal crime rate and its inferior social provision was the perfect setting for the student of criminology.

When he was not acting in a consultative capacity for the Criminal Investigation Department, Holmes continued to improve his knowledge in the areas which he had marked out for special attention as an undergraduate.

To assist him in his studies, he had come to a special arrangement with the staff at St. Bartholomew's Hospital which allowed him a free run of the chemical laboratories there. According to "young Stamford" who was later to introduce him to Doctor Watson:

"He is a little queer in his ideas - an enthusiast in some branches of science. As far as I know he is a decent fellow enough as far as I know, he has never taken out any systematic medical classes. His studies were very desultory and eccentric, but he has amassed a lot of out-of-the-way knowledge which would astonish his professors."

Exactly how and why Holmes was allowed complete freedom to pursue his singular studies in the chemistry and dissecting rooms we shall probably never know. However, Watson's narrative does give us an idea of what constituted his "desultory" experiments. Not only did he dabble with poisons a great deal, but he also experimented with cadavers, "beating (them) with a stick to verify how far bruises may be produced after death."

The decade of Holmes' move to Montague Street had been remarkable, especially for London. There had been the poisoning of Charles Bravo (1876), the execution of the notorious murderer Henry Wainwright (1875) and the curious case of the Stauntons who starved an innocent sister-in-law to death. [8]

In 1881, the year of Holmes' meeting with Watson, Bart's Hospital was already becoming a pioneer in new medical methods. Until 1865 the dissecting rooms had been used every summer for chemistry classes but in that year, it was decided to provide a chemical classroom to accommodate 130 students. In 1870 a new chemical lab was built with a lecture theatre for 100 persons and a preparation room. In 1876 the Medical School was entirely rebuilt, paid for by the Charity Commissioners. The new anatomical theatre held 300 students (it was later destroyed by a bomb in 1940). The dissecting room, where Holmes spent his time beating corpses, was enlarged to twice its original size and a gallery added to it which housed the Anatomical Museum. This unique collection would have afforded particular interest to Holmes the criminologist, for amongst its exhibits was the skull of John Bellingham who in 1812 was executed for the murder of the Right Hon. Spencer Perceval, Prime Minister - a unique case in the annals of British criminal history.[9]

In an attempt to shed some light on Sherlock's attendance (or non - attendance) of lectures during the period 1877-1881, A.N. Griffith has attempted to establish a link between Holmes and Norman Moore (later to become something of a celebrity in British medicine):

'Augustus Mattiessen was the lecturer in chemistry at Bart's from 1870 onwards. Sir Norman Moore recalls that he had two private pupils; one was Moore himself, the other he does not mention. He had been in Strasbourg during the Franco-Prussian war…when a shell passed through his house; Mattiessen was interested in opium and together they investigated its alkaloid properties.'

A connection between Holmes and Moore is more than likely. During Holmes' period of attendance at Bart's, Moore became a lecturer on comparative anatomy, a field which was of special interest to the young criminologist.

---

8. See later..

9 On 11 May 1812, Spencer Perceval, prime minister of Great Britain and Ireland, was shot dead in the lobby of the House of Commons by one John Bellingham, a Liverpool merchant who had a grievance against the government. Bellingham was arrested and, four days after the murder, was tried, convicted and then sentenced to death. Executed at Newgate Prison on 18 May, a week after the assassination and a month before the start of the War of 1812, Spencer Perceval so far is the only British prime minister to have been assassinated. One wonders if Lombroso might have formed an opinion about the murderer's skull and features of it which might suggest his tendency to commit murder. My examination of a drawing of Bellingham revealed this to be likely since his profile reveals his large nose and recessive chin, features according to Lombroso, which were the classic hallmarks of the criminal.

The curious experiments carried out by Holmes on the cadavers of his 'subjects' in the dissecting rooms were conducted under the auspices of John Wickham Legg (1878-87) who was the author of a monograph entitled 'Some Account of Cardiac Aneurysms.' * This work, which occurred three years after the death of Jefferson Hope, must have been of considerable interest to Holmes. (Hope died of an aortic aneurysm, a localized enlargement of an artery due to blood pressure acting on a weak vessel). Another lecturer who may well have brushed shoulders with Holmes in the spacious laboratories at St. Bart's was Thomas Lauder Brunton, a Scot who etched out his career at Edinburgh in the 1860's. Certainly Holmes would have read with interest his authoritative monograph on the overuse of digitalis.

---

* See – Medvei, C.V. and Thornton, J L – 'The Royal History of St Bartholomew'. Published by Barts Hospital. London, 1967. Matthiessen, FRS, (2 January 1831, in London – 6 October 1870, in London), son of a merchant, was a British chemist and physicist who obtained his PhD in Germany at the University of Gießen in 1852 with Johann Heinrich Buff. He then worked with Robert Bunsen at the University of Heidelberg from 1853 to 1856. His work in this period included the isolation of calcium and strontium in their pure states. He then returned to London and studied with August Wilhelm von Hofmann from 1857 at the Royal College of Chemistry, and set up his own research laboratory at 1 Torrington Place, Russell Square, London. He was elected a Fellow of the Royal Society (FRS) in 1861. He worked as a lecturer on chemistry at St Mary's Hospital, London, from 1862 to 1868, and then at St Bartholomew's Hospital, London, from 1868. His research was chiefly on the constitution of alloys and opium alkaloids. He contributed to both physics and chemistry.

In the first chapter of 'A Study in Scarlet', there is a vivid description of the old chemical laboratory at St. Bart's, that dingy room, now immortalised by the meeting of Sherlock Holmes and Doctor Watson:

'It was familiar ground to me, (Watson writes) and I needed no guiding as we ascended the bleak stone staircase and made our way down the long corridor with its vista of whitewashed wall and dim—coloured doors. Nearer the farther end a low arched passage branched from it and led to the chemical laboratory.

'This was a lofty chamber, lined and littered with countless bottles. Broad, low tables were scattered about, which bristled with retorts, test—tubes, and little Bunsen lamps, with their blue flickering flames. There was only one student in the room, who was bending over a distant table absorbed in his work. At the sound of our steps he glanced round and sprang to his feet with a cry of pleasure.

"I've found it! I've found it," he shouted to my companion (Stamford), running towards us with a test-tube in his hand. "I have found a reagent which is precipitated by haemoglobin, and by nothing else.'' Had he discovered a gold mine, greater delight could not have shone upon his features.

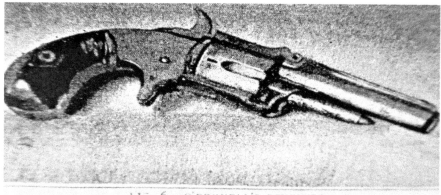

FIG. 6.—O'DONNELL'S REVOLVER.

The small, lightweight, American Webley pistol, which was responsible for the killing and maiming of more victims of crime than any other gun in late Victorian London and the gun used to kill Charles Milverton.

"Dr Watson, Mr. Sherlock Holmes," said Stamford, introducing us. "How are you?" he said cordially, gripping my hand with a strength for which I should hardly have given him credit.

"You have been in Afghanistan, I perceive?"

Why was Holmes so excited at this first encounter and what had he been researching? He described it as "the most practical medico-legal discovery for years" and "an infallible test for bloodstains."

The identification of bloodstains had continued to vex criminologists throughout the nineteenth century. Blood itself could be identified: the problem lay in developing an accurate chemical test which allowed the investigator to match types and to distinguish between human and animal traces. As I have demonstrated before,[9]

'Whatever the method (Holmes used), it is worth noting that the result was the separation of the haemoglobin or its constituted parts by a process of precipitation. Holmes discounts 'the old guaiacum test' ('clumsy and uncertain.') as he also does the 'microscopic examinations for blood corpuscles'. Yet in some ways the Holmes test does resemble the 'old guaiacum test.'

My own theory is that Holmes, having experimented with the known methods and found them wanting, discovered a short cut based on the benzidine reagent process but eliminating its unpredictable tendencies. In this way he would be able to provide certain proof of the existence of haemoglobin.

To have achieved such an important break-through at the outset of a career suggests that Holmes must have spent a considerable amount of his time and energy in that dingy laboratory.

In fact, all the evidence suggests that he was an accomplished chemist. Watson, in listing his friend's limits, described his "knowledge of chemistry" as "profound." Throughout his working life he regarded chemistry as something of an intellectual challenge. In SIGN, IDEN and COPP Watson informs us that Holmes turned to chemical analysis, so as to stimulate his mind when not actively engaged on a case.

---

[9] 'The Making of Sherlock Holmes, Magico Books, NY, 1979. Holmes no doubt had a library of criminological works, files on murderers like Spencer Perceval, and many toxicological studies.

So oblique are the references to Holmes' chemical experiments, that it is difficult to establish what he achieved in the field of organic chemistry apart from the famous test for bloodstains.

The leading nation for chemical investigation in the nineteenth century was Germany, and we can be certain that Holmes, whilst engaged on his European travels, would have made an attempt to consult such authorities as Bunsen, Wohler, Baeyer and Fischer, all of whom specialised in organic chemistry.

One of the most controversial theories around at this time was that of the three-dimensional nature of carbon compounds, propounded by Van Hoff and Bel. We can be certain that Holmes was only too well aware of the revolutionary nature of the theory, which enabled molecular compounds to be seen in three dimensions, for his speciality lay in investigating the alkaloids such as strychnine, opium, belladonna and others, and in his first publicised case he was able to put the knowledge he had acquired to considerable use.

There has been some criticism over the years of Holmes' use of chemical terms, and the validity of several of the experiments he conducted has been questioned. Unquestionably this is because the broadsides have been fired from a modern standpoint, which does not allow for the limited state of knowledge at that time.

The experiments in question (of those which are identifiable) number three. In 'The Copper Beeches' Holmes remarks: "I had better postpone my analysis of the acetones." The compounds which interested Holmes are known as ketones.

Now in 'The Sign of Four,' mention is made of his "dissolving a hydrocarbon" a procedure which is normally a preliminary to further analysis. Why was Holmes pursuing this rather obscure path? The answer is a forensic one. Acetone is a substance which is to be found in blood and wine and the existence of ketone bodies, as the renowned Sherlockian, Christopher Redmond notes, 'is characteristic of certain metabolic disorders, including diabetes, and in cases of high-fat diet.'

More importantly, however, changes in the acetones can be detected immediately following an injection of adrenalin. Since the level of adrenalin is often raised after the absorption into the bloodstream of a harmful alkaloid, this area of research would be of interest to Holmes.

In 'A Case of Identity,' Watson finds:

'... Sherlock Holmes alone ... half asleep with his long, thin form curled up in the recesses of his armchair. A formidable array of bottles and test-tubes, with the pungent cleanly smell of hydrochloric acid, told me that he had spent his day in the chemical work which was so dear to him.
"Well, have you solved it?" I asked as I entered. "Yes,
it was the bisulphate of baryta."

As has been pointed out by the master Sherlockian, Don Redmond, and others, the problem is that there is no such thing as a stable bisulphate of baryta.[10] However, baryta (or barium monoxide) absorbs water and crystallizes to form barium hydrate. This substance is important in the process of sugar refining. Redmond suggests that what Holmes was probably investigating was a case of faulty refining and subsequent food poisoning.

In April 1883, a particularly unpleasant murder came Holmes' way. 'The Adventure of The Speckled Band' brought the first of many innocent female victims to Baker Street, because by now the legend that had become Sherlock Holmes was already widely known throughout England. The matter was of special interest to Doctor Watson for it concerned two sisters, Helen and Julia Stoner, who had been raised in India around the time of the Indian Mutiny. The main protagonist, Helen and Julia's deeply disturbed and disturbing stepfather, was a psychopath who would have attracted Holmes' suspicions the moment he entered the rooms at Baker Street. The last surviving member of one of the oldest Saxon families in England, Dr Grimesby Roylott suffered from a violence of temper which approached mania. In India he beat his native butler to death, whilst at the family home in Surrey he indulged in vicious brawls.

The terrible vulnerability of Helen and her twin sister, Julia, is vividly conveyed in Watson's chronicle of the events and, unlike the Lauriston Gardens mystery, we are led to identify closely with this young woman, huddled about Mrs. Hudson's fire, in "a considerable state of excitement."

'The Adventure of the Speckled Band' served to reinforce Holmes' view of the power and potential corruptibility of the medical profession.

---

[10] D.A. Redmond, 'Some Chemical Problems in the Canon, 'BSJ.,Vol 25, no 4, Dec., 1975, pp 216-7.

"A doc

tor has nerve and he has knowledge. Palmer and Pritchard were among the heads of their profession. This man strikes even deeper."

It comes as no surprise to find that he had little sympathy for Roylott, whose death he inadvertently caused at the conclusion of this bizarre affair. As for the "swamp adder", whose venom disposed of the unfortunate Julia Stoner, this has so far evaded positive identification. The most likely candidate is the Echis Carinata (saw-scaled viper) since its appearance fits perfectly Watson's description of a "peculiar yellow band, with brownish speckles."

The "deadliest snake in India" killed its victim "within ten seconds," according to Holmes. This is something of an overstatement and may well suggest that Watson embellished the account. The Echis Carinata carries a hemotoxic venom which is slow-acting. (We can, of course, assume that he was the victim of an apoplectic attack - see below in the Addenda to this chapter). The other problem lies in Watson's description of the "puffed neck" which immediately suggests the cobra. Clearly the details of the night's tragedy in Stoke Moran had become somewhat vague by the time Watson recalled events some nine years later. However, later in this series, in volume two, we shall examine the entire criminal psychology of Roylott.

ADDENDA.
NOTES REGARDING THE TWO 'DOCTORS IN CRIME.'

1. EDWARD PRITCHARD.

A Glasgow physician who poisoned his wife and mother-in-law with aconite, Pritchard was an egotist of the first order, gave travel lectures about places he had never even visited, became a Freemason and handed out signed photographs of himself. His motive for murder appears to have been a promise he made to a 15 year old servant girl whom he made pregnant, then aborted.

Pritchard would never have been caught save for an anonymous letter sent to the Procurator-Fiscal. He was hanged in July 1865. Holmes' remarks regarding the errant doctor were indeed apt. The Stoke Moran affair (SPEC) took place in April 1883. Only a year before Dr George Henry Lamson had poisoned his 18 year old brother-in-law with a little known vegetable poison, aconitine, contained in a capsule of sugar. He was executed in April 1882

The loathsome and scheming Dr Pritchard, described by Sherlock Holmes as 'the worst of criminals'. This was especially true in Holmes' era, when a G.P. had a high status in the community; and who, unlike many modern doctors, was rarely challenged in the execution of a death certificate.

Palmer's trial took place in 1856. He qualified at St. Bart's in 1846, and he began practice in Rugeley, Staffordshire. He married, had an affair with his servant, and frequently got into debt. He resolved then to poison his mother-in-law so that her estate would pass to his wife and eventually to himself.

Palmer's four children died, then his wife and brother (after they had been insured for very large sums). Palmer was a compulsive gambler and in 1855 attended Shrewsbury Races with a friend, John Cook. Cook won large sums while Palmer lost.

Having collected Cook's winnings for him, Palmer then poisoned his companion. Unfortunately for Palmer, the autopsy showed evidence of antimony poison.

According to the intrepid Victorian crime chronicler, Major Arthur Griffiths, in Vol. 2 of his 'Mysteries of Police and Crime,' (1899) - a book which surely Holmes the astute criminologist would have read from cover to cover - Palmer was a highly devious character who covered his traces very assiduously:

> 'One of the most remarkable cases of the misuse of medical knowledge was that of William Palmer, the sporting doctor of Rugeley, in Staffordshire, whose crimes were many, although he was actually convicted of only one. The physiognomist would have detected nothing in Palmer's face to indicate the secret poisoner. He had an open, rubicund visage, was frank and free-spoken, and generally esteemed a good fellow and a merry companion. He was still young, barely thirty-one, when he paid forfeit with his life, but he looked older. The world had not gone well with Palmer for many years'.

After taking his diploma he set up practice in his native place, Rugeley, in 1846, and married money, as he thought, the following year. His wife was the natural daughter of a Colonel Brookes, of the East India Company's service, who had settled at Stafford on his retirement. He left a fine fortune among his children at his death, but it was claimed and secured by his legitimate heirs.

Very little came to Mrs. Palmer, but the doctor had started extravagantly. Yet now he made no change in his way of life, neglecting his profession, and attending only a few relations and personal friends. He had gone upon the turf, owned racehorses, and was engaged in large betting transactions.

The luck was steadily against him, and within two years of his marriage he must have begun his murderous career, for in 1849 his mother-in-law died quite suddenly when on a visit to him.

Viewed in the light of later events, he no doubt had compassed her death in order to succeed to certain house property in Stafford. Again, in 1850, he appears to have been responsible for the death of one Bladon, a turf man, who stayed a few days with Palmer in Rugeley, but did not leave the house alive. Bladon had but just won a large sum of money, which he carried with him, to his own undoing. He died suddenly and mysteriously, and was buried on the certificate of a friendly old doctor, Bamford, who subsequently figured in the Cook case. Only £15 was found in Bladon's possession, and his betting book, in which Palmer figured as a heavy loser, had also disappeared.

The sheer, outrageous but compelling deviousness of the case with Palmer must have fascinated Holmes, who was, it seems, as much compelled to look at and examine the psychological profiles of murderers as he also was wont to examine the forensic details.

In his summing up of the evidence against the poisoner, the attorney general said of Palmer's conduct at the post-mortem, 'the tampering with the cover of the jar—by whom?—his anxiety to upset Mr. Stevens when in charge of it, because, it had been urged, of 'his prying meddlesome curiosity;' his presents and letters to the coroner; his prompting Cheshire to tamper with the letter from Dr. Taylor; his anxiety to know, and to let the coroner know, that strychnia had not been found; his suggestion to call Smith (what a witness Jeremiah would have made!); his assertions of previous epileptic fits, and his hope "that the verdict to-morrow would be that he died of natural causes, and thus end it," were all dwelt upon: "little things, if taken individually, but taken as a whole," said the Attorney-General, "as I submit to you, leading irresistibly, to the conclusion of the guilt of this man."

In concluding this masterly speech, though in some parts too it must have been rather like fighting for a verdict, the Attorney-General criticised the assertion by Serjeant Shee of his belief of the prisoner's innocence:

"You have, indeed, introduced into this case one other element which I own, I think, had better have been omitted. You have had from my learned friend the unusual, I think I may say the unprecedented, assurances of his conviction of the innocence of his client. I can only say upon that point that I think it would have been better if my learned friend had abstained from giving such an assurance. What would he think of me if, imitating his example, I should at this moment declare to you, on my honour, as he did, what is the intimate conviction which has followed from my own conscience."

Palmer, the sort of man who my dear old mum would have called 'a vile villain' or my dad, a policeman all his life, would describe as something worse than that, was arrested and subsequently hanged in 1856.

BIBLIOGRAPHICAL NOTE TO THE ABOVE

For the most comprehensive account of the famous poisoning cases of Holmes' period, and immediately prior to this, the eager student of Victorian crimes of this sort should consult:

REPORTS OF TRIALS FOR MURDER BY POISONING by Prussic Acid, Strychnia, Antimony, Arsenic and Aconitia, including the trials of Tawell, William Palmer, Dove, Madeline Smith (aka the baby killer - KJ), , Dr. Pritchard, Dr Lamson, and details of the poisons they used. by G Lathome Browne, London, 1883.

(Students of 19th century criminology and the Holmes saga will find the free dogital Internet Archive website copy of this rare book especially useful.)

The famous plaque celebrating the immortal partnership, which commenced at St Bart's. Erected in 1953.

A STROLL TO ST. BART'S

When Watson strolled through the London streets with Stamford on that memorable day to meet the mysterious man his friend had in mind for him as a flat mate, the intrepid and dogged doctor could not have failed to notice the large proliferation of small bookshops down the narrow side streets they passed in The Strand, selling cheap, mass produced photographs of desirable young ladies, often attired in what were in Watson's time known as 'burlesque' costumes. But if he had persuaded his young dresser to examine these in more detail, Stamford would then have seen that some of the women in the photos, like the men they were pictured with, were wearing hardly anything at all, save perhaps a pair of revealing silk knickers and a jaunty hat.

As the two men proceeded onwards, they would alo have passed more young ladies, but this time in the flesh, in groups of often three or more, some looking decidedly the worse for wear through excessive gin drinking, others dressed in cheap, brightly coloured short dresses that revealed to the doctor and his friend, long black French stockings covering their dainty ankles.

Being by nature an observant and red blooded fellow who, as his future flatmate Holmes recalled of him, was someone who had an experience of the fairer sex 'extending over three continents,' they may have been tempted to chat to these ladies, but probably did not, since by now Watson was almost penniless, an embarrassing financial position which he may well have shared with his young friend.

The story of Kitty Winter, which many years later Dr Watson provided an account of, in the story of 'The Adventure of The Illustrious Client,' (published in the Strand Magazine in November, 1904), is fairly typical in its depiction of the attitude of more enlightened members of the male society in Victorian England, like Conan Doyle.

During the early part of the 19th century, women from a lower to a higher working class background had been severely challenged by the effects of the economic and industrial changes within Britain, as society became prosperous for some women, those, for instance, married to successful merchants, but for some, these changes had created poverty and for others, the woeful and desperate stories that were told first-hand to people like Henry Mayhew in the mid-nineteenth century, showed a pattern which was set to continue into the 1880s.

For many impoverished women, especially in the capital, life did not change much over those intervening decades. Of course, not all of the prostitutes that these two friends saw plying their trade in and around the Strand, and no doubt also in The Criterion Bar, where the two men sat enjoying a drink together, would have been prostitutes through force of poverty or necessity. Some women, though it must be admitted, these were not in the majority, did the job because they simply enjoyed it and because it was comparatively well paid, compared to many menial or exhausting factory jobs.

And being a 'gay' lady in 1880's England had it attractions (the term 'gay' at that time didn't apply solely to homosexuals but meant simply a person of loose morality or one who led an abandoned life style). After all, you got to wear fashionable clothes. You could go to the music hall most nights and if you were good at the job, you could work from a rented apartment or even, if you were very good at it, even buy your own house, as was the case of what were in that age termed, by the popular press, 'strumpets,' - the type of harlot that at Christmas, each year, the monarch's son, Edward, provided a specially commissioned train to convey his well attired women 'of easy virtue,' through the lush woods of the Royal Family's great Sandringham Estate, in Norfolk, then disembarking at the little railway station that once stood, concealed among the trees.[11]

Regarding the Sherlock Holmes story of Kitty Winter, nowhere is this predicament more vividly described in terms of male and female sexuality, than in the remarkable, offensive but most authentic account, of one man's obsession with his own sexuality, and his quest to exploit this obsession in working class female London. This 'banned' book, entitled 'My Secret Life ', by an anonymous author who calls himself 'Walter,' began in a very limited edition in Victorian London at the time when Sherlock Holmes was pursuing his career and the Ripper stalked the streets of London for his female prey.

Soon, pirated, but highly expensive copies of it were made and distributed amongst mainly wealthier male members of society, and it became a very wanted book for those of a less prurient mind. The book is, of course, decidedly pornographic in its effects upon the reader, but nevertheless, a significant record of great historical importance, and in my view, essential reading for admirers of the Sherlock Holmes saga. who wish to comprehend the true underbelly of Victorian society and realise the impact it reflects on the subculture of its criminal world.

In this huge memoir, the author describes in immense, explicit detail his attempts, which were on the whole successful, (since he was, by and large, paying for sex), to achieve his ambition: intercourse with thousands of women. This having been achieved over a period of about 40 years, the author was, all the while, keeping a record of these so-called 'Adventures,' exactly as Baron Adelbert Gruner does in 'The Illustrious Client'.

In the narrative of this comparatively later and unusually feminine --centric Holmes story, Kitty Winter tells Holmes that Gruner kept a black book which, she tells Holmes, the businessman and collector of both rare *objets d'art* and females, loathsomely referred to as his 'beauty book'; and which contained 'snapshot photographs.' Presumably these would have been photos of his chosen women posing in the nude, and in compromising positions for him, their addresses and other 'details,' no doubt of the type which the editors of 'The Strand Magazine' would not wish to see published

---

[11] Although the railway at Sandringham hasn't survived, it and its company of 'special gay ladies' was certainly remembered by many Norfolk folk, including my wife's grandfather, a blacksmith who served the adjacent small village of Flitcham and who made the elegant magnifying lens, pictured on page 34.

or referred to explicitly in their glossy magazine, where its pages certainly showed photos of alluring women as illustrated in this book but certainly nothing which might be regarded as pornographic. And significantly, according to Kitty, it was a 'beastly book, which no man could have put together,'

Someone of the same period who certainly may well have kept such a book, was the lecherous and ubiquitous 'Walter'. Walter, a middle-aged, self-described, 'gentleman of private means,' would wander through the streets of London, trying to sate his lust, then in later volumes, travel abroad in search of more vicarious sexual pleasures in the great and prosperous capitals of Western Europe,

The social historian, Steven Marcus, believes that the mysterious Walter's journal is the most important document of its kind about Victorian England, a view which I utterly endorse, and which was the motivation for my republishing the entire work, in six volumes in 2019. In my edition, each volume is accompanied by an extensive biographical introduction, and detailed bibliographical references for this profane, but haunting literary colossus, which runs to over a million crude but illuminating words.

It seemed to me, during the three years I worked on the text and edited it, that if anyone were truly interested in the social narrative of Victorian England, he, and most certainly she, should read this book.

Academic history undergraduates students of the period (I would not, of course. recommend the publication or issuing of a schools' edition) should also understand that it stands far above any work of fiction or, indeed, above any other work of a similar nature, in terms of its unadorned and explicit social commentary, (including the observations and various charity commissioned documentaries, gathered from the poor in the mid-century, by Mayhew and his contemporaries) that are to be found in the literature of Victorian western Europe of this period, regarding the dire poverty of the 1880s, of its exploitative and humiliating nature, endured by so many working class women, but also of the prevailing attitudes which prevailed and were part of a shared mythology, about human sexuality.

For details of prostitution in the Victorian period in Britain, this book is the primary resource of all social history of its nature. Walter, a vain, self-regarding, self - confessed, and idle fantasist, is obsessed, not just by his own frequently tumescent sexuality, but also by the possibility of not having money or spending it all on his exploits; for he knows only too well, that if he does run out of it, he

The Criminal World of Sherlock Holmes, Volume One

will be reduced to grinding poverty. Moreover, Walter associates his occasional impotence with the state of being poor, and frequently uses the verb 'to spend' as a synonym of ejaculation. This association was much in his mind and was, no doubt, in the minds of many men of his own generation, when thinking of sex.

Sexuality between a man and a woman was considered to be, for many Victorians, a transaction, like any financial or commercial arrangement, and this was a key notion in the minds of the late Victorian middle class man, for the pornography of the age, and particularly of the period of the last 20 or so years of the 19th century, reflect this only too well. It was even a shared belief among many male gynaecologists that, in intercourse, women 'came' in precisely the same way that men did, which of course they do not.

To Conan Doyle, Kitty Windsor, who, like the protagonist in Doyle's universally ignored erotic novella, 'The Parasite,' wishes to throw vitriol (sulphuric acid) into Gruner's face, as a premeditated act of revenge for the treatment she has suffered at his hands, this story represents the painful memories of many women, who were the objects of exploitation and who entered into prostitution, at first willingly, but as time passed, unwillingly; then to be further abused by their pimps, who put them onto the street, a highly dangerous place for an unaccompanied female, but more so then, in Victorian England. Inevitably, they became that class of women preyed on by the remorseless psychopath we know as the self-styled slayer of 'drabs' or whores, 'The Ripper', a man who altogether escaped justice, and most probably lived never to divulge his secret.

Another of the Holmes stories that comes close to 'The Illustrious Client,' as a story of female revenge, where again we see Holmes, like his creator, representing the status of abused women, is the rather brief tale entitled 'The Veiled Lodger.'

Again, it's the story of a woman who'd suffered endless beatings and abuse from her violent husband. She conspires with a man called Leonardo to club her husband to death, thus securing her freedom, but unluckily for her, as Leonardo strikes her husband with a large club, embedded with nails, a lion escapes. When she is revived, she then realises her face has been badly mauled by the lion. At the sight of her, her lover deserts her, to thus endure a poverty-stricken fate. So afflicted, she takes a phial of prussic acid to end her sorrows. Apart from prostitution, what other occupation could the abandoned female pursue other than begging?

In 1875, two years before Sherlock Holmes came to London, the Artisans' Dwelling Act empowered the City of London Corporation and the Metropolitan

49

Board to buy up slum property, knock it down and resell the land for working-class accommodation. Ironically, that act profited the landlord, not the tenant, and created thousands more homeless than before.

The stationary type of begging practised by Neville St. Clair in 'The Man With The Twisted Lip' was in fact much rarer than it is now generally supposed. Begging was illegal then, as it is now, and a person who drew a crowd round him in a busy thoroughfare was liable to attract the attention of a constable.

The problem of begging in the Capital had been partly created by the increased vigilance of the municipal police who drove the vagrants of the countryside into the metropolis. In the "paddingkins" or cheap lodging houses of the great city, they could dodge the police much more efficiently, and their anonymity served as an added protection. In the case of Hugh Boone, alias Neville St. Clair, he avoided prosecution by pretending "to a small trade in wax vestas". The competition was fierce and often vicious in those days. To succeed at begging you not only had to contend with the police; you also had to hold your pitch against competitors.

The procedure of 'standing a pad on a fakement' (this involved carrying a card round your neck detailing your claim to charity, tragic past history, etc.) was at the best, risky. The blind beggars (the genuine ones, that is) were best off. Gonorrhoea, for which there was no cure, and smallpox, rife among the lower classes, claimed many victims, and the blind man with his dog became a familiar object of Victorian sentiment. Sham blindness was surprisingly uncommon, mainly because it did not often go undetected for very long. If the police didn't realise it, then your own kind soon would.

Boone faked a limp, according to Holmes, but "in other respects he appears to be a powerful and well nurtured man." Perhaps that was just as well, for he would have attracted little sympathy from his begging colleagues. But it was, of course his unusual and ghastly appearance which drew in the money.

It is against this backcloth, then, that we find Dr. Watson choosing 'less pretentious and less expensive (quarters)'. His state of finance had 'become alarming'. Perhaps the meaning of that statement does not have as much significance now as a hundred years ago, when a person of any station without income and unable to rely upon a welfare state, would soon sink into the quagmire of the seething underworld.

It was then Watson met Stamford, whilst standing at the Criterion Bar, and, as Watson records, 'the sight of a friendly face in the great wilderness of London is a pleasant thing indeed to a lonely man'.

The gaunt, cerebral and rather forbidding man whom Watson shared
lodgings with, in that untidy flat at the address of 221B Baker
Street, one of the most famous fictional addresses in English
Literature. The detective is personified here by William Gillette.
Doyle, when first seeing him in the flesh on an English railway station,
exclaimed, 'You ARE Sherlock Holmes!'

The conventional view of an attractive, and for men, alluring female, portrayed here in The Strand Magazine in the 1890s. Such images were sexually potent for male readers of the magazine.

A rare and empathetic drawing of Holmes by Sidney Paget, (CARD), with body language here, showing a relaxed,receptive style of sitting, with legs apart. Only rarely did the detective show much genuine public sympathy to the plight of the female, but there were certainly notable exceptions. This female and the emotionally distressed Julia Stonor in 'The Speckled Band,' are among the most striking. The young woman is Miss Cushing, who has been the unfortunate recipient of a box containing two severed human ears.

STUDIES IN SCARLET, PART TWO

"There's the scarlet thread of murder running through the colourless skein of life.
- Sherlock Holmes, STUD.

The decade prior to Holmes' move to London and Montague Street had been one of remarkable interest from the point of view of the criminological student. A year before his arrival (1876), all London had been shocked by circumstances surrounding the death of the eminent barrister, Charles Bravo.

On 18 April 1876 Charles Bravo and his wife Florence ate dinner in the company of Mrs. Jane Cox, Florence's companion. About 9:45pm the same evening, Charles was heard calling loudly for his wife. When she got to his bedroom, she saw him standing by the open casement, his face grey and beaded with sweat.

Within three days he was dead.

A post-mortem revealed that he had died of antimony poisoning, administered in a single dose of 20-30 grains.

When questioned, Mrs. Cox said that Bravo told her he had taken poison but when asked about this, Bravo replied that he might have swallowed some laudanum which he had been using to rub against his gums to alleviate his neuralgia.

Despite the two inquests that followed, an open verdict was returned and the cause of Charles Bravo's death, even to this day, remains a mystery.

However, there is a theory that Bravo had intended the poison for his wife and, in an act of carelessness, administered it to himself. It is known that not only did Florence have an affair with an elderly Doctor Gull but that in the event of her death, her entire estate would pass to her husband.

The stuff that killed Charles Bravo was tartar emetic — a salt of antimony and a poison which had figured in two previous classic cases: those of William Palmer (1856) and Dr. Pritchard (for both, see above).

There is no doubt that young Sherlock Holmes studied the Bravo case and its forerunners with intense interest, for later in his career, in that famous comment on doctors and crime, memorably enunciated by the late Jeremy Brett, he was to remark that "when a doctor does go wrong he is the first of criminals. Palmer and Pritchard were among the heads of their profession."

A year before, on 21st December, 1875, the Newgate scaffold disposed of Henry Wainwright, whom Holmes referred to as "no mean artist" (ILLU) later in his career. Holmes was 21 at the time, but undoubtedly the horrific details of the case earned themselves a place in his 'Good Old Index.' Holmes' position as a private consulting agent was one that suited him admirably. Preoccupied and motivated as he was with the process of inductive reasoning, it comes as no surprise to find him despairing of the pettier forms of crime he was asked to deal with, whilst rising with enthusiasm to the fiendish cunning of intellects like those of Dr. Grimesby Roylott or his finest adversary, Professor Moriarty. It is interesting, therefore, to find Charlie Peace and Henry Wainwright given the highest accolade in Watson's account of "The Illustrious Client."

Holmes' remarks are also perplexing to the student of 19th century criminology. Firstly, it is rather disputable whether Peace was really ever possessed of "a *complex* mind." Secondly, the reference to Wainwright is either a misspelling by Watson's literary agent, or a real case of confusion on Holmes' part. The almost legendary Sherlockian scholar, William S. Baring-Gould refers, in his 'Sherlock Holmes' (and again in 'The Annotated Sherlock Holmes'), to the case of Thomas Griffiths Wainewright (1794-1852), the compulsive poisoner.

On the face of it, Baring-Gould would seem to be correct in his assumption that this is the "Wainwright," for T. G. Wainewright, who was suspected of poisoning his grandfather with strychnine, in order to inherit his wealth, and was a dandy who took up painting and writing. During his lifetime he became friendly with De Quincey, Hazlitt and Lamb. A spendthrift, he forged the signatures of the trustees who controlled his stock, and illegally procured £2,000 which he subsequently spent in gambling clubs. When Wainewright found that his grandfather's estate hardly cleared his debts, he then dutifully poisoned his mother-in-law, Mrs. Abercromby (although this was not positively proved). In 1830 he insured his 20-year-old sister-in-law. In December of that year, she then died after a bout of severe vomiting. Wainewright fled the country but was arrested on his return to England in 1837. The evidence was only sufficient to try him for forgery (forensic medicine was then in its infancy) and he was transported to Tasmania. He later in his trial stated that he murdered Helen Abercromby because he objected to her thick ankles!

It is most probable that Holmes, in recalling this affair, confused T. G. Wainewright with the more recent Henry Griffiths Wainwright (1875). This other Wainwright case received sensational coverage in the popular press of the period, so that the 21-year-old Holmes would undoubtedly have remembered its details. Since Baring-Gould does not even deign to mention this case, it seems appropriate to give the facts in detail, for we may be assured that Wainwright held an honoured place somewhere among the W's of the Baker Street Index.

As already noted above, Holmes' connection with Charlie Peace is also intriguing. Arthur Griffiths ('Mysteries of Police and Crime') records that, in 1876, Peace was busy organizing several burglaries in the East Riding of Yorkshire. It is just conceivable that the 22-year-old Holmes may have met the man when he was visiting his parents in the East Riding. (How else would he have known Peace was a violin virtuoso?) Peace, according to Griffiths, who knew him personally, was a very cunning and direct man of a practical turn of mind, but it is difficult to see how Holmes' adjective of 'complex' could really apply. He was arrested in dramatic circumstances at a house in Blackheath (a favourite courting place for Doyle when he met his second wife, Jean Leckie), when Holmes was at the height of his career (1878):

'By then (Griffiths tells us), Peace was a wanted man, having murdered his neighbour, Mr. Dyson, two years previously. Peace had amorous designs on Dyson's Sheffield wife and was warned off by Dyson. Undaunted, Peace began to harass Dyson, and eventually he shot him through the temple in his own back garden. He later shot a policeman in a village near Manchester, a crime for which another suspect, William Habron, was wrongly convicted'.

After Sheffield, Peace moved to a house in the East Riding and then moved again to Nottingham, where he carried out daring warehouse robberies. When things got too hot for him he then moved to Lambeth, London, to continue his burglaries. Then he relocated to Greenwich, and thence to Peckham, to a bigger house, furnished with the proceeds of his countless break-ins. The contents of his drawing-room, comprising a walnut suite (50 guineas – a fortune in those days), ornate mirrors, Turkish carpets, a bijou piano, a Spanish guitar, and fine Cremona fiddles, would have amused the inhabitants of 221B, Baker Street. (Did Holmes obtain his Stradivarius via Peace? The whole matter remains an enigma.)

Peace was an accomplished criminal, who possessed both pluck, and daring. Maintaining a respectable veneer, he employed several impeccable matrons at various rented addresses to guard his "valuables." One aspect of his character would have earned the detective's admiration when as a master of disguises, he appeared often in Peckham as a one-armed man with a hook, and in Greenwich as a kindly churchwarden.

On November 17, 1878, Constables Robinson and Girling were on watch outside No. 2, St. John's Park, Blackheath (the original house still stands and is a mere stone's throw from the Cedars of TWIS fame). The night was dark and still, so that when Robinson saw a candlelight flickering in the kitchen, he knew his chance had come to earn himself some promotion.

Peace put up a good fight. After firing five shots, he attempted to stab Robinson with a sheath knife, but he desisted once the "bracelets" were clapped about his wrists. Once arrested, the constables saw that his face was stained with walnut-juice and he claimed to be an American half caste, John Ward by name.

After a fortnight, this alias yielded to another. This time he was a man called Johnson who lived in Peckham. A search of his clothing yielded several pawn tickets which, when followed up, indicated the proceeds of his recent burglaries.

When he was removed from Pentonville to the Leeds Assizes, Peace attempted a daring escape from a railway carriage, but succeeded only in breaking his legs. He was a true professional, as his collection of picks and skeleton keys in the Black Museum testifies. Nor was he without a sharp sense of humour. Griffiths recorded this story when he visited him in prison, shortly before his execution:n, for he was by that stage ready to meet his maker, having successfully evaded capture for years, thus earning for himself an accolade in the annals of British crime folklore.

"What is the good of telling the truth? No one believes you when you do. ... When I was Mr. Johnson of Peckham, I went into the chemist's one morning, smoking an excellent cigar. The chemist observed: 'That is very good tobacco. Where do you get your cigars?' 'Steal them,' I replied, perfectly frankly and truthfully. "It was the absolute fact. I had stolen the cigars. But my friend, the chemist, thought it an excellent joke. He roared with laughter.... "I wish you'd steal me a few of the same kind,' he said. ...

Some weeks afterward I came across a very fine lot of Havanas in a house I visited rather late at night, and I secured them. The chemist got a box of them.

'There, Mr. So-and-So,' I said, 'I have stolen you these. I hope you will like them.'
"Again he laughed loudly, and he no more believed me than before."

Dr Watson questions the miserly Josiah Amberley about the disappearance of his wife in Lewisham. Nearby Lee was the location of TWIS; also close at hand in wealthy Blackheath, was where Charlie Peace, the master burglar, attacked a PC, when discovered escaping from a burglary, and it was where Druitt, one of the Ripper suspects, worked at a boys' prep school, prior to his sudden and unexplained dismissal.

But perhaps the most bizarre case of that decade to command the young detective's attention was that of the Stauntons, mentioned earlier in this volume. It was in July 1877 that Holmes took rooms in Montague Street. "Months of inaction followed" he later told Watson, during which time he no doubt followed the sensational trial of the Stauntons with avid interest.

In the September of that year Louis Staunton, his mistress, Alice Rhodes, along with his brother Patrick and Patrick's wife, were charged at the Old Bailey with the murder of Harriet, Louis' wife. Other Stauntons were to grace the pages of Holmes' Index: "Arthur H. Staunton, the rising young forger... and there was Henry Staunton, whom I helped to hang." (MISS) But surely the case of the Stauntons took pride of place in Holmes mind for this sensational case was about the injustice suffered by the vulnerable and we know he had strong views about the subject.

In 1875, Harriet, described in the Press of the time as a 'simple-minded girl', married Louis Staunton, an auctioneer's clerk. In our own century, if we had met Harriet Staunton herself, we would probably describe her as a young, rather plain faced, genial, middle - class woman who suffered from quite severe learning disabilities. In Victorian days there were no schools that persons in that category or condition might be able to attend. If you were blind then maybe you learned Braille but there were few blind schools in London where you might be able to receive even a basic education. Harriet was not blind, but neither, it seems, did she have much confidence. She was just 'simple.' She was labelled by the public as 'a simpleton.'

Harriet had an endowment of £3,000, and when an anxious mother went to visit her daughter in Brixton, she was given a hostile reception by the Stauntons. Soon afterwards they moved to Cudham, a small village in Kent, where Louis began an affair with his sister-in-law, Elizabeth. On 8th April, Patrick and Elizabeth visited Guy's Hospital in London, where they deposited Harriet's child, in a weak and emaciated condition. And within three weeks the baby was dead.

On 12th April, Louis rented a house in Penge where Harriet was moved and subsequently died. The doctor who examined her found her in a filthy, louse-ridden condition. She weighed only 5 stone 4 oz.

The only known surviving photo of Harriet Staunton. P. Domain,
from A. Ayers' account of her in 'The Stauntons','Great British
Trial Series.'

The poignancy of Harriet's plight struck a chord of sentiment in the
minds of the Victorian public. She was seen as a helpless victim, like the
unfortunate Lady Frances Carfax who Holmes, unlike Harriet, managed to
wrest from the hands of her oppressors later in his career, but only when,

after exploring every legal avenue known to him, he had to commit a felony and break into the house of the conman and fraudster, the most irreverent 'Reverend Schlessinger,' aka 'Holy Peters and his female accomplice. The two conspirators had kidnapped her, bound, gagged and chloroformed her, prior to entombing her in a larger than average coffin, which they had intended should share for all eternity with the corpse of a recent workhouse corpse.

There is a distinct parallel here for the reader of the Sherlock Holmes crime files, for in Dr Watson's account, entitled 'The Disappearance of Lady Frances Carfax', these criminals were, like the Stauntons, fraudsters who were at the centre of a high profile and controversial trial at the Old Bailey in the 1870s. As a result of their individual and conspired cunning in order to take advantage of the sister in law's weaknesses and vulnerability, they thereby intended to profit from her death. As things turned out, however, they were confounded by the timely intervention of a well meaning and concerned relative. As a result, when it came to sentencing the conspirators, the trial ended, the jury were unanimous in arriving at their guilty verdict, and consequently, Judge Hawkins passed the death sentence on 26 September, 1877.

However, it was not long after sentence had been given, that a campaign for the Stauntons' reprieve was begun. There were petitions and public meetings held, including questions about the draconian nature of the sentences that had been meted out; so that on 14 October, only two days prior to their hangings, the Stauntons' mother, Mary, journeyed to Balmoral in the hope of asking the monarch Herself to intervene.

However, it was not the Sovereign, but a leading article in the Lancet on 6 October that changed the conspirators' fate.. The piece referred to the medical evidence, which they claimed flew in the face of the other, mostly circumstantial evidence, and of course, in strictly rational and forensic terms their objections were entirely reasonable; and we may be sure that if Sherlock Holmes did follow the trial in detail, he would have been certain to agree with them, was highly prejudicial.

Holmes certainly would have noted the judge's rash dismissal of medical evidence, which suggested that Harriet had died not actually from starvation but from cerebral disease, or tubercular meningitis. The Stauntons, the doctors insisted, were guilty of criminal neglect, but surely not of murder.

Many members of the BMC added their names to a "memorial," to be submitted to the home secretary. Seven hundred doctors went on to sign this petition, among them a leading member of the medical fraternity, Sir William Jenner. The home secretary felt that he could no longer ignore the pressure of the medical lobby, and so, on 14 October, the Stauntons' sentence was commuted to penal servitude for life. Alice Rhodes, meanwhile, was pardoned and released.

But surely, Sherlock Holmes would have asked the jury, did not Elizabeth Staunton and the others deliberately starve Harriet to death? Some believe they did not, pointing to the evidence of Clara Brown, the Stauntons' servant, who said nothing of her employers' abuse of Harriet at an initial inquest, but then, at the Old Bailey, contradicted herself by giving a detailed account of their cruelty.

The trial and verdict of the Stauntons' Case, a cause celebre in the history of British trials. remains a contentious affair and its distinct legal ambiguity most probably irked Holmes. The Case of Lady Frances Carfax certainly irked him, for here, rather like the Staunton case, there was certainly conspiracy, fraud, and quite possibly intended manslaughter at work, yet he felt powerless to act within the confines of the law. In both these cases we see the exploitation of vulnerable members of Victorian society, on the one hand a 'rather pathetic figure,' a wealthy widow, whom Watson describes as 'beautiful…still in fresh middle age yet… the last derelict of what only twenty years ago, was a goodly fleet,' falling prey to the attentions of a highly determined predator who is determined to kill her and profit from her fortune; and in the trial of the Stauntons, a transparent reflection of the unambiguously dismissive way in which Victorian society regarded those highly vulnerable people who had severe learning disabilities.

It is patently obvious, reading from the trial accounts today, that had the concerned neighbour not acted in the way she did, and not drawn the attention of the authorities to the disappearance and death of the sister in law Harriet, no one would ever been have been the wiser as to her precise whereabouts for many years after her death. The fact that the case came to the attention of the police, and that a subsequent prosecution was raised, these points all suggest that the police had a strong regard for the plight of the young woman concerned. After this trial was finally completed, the authorities slowly became more accustomed to the position of those who had learning difficulties. And it is doubtful whether from that time onwards, fraudsters like the Stauntons would have imagined they might succeed in such a malicious plan.

The sentiments of many of the public regarding the Staunton affair were much like those of the judge who, in his summing up, referred to the murder of Harriet as a "cruel and barbarous" plot.

This short deposition at the trial by one of the witnesses, speaks volumes regarding her plight and subsequent death:

"I am a porter at Bromley Station. I remember seeing a lady helped into a first-class carriage at 8.26 on 12th April; she was not able to walk; her feet dragged. I picked up a list slipper lying between the rail and platform the next morning."

The plight of a weak and defenceless woman preyed upon by the calculatingly criminal, was an example Holmes was to see enacted many times in his long career, especially in the account Watson chronicled subsequently in 'The Strand Magazine' as 'The Tiger of San Pedro.'

And only two years after 'A Study in Scarlet,' he was to encounter the insidious Dr. Roylott, who cold-bloodedly planned the execution and murder of his stepdaughters.

DEADLY WERE THE POISONS

(POISONS, POISONERS AND THOSE WHO WERE POISONED IN THE SHERLOCK HOLMES STORIES)

According to the OED, a poison is 'any substance which, when introduced into or absorbed by a living organism, destroys life or injures health.' Sherlock Holmes once observed that he dabbled in poisons a great deal ('A Study in Scarlet').

Holmes, was, according to Watson, 'well up' in his knowledge of poisons, and poisons featured in a number of his cases, including 'The Devil's Foot', 'The 'Greek Interpreter', 'The Sign of Four', 'Silver Blaze', 'Lady Frances Carfax', 'The Retired Colourman', 'The Speckled Band', 'The Golden Pince - Nez', 'The Creeping Man', 'The Dying Detective' and 'The Sussex Vampire'.

Types of poisons encompassed by those cases reported by Watson include curare, snake venom, coal gas, strychnine, opium, and chloroform. Holmes also define himself as a 'self - poisoner' by cocaine and tobacco.

The last two decades of the 19th century were crucial to the scientist and criminal investigator regarding poisons. They were pioneering years both in Europe and America. Before the 1880s, the weight of evidence which went to condemn a murderer to the gallows often depended on eyewitness reports. By the turn of century, the whole *modus operandi* of the criminologist was starting to transform Scotland Yard and the French Surete. These were the virgin years, during which, a number of isolated pioneers dominated the literature of the scientific journals. Toxicology, the study of poisons, had remained largely unchanged since the era of Matthew Orfila, the "father of toxicology", who, in the 1840s, had played such a vital part in the Lafarge case.

There was, even in the later years of the 19th century, a great deal of mystery and confusion surrounding the subject of poisons, so much so, that when Dr William Guy published his "Principles of Forensic medicine", in 1861, he declared that "the term poison does not admit of strict definition". This is true even now, for the effects of the poison depends purely on its dosage, and what will kill one man may have even beneficial effects upon another.

The pioneering work carried out by Orfila (particularly in the field of arsenic examination) was continued by one of his pupils, Sir Robert Christison in (1797 to 1882), who was appointed to the chair of forensic medicine in Edinburgh. In 1829, he published his seminal "Treatise On Poisons", which was to remain for many years, the most authoritative English work on the subject of poisons. Christison's breakthrough was in establishing that, despite the problem of definition, poisons all had one thing in common: they were all substances which caused chemical and psychological changes in the body, sometimes resulting in tissue damage and malfunction of the nervous system.

He was also able to classify poisons into four main categories: A) poisons which cause an interruption to the oxygen-carrying capacity of the blood (cyanide, carbon monoxide) B) poisons which cause corrosive damage (acids, alkalis), C) systemic poisons, which are absorbed through the skin or intestinal tract and which cause damage to the main organs (arsenic, antimony). This category includes the vegetable alkaloids (strychnine, morphine, etc,), which affect the central nervous system and its operation, and a further category of poisons, which leave no trace of entry, but which cause destruction after absorption (ricin, arsine, etc,.)

By the time that Sherlock Holmes had abandoned rural existence for the investigation of crime at Bartholomew's Hospital, advances in toxicology in England had been piecemeal but far from comprehensive. Even so, the latter part of the 19th century saw the appearance of many remarkable names in the field of scientific and medical examination. Many of these names the aspiring criminologist like Sherlock Holmes would have found familiar. There was Joseph Lister, whose development of antiseptics was revolutionising the work of the surgeon, both in Edinburgh and London. He had come to London in 1877, taking with him four of his faithful assistants to help him in his crusade. All over the world, except in London, surgeons were now adapting his new ideas. Asepsis is now used in hospitals throughout the world, but in those far-off days of the 1870s and 1880s, the operating theatre was often far from spotless, and the death rate from post-operative infection was too high.

As the Lister revolution spread, Joseph Lister gained universal acknowledgement as the leading surgeon of his age, so much so, that by 1883, when he was 56, Queen Victoria awarded him a baronetcy.

Another name familiar to the lean faced figure, bent over the retort stand in that dingy chemical laboratory at Bartholomew's Hospital, was that of Louis Pasteur. In many respects, advances in medicine moved at a greater pace than in the somewhat more conservative field of forensic sciences. In Britain, investigatory work was the province of the coroner rather than the police surgeon, and it was not until Professor Hans Gross published his Criminal Investigation (first published in English in 1906), that English police began to accept a more scientific approach to crime investigation. Again, it was Europe rather than Britain that led the field of contact trace examination with the work of Edmund Locard (1910). And it was the University of Lasalle in Switzerland, rather than an English university, which offered the first course in criminalistics for students (1902).

Young Stamford, who acted as a dresser under Watson while at Barts, makes an illuminating comment about Sherlock Holmes: "Holmes is a little too scientific for my tastes – it approaches to cold-blooded nests. I could imagine his giving friend a little pinch of the latest vegetable alkaloid, not out of malevolence, you understand, but simply out of the spirit of enquiry in order to have an accurate idea of its effects. To do him justice, I think that he would take it himself with the same readiness. He appears to have a passion for definite and exact knowledge." (A Study In Scarlet.)

Elsewhere, while citing Sherlock Holmes' limits, Watson observes that his companion is "well up in belladonna, opium and poisons generally".

The suggestion in both these passages is that Sherlock Holmes had made, and was making a particular study of the alkaloids. This is not really surprising, since Victorian England was littered with victims of alkaloidal poisons. The age of the manufactured synthetic poisons (barbiturates, for example) was yet to arrive. To the Victorian gentleman, the most unobtrusive method by which to dispose of his spouse or business rivals, was to obtain one of the readily available mixtures, which, in that era, could be bought freely over the shop counter of a chemist. Some of these were prepared for household, and some for veterinary and some for garden use: weedkiller, rat poison, fly killer, etc. There were a great number of standard medicines which also held poisonous ingredients and which could be obtained without trouble: Fowler's solution (arsenic), Easton's syrup (strychnine) and of course, laudanum (a solution of morphine). Attempts to regulate these poisons did not actually begin until the Arsenic Act of 1851, but even then, it was only required that the purchaser of the poison should be known by the seller.

It was not until 1868, that the range of controlled poisons was broadened and pharmacists were compelled to keep a note of their sale. Even then, it was possible for the enterprising poisoner to obtain his or her poisons by devious methods.

Britain had to wait until 1933 (Pharmacy and Poisons Act) for the first truly comprehensive system which governed not only the sale but also the labelling, storage and the transportation of drugs.

In studying the alkaloid poisons, Holmes chose to investigate the oldest group of drugs known to man. However, since the last century the crude vegetable drugs like strychnine, to which this variety belong, has declined (except for digitalis [10] which is still used for the treatment of heart conditions), and the synthetic drugs have come to the fore. In this monograph, Holmes describes in detail the alkaloids, basic substances that can combine with acids to form salts (e.g. morphine tartrate, atropine sulphate et cetera). Their composition is constant and their action consistent. In the 1880s, toxicology was a minor branch of pharmacology, which itself was the development of the study of the *materia medica* (some chairs of pharmacology are still called chairs of Materia Medica – especially in Edinburgh.) The student was expected to have a good general grounding in botany (Watson refers to Holmes' knowledge of botany as variable), so that
he could check the medicines and their preparation.

In the second half of the 19th century, there was a developing interest in the efficiency of plant preparations and a number of experiments were carried out by researchers often on themselves. The results of these often hazardous experiments were published regularly in the British Medical Journal (Conan Doyle was known to have used himself as a guinea pig

---

[10] The history of digitalis is interesting The first use is usually attributed to William Withering and his study on the foxglove published in 1785. However, some knowledge of plants with digitalis-like effects used for congestive heart failure (CHF) was in evidence even in Roman times.

regarding the use of the drug known as Gilsemium). The great inquisition into both the useful and harmful plant preparations was well advanced by the 70s and Sherlock Holmes was evidently part of this tide of great enthusiasm. With the new drugs came new poisons, and the study of toxicology grew more complex.

For Sherlock Holmes, the vegetable derived substances were invariably used on victims he encountered. Hence the long hours spent in the old chemistry laboratories in Bartholomew's Hospital provided him with the groundwork necessary for a criminologist of his stature. As Stamford put it to Watson: "he is a first-class chemist. His studies are very desultory and eccentric, but he has amassed a lot of out of the way knowledge which would astonish his professors." – A Study in Scarlet.

What precise knowledge regarding poisons would Holmes have based his assessment of poisons on? Holmes would have known, for example, that the repeated drinking of a decoction of hemlock produces no symptom of poisoning, but that the individual to whom it has been administered is destined to certain death with all the symptoms of consumption; so that in any specific case if the suspected guilty person has told the witnesses that the deceased certainly died of consumption, while there are no other grounds for suspecting that disease, that alone would be a reason for suspecting him of the crime of poisoning. A similar case occurred in Bohemia, according to the indefatigable Austrian judge and criminologist, Hans Gross. He relates he case in his pioneering work, 'Criminal Investigation. Hans Gustav Adolf Gross (26 December 1847 – 9, December 1915) was an Austrian criminal jurist and the "Founding Father" of the system later described as 'criminal profiling,' which in Britain, did not make its appearance until the Ripper murders in the late 1880s. Throughout his life, Hans Gross made significant contributions to the realm of scientific criminology, having noticed the failings in the field of law regarding the investigation of serious crime. A man had poisoned with dried poisonous mushrooms the whole of a family of peasants. Among the victims was a daughter of the criminal, who was a servant in the family. This circumstance was decided in favour of the accused, but served only to corroborate the suspicion against him when it was found that, in the part of the country from which the accused came, it was a universally believed opinion that poisonous mushrooms were perfectly harmless to young women. In such a case, Gross advised that:

'Besides such scientific knowledge, the Investigating Officer ought to have at least an approximate idea of the effects of poisons, but this he can only acquire by careful study of some first class manual of toxicology. Here only the most striking points can be noticed. All cases of death are suspicious which follow a sickness of which the cause is unknown, presenting symptoms not agreeing with the usual symptoms of a natural illness. Undoubtedly such an indication is very vague and still further loses in value when it is remembered that the classic symptoms of poisoning, such as vomiting, diarrhoea, giddiness, etc., do not necessarily accompany all poisons; and that on the other hand the sudden appearance of these symptoms does not conclusively indicate a case of poisoning. It is exactly the people who are circumspect, and therefore the most dangerous, who know how to make use of a slow and creeping poison, producing only a sickness marked by long continued weakness without any of these alarming symptoms.'

As regard the methods of the examination of poisonous substances, he advised the following procedure which was much in evidence in the case of the investigation of Palmer, about whom Holmes quotes.

'In a case of poisoning therefore, even more than in cases of another nature, the Investigating Officer should endeavour to be in close communication with the experts, to communicate every information he has on the matter, and to endeavour if possible to have a conference between the medical men who treated the deceased, those who made i.e., post-mortem and the chemical examiner.

Gross concluded that:

'It may be necessary to decide in what direction inquiries should be made, whether it is necessary to call in the aid of microscopists or botanists, whether any particular portions of the body should be preserved for further examination; and lastly, if, in view of the statements of the witnesses or other indications, it appears necessary to start fresh inquiries. As a general rule, such conferences should always be arranged; they frequently give important results and they ease the conscience of the Investigating Officer. He has the consolation of having done everything it was humanly possible for him to do'.

'When the least suspicion of poisoning exists and conforms to instructions, the stomach and its contents should be removed by the nearest available medical man, generally an hospital assistant or apothecary, and preserved for the purpose of putting them at the disposal of the Court and the Chemical Examiner. Then one should scrutinise on the spot, with the aid of the medical man and the assistance of a good magnifying glass, and without avoidable disturbance, the stomach and intestines, etc., to see if any plants, or fragments of plants, suspicious foreign bodies, etc., are to be seen. If there are, they should then be examined, to see if they are poisonous.'

Again, with reference to the case of Palmer but also to that of the man found on the floor at Lauriston Gardens, Brixton, Holmes' first recorded case by his amanuensis, Dr Watson, (in STUD) Hans Gross declares:

'In general, poisoning and particularly arsenical poisoning may be suspected when there are found vomiting, have a violent thirst, sensation of burning in the throat, pains in the stomach, diarrhoea, and cramp in the calves of the legs, or some of these symptoms. Many believe that the perspiration and respiration of persons poisoned by arsenic have an odour of garlic, like that disengaged when arsenic is sprinkled on burning charcoal, but it appears that this odour is found only in cases of chronic poisoning'.

Gross was one of the first criminologists to point out how closely the symptoms of cholera resemble those of poisoning by arsenic. Arsenic then was largely used as an antidote to fevers of all kinds, as an aphrodisiac, in cases of rheumatism, gout, and syphilis, and externally for skin diseases such as itch and eczema. It was also employed for many industrial purposes, as in curing skins and gold-working; and preserving roofs, floors, and walls of buildings from the ravages of vermin and particularly white ants. For the latter purpose it was commonly mixed with tar and brushed into cracks and holes.

The arsenical oxide or common white arsenic of the bazaars was also commonly used for all these purposes, Gross goes on to say, 'for homicidal employment. It is frequently mixed with coarse sugar and made up into a sweetmeat. It is sold either as a white powder or as a solid white mass resembling enamel; in the latter form it must of course be pounded before use. Traces of pounding should therefore be looked for. Like arsenic, yellow arsenic or ointment, is also occasionally employed, generally mixed with a proportion of white arsenic.'

Gross then goes on to list the possible alternatives a detective might look for in his examination of the afflicted victim or the body of the deceased:

'In poisoning by phosphorus there is pain in the stomach, vomiting, feeble pulse and collapse; in chronic cases there may be yellowing of the skin, and slight bleeding from nose, mouth, and bowels. The phosphorus for poisoning is ordinarily obtained from the ends of matches, and the phosphorus from sixteen matches has been found sufficient to poison an adult. In homicidal and suicidal cases, mercury poisoning mostly takes the acute form. The agent is chiefly corrosive sublimate, or mercuric chloride, a white crystalline mass or crystalline powder'.

The Austrian judge also has a great deal to say about the effects of opium, which undoubtedly Holmes would have found absorbing, since in 'The Man with the Twisted Lip,' Watson finds the detective in an opium den where his flatmate has been for quite some while.

'Opium as already pointed out, is the favourite medium of suicidal poisoning, and can generally be at once detected by the characteristic odour. Opium both in its solid form and as a decoction is so universally used, especially as a febrifuge. It is also commonly available in the form of laudanum'.

The opium den, with all its mystery, danger and intrigue, appeared in many Victorian novels, poems and contemporary newspapers, and fuelled the public's imagination. Here are two examples, one of which was written at the period, some while after TWIS appeared in 'The Strand Magazine' (see Appendix to this volume).

"There were opium dens where one could buy oblivion, dens of horror where the memory of old sins could be destroyed by the madness of sins that were new."

Oscar Wilde in his novel, 'The Picture of Dorian Gray' (1891) conveys this rather over-stereotypical, and melodramatic picture of the opium den: "It is a wretched hole… so low that we are unable to stand upright. Lying pell-mell on a mattress placed on the ground are Chinamen, Lascars, and a few English blackguards who have imbibed a taste for opium."

The article above that of Oscar Wilde's is a description reported in the French journal 'Figaro', describing an opium den in Whitechapel in 1868. The first of these descriptions is by Wilde, who had written his novel as a response to an invitation both he and Conan Doyle had received from the agent who subsequently printed their work in Lippincott's Magazine. Intriguingly, Wilde chose to write about the gradual erosion of the self, experienced by his protagonist through the use of drugs and a libidinous lifestyle.

'The Sign of Four,' which Doyle submitted, is also much preoccupied with drugs and drug taking. Indeed, the first chapter of Watson's narrative is almost entirely devoted to Homes' explanation of why he uses cocaine and morphine.

Readers at the time would have regarded both Dorian Gray and Holmes as 'Bohemians', a widely used concept which had connotations of decadence, self – indulgence, 'art for art's sake' and the 'fin de siècle flirtation with all that was seen as slightly suspect, morbid and self-regarding. Wilde himself believed that he was witnessing the end of European civilization, and that he was living now in the waning, twilight years of a once great Empire in a period of decadence, much like the latter days of the Roman Empire. Apart from drugs and art, what else was there to enjoy during those declining days of an Empire which had grown glutinous and terminally exploitative?

The general public must have shuddered at these descriptions and imagined areas such as London's docklands, and the East End, to be opium-drenched, exotic and dangerous places. The den visited by Holmes and Watson was situated in Upper Swandam Lane, in Rotherhithe. As a youth, I often cycled from my home in Lewisham to Rotherhithe, which was then a place of gaunt red brick warehouses, interspersed with small public houses and residential buildings. Here I discovered several likely contenders for the opium den of TWIS, several with a basement and upper floor at the back of which, doors opened to convey goods onto barges. What puzzled me at the time when I first read Dr Watson's account, in TWIS, and what still intrigues me now, is Holmes' comment to about his familiarity with the opium den:

'Had I been recognised in that den my life would not have been worth an hour's purchase; for I have used it before now for my own purposes, and the rascally Lascar who runs it has sworn to have vengeance upon me. There is a trap door at the back of that building, near the corner of Paul's Wharf, which could tell some strange tales of what has passed through it upon the moonless nights.'

Exactly what does Holmes mean by telling Watson that he has used the place *'before now for my own purposes'*? Does it mean that he has used the den for recreational opium smoking? Or is he referring to some undercover work which in the past has necessitated his visiting the den in a disguise? Both would imply that he stayed on the premises, smoking amounts of opium in unspecified amounts.

Even more curious is the fact that in the June 1891 edition of the then relatively new Strand Magazine an entire article appeared, graphically illustrated, and entitled 'A Night In An Opium Den.' The anonymous author describes in some detail the sordid den he visited in the Ratcliffe Highway.

'The Sign of Four,' the second Holmes novel, which Doyle submitted to be serialised in Lippincotts' American Magazine, following that memorable meal with the American agent, is also much preoccupied with drugs and drug taking. Indeed, the first chapter of Watson's narrative is almost entirely devoted to Homes' explanation of why he uses cocaine and morphine. Readers at the time would have regarded both Dorian Gray and

In the story of 'Silver Blaze', opium is used to subdue the servants as John Straker Plans to maim the race horse. The administration of opium or laudanum was a Poular tool used by burglars if they had a link to someone in the household.

Holmes as 'Bohemians', a widely used concept which had connotations of decadence, self – indulgence, 'art for art's sake' and 'fin de siècle.'

The public must have shuddered at these descriptions and imagined areas such as London's docklands, and the East End, to be opium-drenched, dens of iniquity and moral depravity, a notion the 'Strand' article surely suggests.

Here, with the Ratcliffe Highway murders, we come full circle with De Quincey, quoted in TWIS by Dr Watson.

As Nick Louras points out in his intriguing article about De Quincey and Doyle, (BSJ Vol 69, No. 3): 'De Quincey wrote at length about the Ratcliffe Highway Murders which occurred in Wapping East London.' On December 7, 1811, a family known as the Marrs were found brutally murdered in their East End shop. In less than a fortnight another murder occurred. This time, the victims were the landlord and his wife in a pub in Gravel Lane. Four days later an Irish sailor was arrested on suspicion of the murders. His name was Williams. At first, the evidence was hardly convincing. Fresh evidence, collected from witnesses who knew the publican, was only circumstantial (for instance, a laundress, who washed William's linen, stated he had given her a shirt to wash which was torn and bloodstained.) While the inquiry was still in progress, Williams hanged himself in his cell at Coldbath Fields prison. Although Williams' and Marrs'

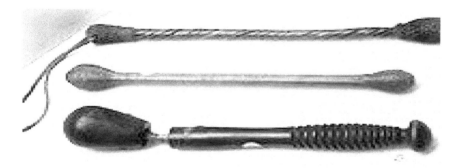

Holmes' world was one where violence lurked on every street corner. To survive, gentlemen would often carry a stout stick or a 'life preserver' as above.

pasts were connected, no real motive for the murders of the victims was satisfactorily established.

It is curious to find mention of the Ratcliffe Highway murder in The Strand article. In the opening paragraphs of the article, the name of De Quincey is mentioned twice. The author claims that his efforts to describe the effects of the drug are not as effective as those literary descriptions of Coleridge or De Quincey. The den hosts several Chinese operatives and, like the Swandam Lane establishment which has a 'Lascar' in charge of operations, – an East Indian sailor, army servant, or artillery trooper during the era of European colonialism in Asia). The Ratcliffe Highway den also has an obligatory 'Malay – a person from the east Sumatran peninsula. In the Strand account, the Chinaman in charge is described in grotesque and caricatured terms:

'The smile became even more rigid, when I explained that I was anxious to smoke a pipe of opium. The way in which he turned his face upon me was…for all the world like the turning on by a policeman of a bull's eye lantern. With a final grin which threatened to permanently distort his features, he bade us follow him…'

In a similar article to the Strand Magazine piece, published in 'Tit-Bits' on 31st October 1891, the anonymous author describes a visit to an opium den near the East India Docks, 'within the sound of the big bell of St Paul's (cathedral),' where the author explains how 'we turn(ed) down a dreary side street, at the corners of which are loafing some rather ugly customers of the Lascar type' and then reach 'what appears to be a shop. Within lies the kitchen with a tin pan on a fire of coke and coal in which the opium is prepared; a staircase leads up to a pair of rooms' where the customers 'wander through scenes which none but a De Quincey can portray.'

The close resemblance of the Ratcliffe Highway den to the one in Upper Swandam Lane poses the question: in writing up the narrative of TWIS, did Watson simply reinvent the former location, basing it upon these contemporaneous accounts? If so, one is led to the conclusion that Watson had never before the night he volunteered to 'rescue' his friend, Isa Whitney, actually visited an opium den and that the opium den episode is simply a poetic elaboration, or a piece of sensationalism, designed to intrigue and entertain readers of The Strand when the story appeared in its pages in the latter part of that year.

The links between De Quincey and Conan Doyle are intriguing. As both Nick Louras, (q.v.) and Michael Harrison in his 'A Study In Surmise' suggest, Doyle had read De Quincey closely and the De Quincey book also comes up in a non-Holmes story entitled 'The Silver Hatchet,' where De Quincey is the name of a character. Harrison notes in his book that there was an 1888 edition of the De Quincey book in Doyle's house at 1 Bush Villas, Southsea, where he conceived many of the initial Holmes tales, and later to appear in the first Holmes short story collection, entitled 'The Adventures of Sherlock Holmes'.

And now we come to that most favoured of killing substances which often featured widely in the deadly tool kit of the Victorian poisoner. and which formed the basis for the Jefferson Hope affair. Strychnine causes death by convulsions and immediately renders the corpse rigid, a rigidity which sometimes remains for weeks. In his master work, 'Criminal Investigation,' Gross is at pains also to point out:

'Datura, the poison of the thuggees[11] in India, is still used mainly to facilitate robbery. It has been pointed out that as datura is popularly

---

[11] Thuggees, - a Sanskrit word actually meaning concealment - were an organized gang of professional assassins – who operated from the 13th to the 19th centuries in India. Members of the fanatical religious group, infamous for their ritualistic assassinations carried out in the name of the Hindu Goddess Kali, were known as Thugs, a word that passed into common English during the British occupation of India. Thuggees worked by joining groups of travellers and gaining their trust before surprising them in the night and strangling, or, garrotting them with a handkerchief or noose, a quick and quiet method, leaving no blood and which required no special weapons. They would then rob their victim and bury them carefully in order to avoid all trace of their crime. During a 1906 meeting of the Royal Society of Edinburgh, Sir William Turner submitted part three of his research "Contributions to the Craniology of the People of the Empire of India." Included were the photographs of individual skulls from a group who the British Medical Journal said "made it their business to frequent the great highways of India and become friendly with travellers, with a view to setting upon them and strangling them." The novel Confessions of a Thug, by Philip Meadows Taylor, 1839, quickly became a best-seller in England and was instrumental in introducing the word "thug" to the greater population. Taylor's novel was a first-person narrative by Ameer Ali, as he lays bare the secrets of his life and his crimes.

supposed not to be poisonous to death, the fatal result is due to the overdose which is necessary to put the robber on the safe side. The datura seeds whole or broken up are commonly mixed with sweetmeats or food, and whole seeds or fragments may consequently be found in the stomach or the remains of the meal.'

Finally, when perusing the pages of his copy of Gross's work, one can but hope (but is perhaps surely quite unlikely) that Holmes may have observed the following note of advice and caution when it came to nicotine:

'Santonine is commonly used for extirpating worms, and as infants are extremely sensitive to this medicament, its absorption is at times followed by sudden death. In poisoning by santonine, the urine is yellowish green. The use of other poisons such as sulphuric acid, oxalic acid, etc., is not so frequent as to necessitate more than a passing reference here. In cases of poisoning by organic substances generally, the medium cannot, as explained above, be readily detected by chemical or microscopical analysis but the absorption of organic substances has been frequently noted to produce brain affections, sometimes rising to furious delirium. Such substances are cantharides, henbane hemlock, datura, belladonna, digitalis, absinthe, opium, hashish, and poisonous mushrooms'.

Caesar Lombroso, a leading theorist of European criminology, who heavily
 influenced Sherlock Holmes' understanding of the root causes of criminal
behaviour with his ideas about atavism.

Sherlock Holmes, the forensic consultant and analyst, posed here by popular American actor, William Gillette, in a publicity - shot postcard, advertising his and Conan Doyle's play, based upon 'The Speckled Band.'

Alphonse Bertillon, the French criminologist, and inventor of the criminal measuring system, 'bertollinage,' whom Holmes regarded, and with some impatience, as something of a rival. Public domain photo.

One of several letters, sent to the Central Press Agency, purporting to have been written by Jack the Ripper. Police believed they knew which of the many letters received by themselves and the Agency were genuine, but never publicised their results. C. 'Jack The Ripper: Letters from Hell.'

'Putting on the darbies' was the police slang for this handcuffing. Sidney Paget drawing from 'The Adventure of the Cardboard Box,' taken from my 1908 edition of 'The Memoirs of Sherlock Holmes.'

Police, summoning assistance and finding the odds against them among down - at - heel, rioting residents of Whitechapel. Such conflicts were common in this lawless area of London during the 1880s. From 'The Illustrated London News,' for 1888. Below, a mob attack truncheon - wielding pre-Peel police near Coldbath prison in 1833. (From Griffiths' 'Mysteries Of Police And Crime.' Truncheons of that period were ebony and lead weighted.

The Coldbath Fields riot of 1869..

The Thames, the perfect getaway for The Ripper, where often an
Impenetrable darkness prevailed at night. From 'The Strand
Magazine,'

Whitechapel, 1888. Another 'drab,' or prostitute discovered
murdered. From 'Police News.'

Dr. A. CONAN DOYLE.
87 UNION SQR., N. Y

A young Conan Doyle. He reinvented the crime story but
disliked Holmes' popularity.

House breaking tools, of the type that Holmes admitted to having in CHAS. From a series of articles in 'The Strand,' entitled 'Crime And Criminals.'

Holmesian crime scene, where Tonga is depicted on the ladder,
making his escape in 'The Sign of Four, here illustrated in the 1908
Edition, drawing by F. H. Townsend.

Fred Abberline, detective in charge of the longest stretch
of the Ripper hunt.

The chairman of the intrepid Whitechapel Vigilance Committee, George Lusk, who received a portion of a human kidney of one of the Ripper victims. The parallel with 'The Cardboard Box' story is an interesting one.

A young Charlie Peace, ambitious master criminal whom
Holmes described as his 'old friend'. Courtesy, 'Charlie Peace,'
by Ben W. Johnson, Pen & Sword Books, 2016.

Gruesome murder scene, followed by ear decapitations, depicted by Paget here in 'The Cardboard Box,' Strand Magazine, but not in the 1st edition of 'The Memoirs' because of its visceral and explicit content.

Holmes follows the creosote trail with Toby in SIGN. Holmes
wrote a monograph on 'The Use of Dogs in Crime Detection'.
Drawing by F.H. Townsend in the 1908, 2nd edn.

Holmes conducting a chemical analysis in the Baker Street
lodgings. Illusn. By Sidney Paget, Strand Magazine, December 1893.

European opium addicts entering an opium den. From
an article in 'The Strand' . See appendix.

The Victorian convict, Jack Prendergast, with shaven head and
arrowed suit depicted here by Paget, from 'The Gloria Scott,'
1908 edn,. 'Memoirs of Sherlock Holmes.'

Sir Francis Galton, who revolutionised fingerprinting techniques in Britain.

Neville St Clair who gave up a job in The City to become a stationary beggar because it was more profitable. From 'The Man With the Twisted Lip,' Paget drawing to 1908 edn., of 'The Memoirs of Sherlock Holmes.'

The Cedars, Lee. Home of Hugh Boone, alias Mr Neville St Clair. Conan Doyle played cricket here in the grounds, as also did one of the Ripper suspects, Did they meet each other? Photo c. of Lewishan Public Libraries.

SHERLOCK HOLMES: THE MURDERED AND THEIR MURDERERS

The detective's own wide knowledge of classic murder cases and of the circumstances of their victims' demise certainly assisted him in the detection of crime and the speed with which he reached his conclusions. Later in that same account by Dr. Watson, Holmes mentions that "The forcible administration of poison is by no means a new thing in criminal annals. The cases of Dolsky in Odessa, and of Leturier in Montpellier, will occur at once to any toxicologist."

One suspects that the Commonplace and other books which cluttered the interior of 221B Baker Street, far from gathering dust, were stuffed to the brim with excerpts from 'The Police Gazette' and cuttings from the newspaper reports of sensational murder trials of the period. And Holmes's brain was, we recall, like an attic (LION), from which all types of useful data could be extracted in order to provide a useful comparison.

Holmes recommended that the most practical thing a detective could do was to "shut yourself up for three months and read twelve hours a day at the annals of crime" (VALL), and pointed out that "It's all been done before, and will be again." (VALL). For that reason, he spent much of his professional career absorbing and becoming expert upon a wide range of specialised knowledge, including tobacco ashes (BOSC, STUD, SIGN), cryptography (DANC, GLOR, REDC, VALL), newspaper typefaces (HOUN), perfumes (HOUN), toxicology (STUD), the dating of documents (HOUN), the typewriter and its relation to crime (IDEN), bicycle tyres (PRIO), tattoos (REDH), footsteps (SIGN), the influence of the trade on the form of the hand (SIGN), and the names and trademarks of the world's major gun making firms. He also showed considerable interest in anatomy, an interest which Watson described as "accurate but unsystematic," and twice applied this knowledge in the form of practical experiments (BLAC, STUD).

Although he claimed to have investigated over five hundred cases in the course of his career, a surprisingly small number (38%) dealt with murder. In fourteen of these, 23 resulted in the murderers being arrested or killed, three involved non-human agents (LION, SILV, SPEC), and in all fourteen, Holmes made a successful analysis. In five other cases, Holmes succeeded in identifying the criminal but the murderers escaped the reach of the law (FIVE, GREE, MUSG, RESI, WIST), and in four other cases Holmes gave the murderers their liberty, (ABBE, BOSC, DEVI, VEIL) because there were extenuating circumstances involved.

Today's forensic scientist would have found the range of murder cases fascinating. Among the causes of death were gassing, poisoning, asphyxiation, and death from head injuries, comprising a variety of blunt instruments and guns. In the vast majority of these cases, a quick eye for detail at the scene of the crime led Holmes to the murderer with remarkable rapidity. The principles he espoused in the detection of crime are no different today than they were, or in the case of some police detectives, should have been in 1880: the power of observation, the power of deduction, and a wide range of exact knowledge (SIGN).

In a period when forensic science was still in its infancy, and, surprisingly, behind that of the great Indian Empire, (Queen Victoria's 'jewel in the crown,') Holmes was a man at the top of his league, and this accounts for much of his success as an investigator. He made full use of many of the forensic fields now permanently established: toxicology, ballistics, document examination, even graphology. One of the most useful areas of forensic investigation is that of contact traces, which encompasses the principle that an encounter between victim and murderer leads often to small traces of contact, e.g. blood, fibres, hair.

One recalls that one section of the rooms at 221B was devoted to the chemical retort and the microscope especially for this purpose. These days, of course, no one man or woman investigates the causes and effects of a murder. The whole thing is a complex process, involving a variety of experts. In Holmes' day, there was no alternative but to become Jack of All Trades. He was sometimes called upon to be police surgeon, forensic analyst, and detective, all at one time. That he did this with such a measure of success places him in a unique position in the annals of crime. In the field of criminal investigation, he has never been matched.

(NOTE: The Dossier of Victims that now follows includes (a) persons who were the victims of attempted murder, (b) murdered persons, (c) suicides, and (d) accidental deaths. The list therefore comprises the range of cases which would come to the attention of the modern pathologist. The majority of these cases involved a premeditated attempt at murder. Throughout I use the 4 letter acronyms invented by J. F. Christ, to denote the stories.

THE INDEX OF VICTIMS

A
Abergavenny Murder, The
Abernetty Family, The
Achmet
Adair, Hon. Ronald
Amberley, Mrs. Josiah
Armitage, James
Atkinson Brothers, The

B
Baldwin, Ted
Barclay, Col. James
Baskerville, Sir Charles
Baskerville, Sir Henry
Beddington
Blessington
Brackenstall, Sir Eustace
Brunton, Richard

C
Carey, Captain Peter
Carfax, Lady Frances
Cubitt, Hilton
Cushing, Mary

D
Dolsky,
Drebber,

E
Enoch J.
Ernest, Ray

F
Fairbairn, Alec
Ferguson, Jnr.
Fournaye, Henri

G
Garcia, Aloysius
Gibson, Maria
Giorgiano, G.

H
Hatherley, Victor
Hayling, Jeremiah
Heidegger
Holmes, Sherlock

K
Kirwan, William
Kratides, Paul

L
Leturier
Lucas

M
McCarthy, Charles
McPherson, Fitzroy
Milverton, Charles Augustus
Murillo, Don Juan

O
Openshaw, Colonel Elias
Openshaw, John
Openshaw, Joseph

P
Pinner, Harry P
Prescott, Rodger

R
Ratcliff Highway Murders
Ronder, E
Roylott, Dr. Grimesby

S
Savage, Victor
Straker, John
Sutton

T
Tarleton Murders,
The Tobin
Tregennis, Brenda
Tregennis, Mortimer
Trepoff Murder, The
Trevor Senior

V
Venucci, Pietro

W
Watson, Dr. John
West, Arthur Cadogan

THE J. FINLAY CHRIST ACRONYMIC LIST
OF SHERLOCK HOLMES STORY TITLES

Invented by the American Sherlock Holmes chronologist and scholar, J Finlay Christ, as a useful list of abbreviations of the Holmes stories' titles and for quick reference. These acronyms, though not obligatory, are currently used by most Sherlockians.

The Adventures Of Sherlock Holmes
A Scandal in Bohemia SCAN
The Red-Headed League REDH
A Case of Identity IDEN
The Boscombe Valley Mystery BOSC
The Five Orange Pips FIVE
The Man with the Twisted Lip TWIS
The Adventure of the Blue Carbuncle BLUE
The Adventure of the Speckled Band SPEC
The Adventure of the Engineer's Thumb ENGR
The Adventure of the Noble Bachelor NOBL
The Adventure of the Beryl Coronet BERY
The Adventure of the Copper Beeches COPP

The Memoirs of Sherlock Holmes
The Adventure of Silver Blaze SILV
The Adventure of the Cardboard Box* CARD
The Adventure of the Yellow Face YELL
The Adventure of the Stockbroker's Clerk STOC
The Adventure of the Gloria Scott** GLOR
The Adventure of the Musgrave Ritual MUSG
The Adventure of the Reigate Squire REIG
The Adventure of the Crooked Man CROO
The Adventure of the Resident Patient RESI
The Adventure of the Greek Interpreter GREE
The Adventure of the Naval Treaty NAVA
The Adventure of the Final Problem FINA

The Return of Sherlock Holmes
The Adventure of the Empty House EMPT
The Adventure of the Norwood Builder NORW
The Adventure of the Dancing Men DANC
The Adventure of the Solitary Cyclist SOLI
The Adventure of the Priory School PRIO
The Adventure of Black Peter BLAC
The Adventure of Charles Augustus Milverton MILV
The Adventure of the Six Napoleons SIXN
The Adventure of the Three Students 3STU
The Adventure of the Golden Pince-Nez GOLD
The Adventure of the Missing Three-Quarter MISS
The Adventure of the Abbey Grange ABBE
The Adventure of the Second Stain SECO

His Last Bow a.k.a The Reminiscence of Sherlock Holmes
The Singular Experience of Mr. John Scott Eccles*
The Tiger of San Pedro* WIST
The Adventure of the Cardboard Box** CARD
The Adventure of the Red Circle" REDC
The Adventure of the Bruce-Partington Plans BRUC
The Adventure of the Dying Detective" DYIN
The Disappearance of Lady Frances Carfax" LADY
The Adventure of the Devil's Foot" DEVI

The Case-Book of Sherlock Holmes
The Adventure of the Mazarin Stone+ MAZA
The Problem of Thor Bridge THOR
The Adventure of the Creeping Man CREE
The Adventure of the Sussex Vampire SUSS
The Adventure of the Three Garridebs 3GAR
The Adventure of the Illustrious Client ILLU
The Adventure of the Three Gables 3GAB
The Adventure of the Blanched Soldier # BLAN

The Adventure of the Lion's Mane# LION
The Adventure of the Retired Colourman RETI
The Adventure of the Veiled Lodger VEIL
The Adventure of Shoscombe Old Place SHOS

Sherlock Holmes Novels
A Study in Scarlet STUD
The Sign of the Four SIGN
The Hound of the Baskervilles HOUN
The Valley of Fear VALL

DOSSIER OF VICTIMS

ABERNETTY FAMILY, The
Source: SIXN
Biographical details: Not known.

"You will remember, Watson, how the dreadful business of the Abernetty Family was first brought to my notice by the depth which the parsley had sunk into the butter upon a hot day." (SIXN)

Holmes referred to this as one of his "classic cases."

Since what happened to the Abernettys was "dreadful," it may well be inferred that murder was involved. The case seems to have occurred around 1900.

ABERGAVENNY MURDER, The
Source: PRIO
Biographical details: Not known.

"My colleague, Dr. Watson, could tell you that we are very busy at present. I am retained in this case of the Ferrers Documents, and the Abergavenny murder is coming up for trial." (PRIG)

Abergavenny is a town in Monmouthshire. There are no murder cases recorded for the town of Abergavenny in or around the year 1901.

ACHMET
Source: SIGN
Biographical details: An Indian merchant who was murdered, because he was in possession of the Agra Treasure. His attackers, three Sikhs and an Englishman called Jonathan Small (q.v.), were sentenced to penal servitude for life.

ADAIR, Hon. Ronald
Source: EMPT
Biographical details: The second son of the Earl of Maynooth, governor of one of the Australian colonies. Lived with his sister (Hilda) and mother at 427 Park Lane. At one time he was engaged to Miss Edith Woodley of Carstairs. Temperament: quiet, unemotional. Fond of cards. Member of the

Baldwin, Cavendish, and Bagatelle card clubs. Died March 30, 1894.

Circumstances: Adair returned alone to 427 Park Lane at 10 P.M. on March 30, 1894. His servant heard him enter the front room on the second floor of the house. At 11:20 P.M. Lady Maynooth returned and found the door locked on the inside. The body was found lying near the table, the

MR TREMBLE BORROWS A HINT FROM HIS WIFE'S CRINOLINE, AND INVENTS WHAT HE CALLS HIS 'PATENT ANTI-GAROTTE OVERCOAT', WHICH PLACES HIM COMPLETELY OUT OF HARM'S REACH IN HIS WALKS HOME FROM THE CITY.

Amusing illustration in the satirical 'Punch' magazine, showing defensive umbrella mechanism to ward off garrotters.

head horribly mutilated. No murder weapon was found in the room. On the table were two banknotes of £10 value each and £17.1Os. in silver and gold, also a piece of paper with figures on it and names of club friends. The window was open, but there were no signs of footprints or marks on the narrow strip of grass separating the house from the road.

Cause of death: Shot in the head by an expanding revolver bullet. Pistol and revolver bullets are intended to hit their targets at short range and are round-nosed and have a large diameter. In comparison, rifle bullets have longer bodies and pointed tips. The type of bullet which resulted in such severe mutilation of Adair's skull was a dum-dum bullet. Because of the high velocity of this bullet, the energy it set up transferred itself into high pressure waves in the tissues surrounding the bullet track, thus occasioning severe pulping of the brain. This phenomenon is referred to as "cavitation."

The unique feature of this crime was that the bullet was fired not from a revolver but from a high-velocity air rifle. The weapon was constructed by Von Herder, the blind German mechanic (d. Vienna, April 1, 1901). The Blozenbilchse, a breech-loading, air-powered rifle, was used. This was originally intended to shoot darts over a distance of about ten metres, but the feature which distinguished it from other air rifles was its absolute noiselessness. Herder first bored the Blozenbuchse to carry a revolver bullet and then redesigned it in the form of a two-piece, take-down model which could easily be concealed by the murderer, Colonel Sebastian Moran (q.v.) (see Ralph A. Ashton, "Colonel Moran's Infamous Air Rifle," BSJ Vol. X, No. 3, July 1960, pp. 155-59. Also see article in Vol 2 of this edition).

At the time of Adair's death (1894), the science of ballistics was in its infancy, and it was not until 1910 that police forces throughout the world were aware of the forensic possibilities of bullet matching and striation marks. The dum-dum bullet, used by Moran, was first tried out in India in 1897 and was subsequently outlawed by The Hague Convention (1899). Because a dum dum bullet is cut across the top, the effect at the moment of impact is for it to mushroom out, thus causing extensive damage to tissues in the body.

AMBERLEY, Mrs. Josiah
Source: RETI

Biographical details: 1855-1898. Described as a "good-looking woman." Married Josiah Amberley, a colour-man from Lewisham, in 1897. Had an affair with Dr. Ray Ernest, a neighbour of the Amberleys who lived near Belmont Hill, Lewisham. Murdered with her lover at The Haven, Lewisham, in 1898.

Circumstances: Done away with at The Haven and then reported missing by Josiah Amberley. Subsequently, her body was discovered in a disused well, concealed from view by a dog-kennel.

Cause of death: Gassing. Mrs. Amberley and her lover, Dr. Ernest, were presumably lured to the strong room of The Haven. The room had been hermetically sealed with an iron door and shutters. On investigation, Holmes discovered a gas-pipe running along the skirting board outside. This rose in the angle of the wall and ended in the plaster rose of the ceiling. A tap in the join of the pipe outside enabled Amberley to turn the supply on or off. Within two minutes of flooding the room, Mrs. Amberley and her lover would have died, according to Holmes. Amberley cleverly concealed all trace of smell of the gas by painting the house.

The coal gas which killed Mrs. Amberley was a common cause of suicide and murder in Victorian times. The substance which it contains, carbon monoxide, is a poison. It replaces the oxygen normally carried to the brain by the haemoglobin, and death results from oxygen starvation. Death from coal-gas absorption occurs usually in just over five minutes. The hermetic sealing of the room was an essential part of Amberley's plan, since the blood must absorb 20% of the carbon monoxide in order for the victim to show signs of dizziness. Symptoms of carbon monoxide poisoning are a high pink tinge to the face, and the blood often fails to clot. The celebrated H. H. Holmes, America's mass murderer of the 1890s, used coal gas to dispose of a number of his victims by piping it into the rooms of his house.

ARMITAGE, James (alias Trevor Senior)
Source. GLOR
Biographical details: Born 1832. A Norfolk squire, J.P., and man of wealth who lived at Donnithorpe, a hamlet to the north of Langmere, on the Norfolk Broads. As a young man he entered a London banking-house, committed the crime of embezzlement, and was transported at the age of 23

with 37 other convicts, bound for Australia aboard the barque Gloria Scott in the year 1855. The prisoners mutinied and, after a dispute with the leader (Prendergast), Armitage and a few others were put to sea in an open boat. After being rescued by the brig Hotspur, Armitage was safely conveyed to Sydney, where he prospered and whence he returned to England, a wealthy colonial. He was subsequently blackmailed by the sailor Hudson and because of this suffered a stroke.

Circumstances: Armitage suffered an attack of apoplexy after receiving a letter posted in Fordingham. The letter warned him that Hudson (the sailor who had been blackmailing him) had "told all," thereby revealing Armitage's part in the Gloria Scott mutiny years earlier

Cause of Death. Apoplexy. Armitage's mouth and eyelids "were all puckered on one side," a condition which spread, causing paralysis and eventual coma. Apoplexy is a term meaning a stroke of bodily disablement connected with some diseased condition of the brain. In persons subject to heart disease, a clot may form in the valve of the heart and be carried to the brain. The occurrence of this embolism produces the sudden effects witnessed in apoplexy. The person who suffers such an attack becomes suddenly deprived of consciousness and lies in a deep sleep, exhibiting a flushed face and slow pulse. Death may occur within a few hours.

ATKINSON BROTHERS, The (1888?)
Source: SIGN
Biographical details. Not known.
"From time to time I heard some vague account of his doings. . . of his clearing up the singular tragedy of the Atkinson Brothers at Trincomalee..." (SIGN)

The Atkinson tragedy and Holmes' involvement in this episode has been fully chronicled by Lt. Cdr, G. S. Stavert (SHJ Vol. 13, Nos. 1 & 2). Holmes, he speculates, had gone on a long sea voyage to Trincomalee, owing to the grave state of his health. Thomas Atkins, the "young son of Corporal Atkins" of the Argyll and Sutherland Highlanders, was found apparently strangled near the entrance to a Buddhist temple, a few miles outside the village at Trincomalee. On examining the boy's body, Holmes was able to deduce that the boy had fallen under the chariot of "Jagganath" during the festivities held by the Hindis and his neck was then broken by the wheel of the chariot. Colonel Forbes-Robertson of the Argyll and Sutherland Highlanders was indebted to the detective for his clearing up of his mystery, especially since blame had been apportioned to the chief Buddhist monk on the island of Ceylon. Holmes' intervention thus prevented serious religious conflict between the Hindis and Buddhists.

BALDWIN, Ted
Source: VALL
Biographical details: An American, member of the notorious Scowrers, a secret society based upon The Molly Maguires. Imprisoned through the efforts of Birdy Edwards (a Pinkerton detective), he served a ten-year sentence in a penitentiary sometime after 1875. Described as a "handsome, dashing young man of about the same age and build as McMurdo" (alias Edwards). Later he attempted to murder Edwards in England but was himself killed by Edwards, who had fled from Chicago, thence to California and thence to Kent in order to escape assassination attempts.

Circumstances: Baldwin, having spotted Douglas (alias McMurdo, alias Edwards) in Tunbridge Wells, then followed him to his moated house at the nearby village of Birlstone. A fight ensued during which Douglas' sawn-off shotgun exploded at close range in Baldwin's face, killing him. Douglas, acting quickly, changed clothes with Baldwin and then secreted himself in the house. Because of the mutilation of the victim's face, the police assumed the body to be that of Douglas. Close examination of both body and scene of crime by Holmes proved otherwise. The victim's clothes, having been tied into a bundle and weighted by a dumb-bell, were disposed of in the moat and later retrieved together. "The sawn gun was not more than two feet long; one could carry it easily under one's coat. There was no complete maker's name, but the printed letters `PEN' were on the fluting between the barrels, and the rest of the name had been cut off by the saw." Holmes observed that PEN stood for The Pennsylvania Small Arms Company, a well-known American firm.

The whole charge of both barrels had been received in the face and consequently the head had been "blown almost to pieces." The body was found on its back, the limbs outstretched.

At close range, shot enters in a solid mass and blasts a hole through the target. Hot gases and flame expelled from the barrel tear tissues and burn skin at this range. As a result, damage is massive and identification quite impossible if the charge is received in the face.

BARCLAY, Col. James
Source: CROO

Biographical details: A distinguished soldier, Colonel Barclay rose through the ranks of the British Army from sergeant to commander, and, after seeing considerable action at Bhurtee, in India, serving with the 117th Foot of the Royal Mallows, he later settled in Aldershot, where he lived with his wife, Nancy, at a house called Lachine. Died of apoplexy on September 9, 1889. Because of the suspicious circumstances surrounding his death, murder was suspected but not confirmed.

Circumstances: Found dead in the morning-room of Lachine, Aldershot, between 9 and 10 P.M. on Monday, September 9. The maid heard an altercation between Col. Barclay and his wife. She received no reply when knocking and found the door locked from the inside. Hearing screams, the coachman, whom the maid had summoned to her assistance, ran round to the outside of the house and gained entry via the French windows. He discovered Mrs. Barclay, stretched unconscious on a couch and the Colonel lying with his head on the ground near the corner of the fender. A ragged cut was discovered, some two inches long, at the back of his head, caused apparently by a violent blow from a blunt weapon. This surmise was later discovered to be incorrect. Close to the body was a club of hard carved wood with a bone handle. This was later discovered to belong to Henry Wood, Mrs. Barclay's visitor.

Cause of death: Apoplexy. (For details of this condition, see ARMITAGE/Cause of death). Colonel Barclay suffered an apoplectic attack and fell, hitting his head on the fender. Traces of blood and hair were noted there by Holmes.

BASKERVILLE, Sir Charles
Source: HOUN

Biographical details: Died May 1889. Lived at Baskerville Hall, Dartmoor, Devonshire only a short while (two years) before his demise. One of three brothers, both of whom died before him. The youngest, Rodger, died in 1876 in Central or South America. Was groomed as the probable Liberal candidate for the next general election. Regarded as amiable and extremely generous by his neighbours, he made large sums of money in South African speculation. A widower who was something of an eccentric. He suffered from heart disease.

Circumstances: Found dead at the end of the yew alley at Baskerville Hall on May 4, 1889 at 12 P.M. by Barrymore, the butler. Footprints seen at the scene of the death proved that Sir Charles had first walked, then run before collapsing of cardiac exhaustion. No signs of violence were apparent. The face was badly distorted, a symptom of dyspnoea (see below). For some days before his death, Sir Charles had complained of breathlessness and suffered acute attacks of nervous depression, exacerbated by his belief in the legendary Hound of the Baskervilles.

Cause of death: Heart failure. Sir Charles suffered from dyspnoea, which means difficulty in breathing. It is probable that he suffered from an aortic disease. Symptoms of this condition are shortness of breath, causing an inability to lie down, dropsy of the legs and feet, and mental excitability. Aortic disease leads to great dilatation and hypertrophy of the heart and frequently manifests itself later in life. Syphilis is especially likely to lead to a degeneration of the aortic valve.

BASKERVILLE, Sir Henry
Source: HOUN
Biographical details: Son of Sir Charles Baskerville's younger brother, and heir to the Baskerville estate. He first went to America but later made his living farming in Canada. Described as a "small, alert, dark-eyed man about thirty years of age, very sturdily built, with thick black eyebrows and a strong, pugnacious face," he travelled to London, where he stayed temporarily at the Northumberland Hotel. He was the victim of an elaborate murder plot authored by Jack Stapleton (q.v.), whose wife, Beryl, formed a romantic attachment with him. Although attacked by a giant

hound, he survived the ordeal, thanks to the attentions of Holmes and Watson.

BEDDINGTON
Source: STOC
One of two brothers who planned a robbery in the City of London. Beddington kept Hall Pycroft in Birmingham, posing as one Harry Pinner, while his brother, acting as Arthur Pinner, attempted to rob the firm of Mawson & Williams of £100,000 in bonds, murdering a watchman in the process. The Beddingtons attempted this daring crime following their release from five years' penal servitude. On hearing that his brother had been captured, Beddington attempted suicide.

Circumstances: Beddington attempted to hang himself by tying his braces round his neck and suspending himself from a hook behind the door of his inner office at New Street, Birmingham. "His knees were drawn up, his head hung at a dreadful angle to his body, and the clatter of his heels against the door made noise… " Beddington survived because he was cut down before he completely asphyxiated. He had reached the point of unconsciousness and his lips had turned purple, but Dr. Watson was able to resuscitate him.

BLESSINGTON
Source: RESI
Biographical details: A member of the Worthington Bank gang. His real name was Sutton. Died at 403 Brook Street, London, where he lived with Dr. Percy Trevelyan before being murdered. Claimed to suffer from a weak heart and was a man "of singular habits, very seldom going out." The nervous seizures which he exhibited, and which were noted by Dr. Trevelyan, were occasioned by the fear of his discovery by members of the gang, who sought revenge. Turned informer after his part in the Worthington Bank robbery incident, the four other gang members were brought to justice and one of these (Cartwright) was hanged. Three attempts were made on his life, the last of which succeeded.

Circumstances: Found hanging from a hook in the middle of his room. Death was made to look like suicide. He was dressed in a long night-dress, the cord of which had been tied round his neck, thus causing asphyxiation.

Cause of death: Asphyxiation. At first sight, Blessington appeared to have tied a cord about his neck, attached the cord to a hook, and then jumped off a box. "The neck was drawn out like a plucked chicken's, making the rest of him seem the more obese and unnatural by the contrast." The characteristics Blessington displayed are common to asphyxiation resulting from choking and strangulation. Blueness of the skin (cyanosis), congestion of the face, and burst blood capillaries (petechiae) are the characteristic signs. This process may take up to five minutes, during which the face becomes congested, the eyes bulge, and there are general convulsions. Asphyxiation is one of the commonest forms of death encountered by the investigator of homicide. Holmes deduced that Blessington was first given some form of trial by the three murderers. Then a block or pulley was attached to a beam and he was hanged from this.

Gavin Brend (in his enchanting Holmesian study, 'My Dear Holmes') has criticised Watson for not cutting down Blessington's body at once in order to determine if he were still alive. The appearance of the victim's face, however, would indicate that he was already beyond the call of help.

BRACKENSTALL, Sir Eustace
Source: ABBE
Biographical details: 1856-1897. Baronet, who lived at Marsham (near Chislehurst), Kent. One of the richest men in Kent, a confirmed drunkard, who mistreated his wife. Once drenched a dog (his wife's), with petroleum and set it on fire.

Circumstances: Found dead on the hearthrug in front of the dining-room fire. His two clenched hands were raised above his head and a heavy blackthorn stick lay across them. His head had been crushed by a heavy poker which had been curved by the force of the concussion. Lady Brackenstall (nee Mary Fraser) gave a false account of his murder to the police, attributing the crime to burglars who, she claimed, first attacked her and then her husband. But, as Holmes demonstrated, her testimony had to be false since there was blood on the chair where she had sat. The bell-rope, used to tie her up, could only have been cut down by an agile person, and the knots used were those known only to seafaring folk. In fact, the murder was committed by Mary's ex-lover, Captain Jack Croker.

Cause of death: Extensive head injuries. The body was lying on its back, the face "convulsed into a spasm of vindictive hatred." Brackenstall suffered the classic "coup" injury — a direct blow to the head. This results in a shatter fracture of the skull, and pieces of bone are driven into the soft brain matter which lies directly beneath the point of impact. Since the poker was found to be curved, the blow which struck the victim must have been delivered with considerable force, hence the considerable quantities of blood found about the room. The convulsions noted in the face were probably the result of rigor mortis, a condition which sets in within five hours of death and achieves completion after twelve hours. The condition is brought about by the coagulation of protein in the muscles, and the early signs manifest themselves in the eyelids and lower jaw.

BRUNTON, Richard
Source: MUSG
Biographical details: An ex-schoolmaster who was employed at Hurlstone Manor by Reginald Musgrave. Described as a "handsome well-grown" man with "a splendid forehead." Butler to the Musgrave family, he was regarded by Reginald as "a bit of a Don Juan." Since he became widowed, he enjoyed two affairs, one with Rachel Howells, the second housemaid at the manor, the other with Janet Tregellis, daughter of the head gamekeeper. Brunton came across the ancient Musgrave Ritual, and, with Rachel Howells, his accomplice, he located the family treasure in a cellar beneath the manor. Aged forty when he died.

Circumstances: Found crouched over a brass bound, wooden box in a small chamber measuring seven feet deep and four feet square. The chamber had been sealed by a large, heavy flagstone, thus cutting off the oxygen supply.

Cause of death: Asphyxiation. The man was squatting on his hams, with his forehead sunk on the edge of the box and his two arms thrown out on each side of it. "The attitude had drawn all the stagnant blood to his face," which had a "distorted, liver-coloured appearance." As less and less oxygen was available to Brunton, he would have experienced an effect known as oxygen starvation. Since the nerve cells are particularly prone to lack of oxygen (those of the brain start to die after eight minutes), deterioration would manifest itself in signs of dizziness and difficulty in breathing. The usual signs of cyanosis and petechial haemorrhages would account for the appearance of the face as described above. The exact circumstances of Brunton's death remain conjectural, since the flagstone may have shut accidentally or been dislodged from its wedge on purpose by Rachel Howells. We shall never know because Howells was not heard of again.

CARFAX, Lady Frances
Source: LADY
Biographical details: Sole survivor of the direct family of the late Earl of Rufton. Left with limited means, but among her valuables was some Spanish jewellery of remarkable hue. Middle-aged and beautiful in appearance. Disappeared whilst on holiday at Lausanne, Switzerland. Abducted by Holy Peters, who later attempted to murder her.

Circumstances: This was a case of attempted murder which almost succeeded. The circumstances of the crime are uniquely interesting. A coffin was constructed which would accommodate two bodies. In the base of the coffin the body of an old woman, Rose Spender, was placed and a death certificate obtained for her quite legitimately. Lady Carfax was then chloroformed and her unconscious form laid on top of the corpse. Holmes and Watson, acting quickly, were only just in time to prevent Lady Carfax being buried alive. She was revived by artificial respiration and injections of ether. The latter is a common treatment for overdoses of anaesthesia.

Chloroform has often been used to assist robbery, abduction, or rape. Death can result from the forced inhalation of chloroform and may be caused by a build-up of the poisonous fumes and a consequent paralysis of the heart. Lady Carfax would have had to inhale 10 to 15 ml. of chloroform to have suffered death, though this would have taken some hours to achieve. Even so, had the plot against her not been detected when it was, there is little doubt as to her eventual fate.

CAREY, Captain Peter

Source: BLAC

Biographical details: 1845-1895. Known as Black Peter, a seal and whaling captain. In 1883, he commanded the steam sealer Sea Unicorn of Dundee. He followed this with several other successful voyages and in 1884 retired, aged 39, to Woodman's Lee, near Forest Row, in Sussex. Lived there for six years until his murder. Described as a "strict Puritan" and a "silent, gloomy fellow." A violent man, prone to bouts of heavy drinking, he had been known to drive his wife and daughter out of doors in the middle of the night and flog them through the park. Once summoned for a savage assault on a vicar. Swarthy and bearded in appearance. His neighbours were said not to mourn his death. Murdered by Patrick Cairns, who attempted to blackmail him. Suspected of the murder of one Neligan, who disappeared overboard from the Sea Unicorn in August 1883.

Circumstances: Found murdered in a wooden outhouse several hundred yards from the house. Probably the crime took place around 2 A.M., following a dispute between Carey and Cairns over the former's involvement in Neligan's disappearance. At midday on the Wednesday, the maids entered the outhouse and discovered Carey impaled by a steel harpoon which had been driven into the wood of the wall behind him. Carey had died when the harpoon entered his chest. The harpoon was marked "S.S. Sea Unicorn, Dundee" and had been taken down from a rack on the wall. A coarse sealskin tobacco-pouch was found on the table bearing the initials "P.C." Also discovered was a notebook belonging to John Hopley Neligan, the missing man's son, who had twice attempted to enter the outhouse and on the second occasion succeeded, dropping the notebook in the process. As a consequence, he became a prime suspect and was arrested for murder.

Cause of death: Since a harpoon possesses a blunt but wide head, and was driven into the victim's chest with considerable force, injuries would have been extensive, no doubt resulting in haemorrhaging of the lungs and damage to the diaphragm. Holmes established the strength needed to impale Carey by stabbing at a dead pig swung from a meat hook in the back of Allardyce, a local butcher. He found that he was unable to transfix the carcass with a single blow and thus deduced that the murderer was a man of tremendous power and muscular development, used to wielding such a weapon. This ruled out Neligan, who was a rather underdeveloped youth of nervous disposition.

CUBITT, Hilton
Source: DANC

Biographical details: A Norfolk squire who was murdered while attempting to defend his wife. Described as a "tall, ruddy, clean-shaven gentleman." Cubitt's family came from Ridling Thorpe in Norfolk. He travelled to London, where he met Elsie Patrick, whom he married at a registry office. The couple returned to Norfolk, where they lived happily for about a year. By June 1898, Mrs. Cubitt began to receive a series of coded messages from Abe Slaney, a gangster from Chicago. Following a message from Mrs Cubitt, Slaney met her at Ridling Thorpe Manor in the early hours of the morning. Whilst attempting to abduct her, Slaney was surprised by Cubitt, who burst into the room and fired at him. Slaney fired back and shot him dead.

Circumstances: Found in his study, described as a "small chamber, facing an ordinary window." Slaney's revolver had been fired from the front and had penetrated the heart. Death was instantaneous. No powder marks were found either on the victim's dressing-gown or his hands. This ruled out suicide. Holmes deduced that the gun was fired from outside the room since he discovered a hole drilled through the lower window sash. Beneath the window a brazen cylinder was discovered which matched the ammunition in Slaney's gun.

Cause of death: The appearance of the wound on Slaney's body would have led Holmes to suspect a third person at the scene of the shooting, apart from other considerations. The neat round hole on the left of Cubitt's chest would indicate that Cubitt was facing the direction of the firearm when he was struck, and the absence of powder marks would suggest that the gun was fired at a distance much greater than eighteen inches. At the time of Cubitt's murder, firearms examination and ballistics were in their infancy, although, nine years before, Professor Lacassagne had made the first advances in bullet and gun-barrel comparison. It was not until the 1920s that the first comparison microscope was developed. Holmes's simple analysis, however, quickly proved that Cubitt must have been shot by an outside agent and the window closed after his departure. It would have been impossible for Cubitt to have committed suicide or for his wife to have shot him.

CUSHING, Mary
Source: CARD
Biographical details: One of three sisters who lived in Liverpool. Aged 29 when she married Jim Browner, a sailor who worked on packet steamers. Through her sister Sarah, she met Alec Fairbairn, who then became her lover. Fairbairn and Mary were murdered by Browner in a rowing boat at New Brighton, a popular coastal resort near Liverpool, probably sometime between the years 1885 and 1891.

Circumstances: Mary Cushing and her lover, Alec Fairbairn, hired a rowing boat at the New Brighton Parade, A mile from the shore, Browner attacked Fairbairn and fractured his skull with a blow from an oar. He then murdered his wife, tied both bodies to the boat, and sank it,"

Cause of death: Mary probably died of knife wounds. After he had committed the double murder, Browner severed one ear from each victim and posted them to Sarah Cushing, the intended target of his revenge. Unfortunately, the package was mailed to the wrong address. The idea of sending parts of a murder victim through the mails in order to shock was used by Jack the Ripper, who was suspected of posting one of the kidneys of his fourth victim to the police. Since the Ripper case took place in the late 80s it is conceivable that Browner had the Ripper in mind.

Holmes' examination of the ears showed a familiarity with anatomy. Since the ears had not been kept in carbolic or rectified spirits but in rough salt, the evidence pointed to a serious crime rather than a practical joke by a medical student, as first supposed by the authorities.

Holmes had written two short monographs on the subject of the human ear which had appeared in the Journal of Anthropology, A few months after the publication of CARD, The Strand Magazine reprinted the study under the title "A Chapter on Ears."

DOLSKY
Source: STUD
Biographical details: A man who was murdered at Odessa, a Russian seaport on the Black Sea. He was forced to take poison. Holmes compared the case to that of Enoch J. Drebber (STUD).

DREBBER, Enoch J.
Source: STUD
Biographical details: Son of one of the four elders of the Mormons of Utah. He persecuted and was responsible for the murder of John Ferrier, whose daughter Lucy became his eighth wife, He fled to Britain sometime between 1878 and 1886 with his secretary Joseph Stangerson but was eventually murdered by Jefferson Hope, probably on the 3rd of March at No. 3, Lauriston Gardens, Brixton. Aged 43 or 44 when he died, he was middle-sized, broad-shouldered, with crisp curling black hair and a short, stubby beard.

Circumstances: Drebber was found in a large, square, dilapidated room in a house off the Brixton Road. The body was on its back, the hands clenched and the arms thrown outwards. The legs were interlocked and the face distorted. A wedding-ring was found underneath the body, and about the body lay a number of blood splashes which did not come from the victim. In one corner of the room, across the plaster, was scrawled the word RACHE, which Holmes interpreted as the German for "Revenge." From evidence left at the scene of the crime, Holmes deduced that the murderer was a man more than six feet high, wearing coarse, square- toed boots and smoking a Trichonopoly cigar. He arrived at the house in a four-wheeled cab, had a florid face, and the fingernails of his right hand were extremely long. These conclusions were based upon an examination of (a) the road outside the house, (b) footprints, (c) the height at which RACHE was written, (d) marks on the plaster, and (e) cigar ash.

Cause of death: Holmes knew by smelling the dead man's mouth that an alkaloid poison had caused his death. The post mortem appearance of the risus sardonicus would also suggest a powerful alkaloid. The alkaloid paralyses the central nervous system, thus resulting in the "malignant and terrible contortion" exhibited by Drebber. Jefferson Hope related how, as a janitor at a laboratory at York College,. U.S.A., he obtained "some alkaloid. . . extracted from some South American arrow poison." This poison he worked into small pills. Various suggestions have been offered as to the identity of this poison. Even nicotine has been suggested. There are two realistic possibilities: (a) a South American alkaloid, (b) one that produces risus sardonicus. That said, our choice lies between curare and strychnos. Of the two, strychnos or chondodendron is most likely, since, although curare paralyses the muscles, it does not produce the facial distortions exhibited by Drebber. With strychnine (or strychnos), a small overdose produces violent contortions. The drug bends the victim double, while his face is twisted into a hideous grin. Convulsions such as this may last up to fifteen minutes, and death results from respiratory suffocation, The South American Indians collected this poison from the outer bark of the tree which produces it. The chondodendron tomentosum, obtained from a South American woody vine, produced an even stronger poison. It is probable that either of these poisons killed Drebber.

ERNEST, Dr. Ray (cf. AMBERLEY, Mrs. Josiah) Source: RETI
Biographical details: A doctor and chess-player who lived at
Lewisham. Murdered by Josiah Amberley because of his relationship with Amberley's wife.

Circumstances: Lured to the strong-room of The Haven, Amberley's house, and there murdered by coal-gas poisoning. Later, his body was dumped in a well in the garden.

Cause of death: Gassing. Carbon monoxide is the chief constituent of coal gas and is particularly dangerous because it has 300 times the affinity for oxygen that haemoglobin has. It converts haemoglobin into carboxy-haemoglobin and thereby deprives the tissues of the body of oxygen. The chemical has a special action on the ganglia at the base of the brain and the result is that permanent damage is often done in the early stages of intoxication.

FAIRBAIRN, Alec (cf. CUSHING, Mary)
Source: CARD

Biographical details: A sailor described as a "dashing, swaggering chap, smart and curled, who had seen half the world," whose affair with Mary Cushing cost him his life.

Circumstances: Murdered in a rowing boat along with his lover, Mary Cushing, at. New Brighton, Liverpool. Cause of death: Cranial injuries caused by several blows from an oar.

FERGUSON, Junior
Source: SUSS
Biographical details: Infant son of Robert Ferguson, tea broker of Mincing Lane and erstwhile associate of Doctor Watson. His mother shielded her step-son, Jack, despite witnessing an attack by him on her baby, and saved the infant by sucking poison from his wound. Circumstances: Scratched by a poison-tipped arrow for use with a small South American bird-bow. The poison was curare, a common poison used for hunting by South American natives. Its use was first noted by Sir Walter Raleigh. The type of bow and arrow in Ferguson's study still survives in museums. The arrow is approximately five feet long and has a detachable tip. Curare operates by blocking the impulses from brain to muscle, thus causing asphyxiation. The spaniel, which Holmes noted had been used as Jack's first victim, should have died from its effects. Claude Bernard, who investigated the poison in 1844, discovered that animals shot with curare-tipped arrows died within minutes. Curare has been used in small doses to relieve convulsions and to assist abdominal operations, although it is now rarely used.

FOURNAYE, Henri (alias LUCAS)
Source: SECO
Biographical details. An international agent, 34 years old, who lived two lives, one as Eduardo Lucas in London and the other as Henri Fournaye in Paris, where he lived with his French wife. He blackmailed Lady Hilda Trelawney Hope into stealing a Government document of international importance from her husband's despatch box. Murdered sometime between 1886 and 1894 by his wife at 16 Godolphin Street, Westminster, where he had lived for some years.

Circumstances: Murdered sometime after 10 P.M. The body was discovered at 11:45 P.M. by P.C. Barrett who, noticing the door of No. 16 ajar, entered and found the sitting-room in a state of disorder, the furniture being swept to one side and one chair lying on its back in the centre. Beside the chair, and grasping one of its legs, lay Fournaye.

Cause of death. Stabbing. A curved Indian dagger, plucked from a trophy of Oriental arms on the wall, had been plunged into Fournaye's heart. There were no signs of burglary in the room. A coroner's jury brought in a verdict of "wilful murder" and Fournaye's valet was arrested, but no case could be brought against him, since he had an alibi. Three days after the murder, Mme. Henri Fournaye was reported to the authorities in Paris as being insane. The police discovered that she had been in London at the time of Fournaye's murder, and a motive was subsequently established. This was further substantiated by the evidence of Lady Hilda, who was an eyewitness to the murder. Mine. Fournaye killed her husband in an insane fit of jealousy because she suspected he had committed adultery with Lady Hilda.

GARCIA, Aloysius
Source: WIST
Biographical details: Son of a high dignitary of San Pedro, South America, wronged by Don Juan Murillo. He tried to murder Murillo in England but was himself murdered by Murillo, who was living under the alias of Mr. Henderson, of High Gables, near Esher. The crime took place sometime between 1896 and 1902. Garcia was one of a number of revolutionaries who banded together to seek vengeance on Murillo when the latter escaped from South America. Garcia was of Spanish descent and was living temporarily at Wisteria Lodge, a large house situated about a mile from Oxshott Common.

Circumstances: Garcia's body was found on Oxshott Common, nearly a mile from his home. He was lured to Murillo's house and murdered as he approached the front door by Murillo himself, who had taken refuge in some gorse bushes. The body was then taken to Oxshott Common and there dumped. When found by the police, it was noted that the head had been smashed to pulp by heavy blows from a sandbag which had crushed the skull but caused no wounding. He had been struck down from behind and the majority of blows administered after death. No attempt had been made to rob the victim, and no footprints were discovered at the scene of the discovery.

Cause of death: Blows to the head from a blunt instrument such as a sandbag are extremely common in the annals of crime. The head is frequently a target, as are the knees and elbows. Blunt, round-headed weapons tend to cause star-shaped wounds, and, when administered to the skull, a weapon such as a sandbag causes a range of fractures, depending on the strength of the blow and the area of impact. Haemorrhage and brain damage are the immediate consequence.

GIBSON, Maria

Source. THOR

Biographical details: Formerly Maria Pinto, Brazilian by birth, and daughter of a Government official at Manaos. Past her prime when she married J. Neil Gibson, an American senator and gold-mining magnate. Lived with her husband in a manor house at Thor Place near Winchester. Committed suicide in such a manner as to implicate her governess, Miss Grace Dunbar. Died in October of 1900 or 1901.

Circumstances: Found in the grounds of Thor Place estate, nearly half a mile from the house, clad in her dinner dress. A revolver bullet was found in her brain, but no weapon was found near her. Her governess was considered a prime suspect since a revolver was found in her wardrobe with a calibre which corresponded to the bullet in the victim's brain and one discharged chamber. The shot was fired from close quarters (just behind the right temple). The body lay on its back, and there were no signs of a struggle. A short note from the governess was found in the victim's hand, asking for an appointment with her by Thor Bridge. A chip in the stonework of the bridge suggested a complex suicide to Holmes, who proved that the revolver had been attached by a piece of string to a heavy stone and once discharged, was then whisked over the edge of the bridge into the waters of Thor Mere.

Cause of death: Suicide by shooting. The revolver placed by Mrs. Gibson in Miss Dunbar's wardrobe was probably an ivory-handled

Whitneyville armoury revolver, taking a standard .22 rim-fire short case, first developed by Smith and Wesson in 1856. The revolver used by Mrs. Gibson to kill herself was a Webley hammerless .320. It had six chambers, a stirrup catch without the familiar thumb-lever, and a shotgun type safety catch.

Mrs. Gibson would have sustained a contact wound, in which the muzzle of the gun is placed directly against the skin. Often in cases such as this, an imprint of the gun-muzzle is found as a bruise and scorching is exhibited around the entry wound. Powder tattooing is common, together with grease particles and pieces of lead stripped from the bullet. The absence of a struggle in the vicinity of the body would suggest possible suicide to the investigator. A detailed examination of the barrel of the weapon found in Grace Dunbar's wardrobe and a comparison with the bullet taken from the victim's brain would clear her of suspicion in a modern murder investigation. In 1900, however, the science of ballistics had yet to be properly established.

GIORGIANO, Giuseppe
Source: REDC
Biographical details: The leader of a notorious Mafia-type Organisation known as the Red Circle. A man with the body of a giant, he earned the name of "Death" in Southern Italy and emigrated to America to escape the Italian police. He was known to have committed at least fifty murders, his victims comprising rich Italians whom the Red Circle attempted to blackmail. Came to England in pursuit of Gennaro Lucca, another member of the Circle who had taken part in a conspiracy to murder Castalotte, an Italian businessman. Lucca pre-warned Castalotte and thus became a target of Giorgiano's vengeance. Murdered by Lucca in a flat in Howe Street in 1893.

Circumstances: Giorgiano was found in a flat on the third floor of a house in Howe Street, London. The body was lying on its back, the knees drawn up, the hands thrown out, and a knife projecting from his throat. By his right hand lay a horn-handled, two-edged dagger and beside it a black glove. Outlined on the bare boards were a number of footsteps, etched in blood.

Cause of death: Stabbing. Since the knife was found still in the throat, the blow was probably delivered with some force. The considerable quantity of blood discovered around the body would suggest that the carotid artery had been severed. Death would occur within minutes.

HATHERLEY, Victor
Source: ENGR
Biographical details: Born 1864, an orphan and bachelor of 16A Victoria Street, London. By profession, Hatherley was a hydraulic engineer. In 1880, he was apprenticed to Venner and Matheson, a Greenwich firm, and in 1887, following an inheritance from his father's death, Hatherley set up his own business in Victoria Street. In 1889, following limited success, he was approached by "Colonel Lysander Stark," a forger working under an alias at a house in Eyford, Berkshire. Hatherley was described as a young man "quietly dressed in a suit of heather tweed" and with "a strong, masculine face" of about 25 years of age.
Circumstances: Hatherley was asked to examine a fault in the mechanism of a hydraulic press which had been used for coining. Realising that Hatherley's suspicions had been aroused, Colonel Stark attempted to crush Hatherley in the machine. Hatherley escaped through a small partition in one of the wooden walls of the press room. He later suffered an amputated thumb in his efforts to escape from the house.

HAYLING, Jeremiah
Source: ENGR
Biographical details: 1862-1888. A hydraulic engineer who disappeared from his lodgings at 10P.M. one night, presumably in 1888.
Circumstances: Probably murdered by Colonel Lysander Stark of Eyford, Berkshire, since his disappearance preceded the attempted murder of Victor Hatherley (q.v.).
Cause of death: Unknown.

HEIDEGGER
Source: PRIO

Biographical details: A German teacher at The Priory preparatory school, where he took special charge of Lord Saltire, the Duke of Holdernesse's ten-year-old son. Went missing on Wednesday, May 14, 1901, along with Lord Saltire. His bed had not been slept in and his bicycle was missing. Found murdered on a piece of heathland known as the Ragged Shaw. Described as a "silent, morose man, not very popular either with masters or boys."

Circumstances: Heidegger's body was found five miles from the Priory School amongst thick gorse bushes. From the bicycle tracks which appeared on the footpath, Holmes deduced that the rider had fallen sideways, remounted, and then finally collapsed. Bloodstains were found on gorse bushes approaching the spot where the body was discovered, and more traces of blood were smeared across the front of the bicycle. The victim was found lying on his back, wearing shoes but no socks and a nightshirt beneath an open coat.

Cause of death: Haemorrhaging of the brain as a consequence of severe blows to the head from a heavy stick. Heidegger was murdered by Reuben Hays, the landlord of the Fighting Cock Inn, who assisted in the abduction of Lord Saltire.

Death from a stick or club is common in the annals of murder, and the head is a frequent target. Usually, several blows are required to kill the victim because of the rigidity of the skull, As a consequence, the scene of such murders is frequently blood-spattered, as is the murderer's clothing.

HOLMES, SHERLOCK
Source: DYIN, EMPT, FINA, ILLU, REIG
Biographical details: Of mixed French and English origin, Holmes was born probably c. 1854. After a university education, he began his career about the year 1878, advertising himself as "the world's first private consulting detective." By 1889, he claimed to have dealt with five hundred cases of importance, and this had grown to nearly a thousand by 1891. His mid-career culminated with the destruction of Professor Moriarty's criminal fraternity, a feat which led to his temporary disappearance from London (c.1888-94). From 1894 to 1901, he investigated hundreds of cases and achieved such public renown that he was offered a knighthood by King

Edward VII (June 1902). He retired c. 1903 to a cottage on the Sussex Downs and devoted his declining years to bee-keeping. Prior to the outbreak of the First World War, he assisted the British Government by acting as a double agent. His efforts led to the arrest of Von Bork, the Prussian spy.

Circumstances: Because of the nature of his occupation, Holmes frequently risked death in the course of his career. The Cunninghams (REIG) attempted to strangle him on realising that their murder of William Kirwan had been revealed by him; Holmes's cries of help saved his life on this occasion. Baron Gruner (ILLU) hired two thugs to attack Holmes outside the Cafe Royal in Regent Street, London. Armed with sticks, they beat him about the head and body, and Holmes sustained two lacerated scalp wounds and considerable bruising, but managed to protect himself with his stick before the men made off into Glasshouse Street.(see Vol. 2 under Weapons). Culverton Smith (DYIN) sent him an ivory box which, when opened, uncoiled a spring tipped with a bacterial poison; his suspicions already aroused, Holmes was able to lay a trap for Smith by pretending that he had contracted the disease and become its victim.

Three attempts were made on Holmes' life in 1891 by the minions of Professor James Moriarty. He was almost run over by a two-horse van on the corner of Bentinck Street and Welbeck Street. Whilst walking down Vere Street, a brick was hurled at him from the roof of a house, and, in the course of visiting Dr. Watson's consulting-rooms, he was attacked by a rough with a bludgeon. On May 4, 1891, he faced his toughest ordeal when lured to the falls of Reichenbach, near Meiringen, Switzerland, by Professor Moriarty himself. The Professor attempted to pitch Holmes into the precipice but himself became the victim when Holmes used his technique of Japanese wrestling. On his return, incognito, to London, he again faced danger in the form of Colonel Sebastian Moran, an Indian Army officer and Moriarty's chief of staff. Moran fired a dumdum bullet at an effigy of Holmes through the windows of Baker Street in an attempt to assassinate him, an action which led to his immediate arrest.

KIRWAN, William
Source: REIG

Biographical details: Coachman employed by the Cunningham family, who was murdered in Reigate, Surrey, in Z1887. He had served the Cunningham family for years and was described as an honest man. Kirwan lived in a lodge with his mother, who became half-witted after the news of his death was brought to her.

Circumstances: According to Alec Cunningham, Kirwan sounded the alarm in the house at 11:45 P.M. Hearing Kirwan call for help, Alec Cunningham claimed he saw Kirwan struggling with a burglar outside the house. A shot was then fired, and the murderer escaped. Holmes cast doubt on the authenticity of Cunningham's statement since (a) the revolver that killed Kirwan must have been fired from a distance of just over four yards, because there was no powder blackening on the clothes, (b) the "murderer" would not have had time to tear the rendezvous note from Kirwan's hand and make good his escape, and (c) no footprints were discovered in the ditch nearby. Cunningham had lured Kirwan to his death by means of the note because he had witnessed the burglary which the Cunningham father and son had carried out at the Actons' house.

Cause of death: Shooting. Probably Kirwan received the shot in the chest, neck, or head. He may well have died of haemorrhaging.

KRATIDES, Paul
Source: GREE
Biographical details: A young man from Athens who was lured to England by the circumstances of his sister's infatuation with Harold Latimer, "a man of the foulest antecedents." Latimer kept Kratides a prisoner in a house in Beckenham, where he subjected him to torture and starvation in an attempt to force the Greek to sign away his own and his sister's property. Latimer engaged an interpreter to communicate with Kratides, since the latter spoke no English. The interpreter, like Kratides, was overcome by charcoal fumes whilst being held a prisoner but, unlike Kratides, he lived.

Circumstances: Kratides was found in an upstairs room of a house in Beckenham, along with his Greek interpreter, a Mr. Melas. A burner set on a small brass tripod in the centre of the room was burning charcoal. Melas had been struck with a life-preserver (club) and then, like Kratides, tied to a chair. Although Melas recovered from his ordeal, Kratides, who was weak from starvation, did not.

Cause of death: Gassing. Charcoal contains carbon monoxide, and, like gas, it acts quickly as a blood poison, displacing the oxygen which is carried to the body by the haemoglobin. The "blue-lipped" appearance of both men, coupled with their symptoms of "swollen, congested faces and protruding eyes" suggests asphyxia was fairly far advanced. The administering of "ammonia and brandy" to Melas was inadvisable and therefore puzzling. More effective would have been the "kiss of life" treatment which restores oxygen to the bloodstream of the victim.

LETURIER
Source: STUD
Biographical details: Unknown. Holmes mentioned the case of Leturier when discussing the forcible administration of poison (cf. DREBBER, Enoch J.).

LUCAS: see FOURNAYE, Henri

McCARTHY, Charles
Source: BOSC
Biographical details: An Australian farmer who emigrated to England, where for years he lived off the wealth of his neighbour, John Turner, in Boscombe Valley, Herefordshire. In the 1860s, McCarthy was the driver of a gold convoy journeying from Ballarat to Melbourne, which was hijacked by Turner. Turner escaped to England, though three of his companions were shot. McCarthy also returned to England, where he fared badly. A chance encounter with Turner in Regent Street, London, led McCarthy to blackmail Turner and to demand land, money, and property from him. When McCarthy insisted that his son marry Turner's daughter, Turner killed him.

Circumstances: McCarthy was found dead in a wood near the family's home. He was discovered by a girl of fourteen, Patience Moran, daughter of the lodge-keeper, who reported the body to William Crowder, a gamekeeper. McCarthy's son accompanied Crowder and the girl to a small pond, near which they observed McCarthy lying in a pool of blood. His head appeared to have been "beaten in" by repeated blows from a heavy blunt weapon. Further detail was supplied by the police surgeon, who reported that: "The posterior third of the left parietal bone and the left half of the occipital bone had been shattered by a blow from a blunt weapon." Watson "marked the spot upon my own head. Surely such a blow must have been struck from behind. . . . When seen quarrelling [the son] was face to face with his father." Watson's observation is shrewd, for it suggests a third person at the scene of the crime. Holmes observed: "The blow was struck from immediately behind and yet was upon the left side. Now, how can that be unless it were by a left-handed man." The part of the skull with which we are concerned is the base, and the gun-butt would have hit this part, since the man was tall and was struck from the rear. It does not automatically mean, however, that the man was left-handed. For instance, the man could easily have turned to his left and encountered a blow to the parietal and occipital bones, delivered from a rifle held in the right hand.

Cause of death: Brain injury and loss of blood through haemorrhaging. Fracturing of the skull and ruptured blood-vessels frequently result from a blow of this kind.

McPHERSON, Fitzroy
Source: LION
Biographical details: A young science teacher who was employed at Stackhurst's coaching establishment, The Gables, a private school near Fulworth, close to Beachy Head, Sussex. He was a natural athlete, despite suffering heart trouble (a consequence of rheumatic fever). He died in July 1907 whilst swimming in the small lagoon which lay at the base of the Sussex cliffs. Although murder was suspected, he died of natural causes, being the victim of the stings of a jellyfish.

Circumstances: McPherson managed to stagger out of the water and make his way up the cliff path before dying of heart failure. Holmes and Harold Stackhurst (proprietor of The Gables coaching establishment) witnessed his death. He was dressed in an overcoat, trousers, and an unlaced pair of canvas shoes. As he fell forward his back was exposed to view. Holmes noted that it was covered in dark red lines "as though he had been terribly flogged by a thin wire scourge." There were long, angry weals on his shoulders and ribs. The victim had bitten through his lower lip as a result of the agonies he had suffered.

Cause of death: Heart failure, caused by excessive shock to the central nervous system. The agent of McPherson's death was the creature known as *cyanea capillata*. It is described in 'Out of Doors' by J. G. Wood as "a loose roundish mass of tawny membranes and fibres, something like very large handfuls of lion's mane and silver paper." Wood goes on to describe how, when bathing off the Kentish coast, he encountered the creature, which, even at a distance of fifty feet, "radiated almost invisible filaments." He explains: "The multitudinous threads caused light scarlet lines upon the skin which on closer examination resolved into minute dots or pustules, each dot charged as it were with a red-hot needle making its way through the nerves." The effect on the victim is to cause a series of pangs in the chest. After these pulsations, says Wood, "the heart would give six or seven leaps" as if forcing its way through his chest. Wood survived the ordeal, but McPherson, who suffered a weak heart, succumbed. This jellyfish was first identified in 1848 by Edward Forbes, who called it "the terror of tender skinned bathers." Since there has been no recorded fatality attributable to jellyfish poisoning, doubts have been cast on the identity of the Cyanea Capillata. The editors of the Catalogue of the 'Sherlock Holmes Exhibition,' (1951) have suggested that the creature was more likely to have been the deadly Portugese Man-of-War, a close relative of Cyanea and more deadly if encountered. A large specimen would certainly kill a healthy man. When fully extended, its tentacles can reach to fifty feet from the float.

MILVERTON, Charles Augustus
Source: CHAS
Biographical details: A high-society blackmailer, whose speciality was the paying of very high sums of money for compromising letters. Milverton established a network of valets and maids whom he kept in his employ. He once paid £700 to a footman for a note two lines in length (a considerable sum of money in the 1880s). Holmes claimed that he had hundreds of people in his thrall in London. He was described as a man of fifty, with a "large, intellectual head, a round, plump, hairless face, a perpetual frozen

smile and two keen grey eyes." He was murdered at his home, Appledore Towers, Hampstead, by an unknown assailant, probably in 1889.

Circumstances: Shot in his study by a woman passing as one of his contacts. He received several shots in the chest from a range of two feet. Facial bruising was also sustained since the attacker "ground her heel into his upturned face."

Cause of death: Probably died of heart or lung failure, following massive damage to major arteries and organs. The weapon used to kill Milverton was probably a small pistol, like the .320-bore Webley No. 2. This was the smallest (but practicable) pocket weapon of its time. (see Vol2, Weapons).When Holmes referred in SPEC to "an Eley's No. 2," he was probably talking about the same weapon. "Eley" was the name given to the cartridges which fitted weapons of this type, not the gun.

MURILLO, Don Juan
Source: WIST
Biographical details: A South American dictator, also known as the Tiger of San Pedro, responsible for the death of Aloysius Garcia (q.v.). After escaping his pursuers, he was murdered with his secretary, Signor Rulli, in their room at the Hotel Escurial at Madrid. The murderers were never apprehended.

Cause of death: Unknown.

OPENSHAW, Colonel Elias
Source: FIVE
Biographical detail.: Emigrating to America when he was young, Elias Openshaw became a planter in Florida, where he did well. During the Civil War, he fought in Jackson's army, and afterwards under Hood, where he achieved the rank of Colonel. About 1869 or 1870, he took a small estate in Sussex, near Horsham. Described as a "fierce, quick tempered" and "foul-mouthed" man when angry, he was nevertheless of a retiring disposition. When he left the U.S.A., he had in his possession vital documents belonging to the Ku Klux Klan which he refused to return. He was sent a death threat in the form of five dried orange pips. He died in 1883

Opeshaw was found in the garden of his house. A coroner's verdict of suicide was certainly incorrectly applied.

Circumstances: Openshaw was found face downwards in a little, green-scummed pool, at the foot of the garden on the night of May 21, 1883. There were no signs of violence, and the water in which he drowned was only two feet deep.

Cause of death: Drowning. This is an unusual form of murder. Death is caused by asphyxia, a state in which the oxygen is cut off from the brain. It is possible that he may have died of cardiac arrest. The classic signs which Openshaw would have exhibited are froth at the mouth and nostrils. His murderers clearly took great pains to cover their traces, since there were no signs of a struggle at the scene of the crime and the body bore no marks of bruising visible to the coroner.

OPENSHAW, John
Source: FIVE
Biographical details: 1865-1887. Son of Joseph Openshaw, John received the identical message which had been sent to his father. Described as a young man of 22, "well-groomed and trimly clad," John was murdered on his way to Waterloo Station.

Circumstances: A newspaper carried the following account: "Between nine and ten last night Police Constable Cook, of the H division, on duty near Waterloo Bridge, heard a cry for help and a splash in the water. The night, however, was extremely dark and stormy, so that, in spite of the help of several passersby, it was quite impossible to effect a rescue… The body was eventually recovered. It proved to be… John Openshaw… The body exhibited no traces of violence, and there can be no doubt that the deceased had been the victim of an unfortunate accident."

Cause of death: Drowning. There is little doubt that John Openshaw, like his father, was pushed to his death.

OPENSHAW, Joseph

Source: FIVE

Biographical details: Brother of Elias Openshaw (q.v.) and father of John Openshaw (q.v.), who came to live at Horsham, Sussex, early in 1884. On January 4, 1885; Joseph received an envelope containing five dried orange pips and a message which asked him to place certain papers pertaining to the Ku Klux Klan on the sundial in the garden. This he could not do, since his brother had burnt them. On January 7, he visited a friend at Portsdown Hill but failed to return. He was found dead at the bottom of a chalk-pit near Fareham. Circumstances: Openshaw had sustained a shattered skull and was found in a deep chalk-pit, where he had been lying, untended, for some days. A coroner's court returned the verdict of "Death from accidental causes." No footprints were seen near the body, nor were there any signs of violence.

Cause of death: There is little doubt that Openshaw was pushed over the edge of the chalk-pit and fell, suffering severe cranial injuries.

PINNER, Harry: see BEDDINGTON

PRESCOTT, Rodger
Source: 3GAB
Biographical details: Died 1895. A forger and coiner who was shot by Killer Evans in a night-club in the Waterloo Road in January 1895. Prescott, like Evans, was from Chicago, and his banknote counterfeiting plates were greatly sought after by the latter.
Circumstances: Unknown
Cause of death: Shooting. Details unknown.

RATCLIFF HIGHWAY MURDERS, The Source: STUD
Biographical details: Referred to in the newspaper report in STUD, Ratcliff Highway is a road in the London borough of Stepney, subsequently renamed St. George's Street. Holmes, it will be recalled, sent "a couple of messages" to "Sumner, shipping agent" in BLAC. A number of murders took place here in the early nineteenth century.

On December 7, 1811, a family known as the Marrs were found brutally murdered in their East End shop. In less than a fortnight, another massacre occurred. This time the victims were the landlord of a pub in Gravel Lane and his wife. Four days later on, an Irish sailor was arrested on suspicion of the murders. His name was Williams. At first, the evidence was hardly convincing. Fresh evidence, collected from witnesses who knew the publican, was only circumstantial (for instance, a laundress, who washed Williams' linen, stated that he had given her a shirt to wash which was torn and bloodstained). While the inquiry was still in progress, Williams hanged himself in his cell at Cold-bath Fields prison. Although Williams' and the Marrs' pasts were connected, no real motive for the murders of the victims was satisfactorily established.

RONDER
Source: VEIL
Biographical details: Died c. 1889. A showman and circus owner. A rival of Wombwell and Sanger, he was at the top of his profession. His addiction to alcohol turned him into "a huge bully of a man" who "cursed and slashed at everyone who came in his way." Married Eugenia Ronder, whom he mistreated and beat into submission. Prosecuted for assault and cruelty to animals on numerous occasions, his business began to decline and his wife planned his death with her lover, Leonardo, a circus employee.

Circumstances: Ronder was murdered by Leonardo at night whilst on his way to feed one of the circus lions. Leonardo had made a club with a head to which he fastened five long steel .nails. The points of the nails were spread outwards so as to represent a lion's paw.

Cause of death: Cranial injuries. The degree of injury caused by a blow to the head depends on the velocity and weight of the weapon, and the effect depends on the size of the area bearing the weight of impact. In the case of a nail (or series of nails), the tissue will disintegrate and bone fragments will be scattered through the brain, even though the nail itself may not enter the cranium.

ROYLOTT, Dr. Grimesby
Source: SPEC
Biographical details: (see also above). The only son of an aristocratic pauper squire, a member of what was once one of the richest families in

England. Four successive heirs in the eighteenth century, followed by a Regency gambler, diminished the family estates to a few acres of ground and a 200-year-old house at Stoke Moran, on the western borders of Surrey. Grimesby Roylott obtained a medical degree and emigrated to Calcutta, where, by his professional skill and force of character, he established a large practice. Whilst in India, he married Mrs. Stoner, the young widow of a major-general in the Bengal Artillery. The family emigrated to England and lived in the ancestral home. Dr. Roylott's wife died in a railway accident at Crewe, although she left a considerable annuity for her two daughters, Helen and Julia. Roylott, who had psychopathic tendencies and a taste for sadism, indulged in numerous brawls with local people, including the blacksmith, whom he hurled into a stream in a fit of anger. Whilst in Calcutta, he beat his native butler to death and narrowly escaped a capital sentence. He died in 1883 whilst attempting to murder his youngest step-daughter, Helen.

Circumstances: Roylott had contrived to kill his stepdaughter Julia by training an Indian swamp-adder to enter her room via a ventilator in the bedroom wall, wind its way down a bell-rope, and then bite her whilst she was asleep. This he succeeded in doing. When he attempted to repeat the crime, this time with Helen as his victim, the snake's temper was aroused by Holmes's attack on it. The creature then returned through the ventilator and bit its trainer, with fatal consequences.

Cause of death: Snake-bite. According to Holmes, Roylott died "within ten seconds of being bitten." There is, in fact, no known snake venom which will kill its victim within ten seconds. It is possible that Dr. Roylott died of a heart attack and that the snake bit him after he was dead. The term "swamp adder" is too vague a description. Since the "speckled band" left "two little dark punctures" in its victims, and it was of Indian origin, it must have belonged to one of two families, the Elapidae or the Viperidie. The Indian viper leaves two puncture wounds in its victim. According to Douglas Lawson ('The Speckled Band - What Was It?', BSJ, 1954, vol. 4,, no. 1), Roylott was killed by the Echis Carinata. This viper has a brown-grey body with three longitudinal series of whitish, black-edged spots, a close approximation to the "yellow with brown specks" of Watson's description. The Echis Carinata carries a hemotoxic venom which invades the haemoglobin. Death from a snake of this type is much slower than from a snake which carries a neurotoxic venom - one that acts on the nervous system.

SAVAGE, Victor

Source: DYIN

Biographical details: The nephew of Culverton Smith, he died of an Asiatic disease administered to him by his uncle.

Circumstances: Unknown.

Cause of death: Bacteriological poisoning. Although the "Black Formosa corruption" and "Tapanuli Fever," either of which Savage appeared to have fallen victim to, are not known by medical science, it could well have been a typhoid culture similar to that used by the Frenchman, Henri Girard, in 1912. It undoubtedly came from the island of Sumatra, where Smith had been a planter.

SELDEN

Source: HOUN

Biographical details: Died 1889. The brother of Mrs. Barrymore, also known as "the Notting Hill murderer." Selden's crime was one in which Holmes took an interest because of the peculiar ferocity of the murder. He was sentenced to death, but the sentence was commuted since there were doubts as to Selden's sanity. According to Mrs. Barrymore, Selden was humoured too much as a child and corrupted by his criminal associates. He was imprisoned at Princetown, Dartmoor, from which he escaped. Here he was able to remain in hiding with help from his older sister until his death. He had an "evil, yellow face, a terrible animal face, all seamed and scored with vile passions," a "bristling beard," and "small, cunning eyes." (see especially article in vol. 2).

Circumstances: Selden had the misfortune to be wearing Sir Henry Baskerville's clothes, a circumstance which led to his death, since the hound kept by Stapleton was trained to pursue Sir Henry. Holmes, in conversation with Stapleton, maintains that Selden "appears to have broken his neck by falling over these rocks." This statement appears accurate until we examine Watson's description. Selden was "face downwards upon the ground, the head doubled under him at a horrible angle, the shoulders rounded and the body hunched together as if in the act of throwing a somersault...The gleam of the match.. . shone upon his clotted fingers and. . . the ghastly pool which widened slowly from the crushed skull of the victim."

The inaccuracy of Holmes' statement to Stapleton now becomes apparent. A man with a crushed skull is far more likely to have died of injuries sustained to the cranium than to have merely "broken his neck." Holmes must have known that Selden's injuries had been sustained as a result of an attack, not from a fall. Perhaps he wished to allay any suspicion Stapleton may have entertained as to the real cause of Selden's death. Cause of death: Since Selden's skull was crushed, he had probably been struck a series of blows from a heavy, blunt weapon from behind, as he stood on the rocks. The position of the body, as described by Watson, indicates that he fell forwards, breaking his neck as a consequence. The considerable loss of blood from the area of the skull suggests that Selden died of cranial injuries.

SHOLTO, Bartholomew
Source: SIGN
Biographical details: 1858-1888. One of two sons of Major John Sholto (d. 1882), an Indian Army officer. Major Sholto was involved in the theft of the famous Agra Treasure and the betrayal of Jonathan Small. Bartholomew and his brother Thaddeus searched for six years for the hidden treasure after the death of their father at Pondicherry Lodge, Upper Norwood. Bartholomew discovered the treasure in a small garret, which had been sealed up, and this he worked out by a process of mathematical deduction. The half-million pounds sterling which the treasure was worth was never enjoyed by Bartholomew, since it was stolen by Jonathan Small and his native assistant, Tonga.

Circumstances: Sholto was found sitting in a wooden armchair inside a locked room. He had been dead for several hours. His head was sunk on his left shoulder and his face was twisted into "an inscrutable smile." On the table beside him lay a brown, close-grained stick with a stone head like a hammer. Beside it was a piece of paper bearing the words "The sign of the four." A long, dark thorn was found stuck in the skin just above the victim's ear. Marks of a wooden stump were found on the floor of the room and a boot-mark on the windowsill. Small's ally, Tonga, gained access to the room via a trap-door in the roof, and prints of a small, naked foot were found in the immediate vicinity of the garret.

Cause of death: Sholto died as a result of poisoning. His features were set in an unnatural grin. Holmes observed that "The muscles. . . are in a state of extreme contraction, far exceeding the usual rigor mortis," suggesting "Death from some powerful vegetable alkaloid ... some strychnine-like substance which would produce tetanus." The thorn which Watson examined was "long, sharp and black, with a glazed look near the point as though some gummy substance had dried upon it." It came from a blow-pipe described as "a short, round piece of wood, like a school-ruler," and we have Holmes's word for it that "the poison acts so quickly that the man was dead before Jonathan Small ever. . . reached the room." If, as it appears likely, Sholto died in about five minutes, then it is unlikely that the poison employed was strychnine, for this takes up to fifteen minutes to kill its victim. The Upas (a member of the mulberry family,) grows in Ceylon, Java, Burma, Borneo, and India. The gum extracted from it has been described as "thick, dark-brown," and "resinous." The poison it contains, known as antiarin, can kill within a few moments of entering the bloodstream. The natives who employed the substance used arrows with a detachable, sharp point which would stay in the flesh for some moments. The effect of the poison was to produce violent tetanus convulsions, leading to paralysis of the central nervous system and respiratory failure. The circumstances of Sholto's murder suggested parallel cases to Holmes, from India and Senegambia.

SMITH, Willoughby
Source: GOLD
Biographical details: Died 1894. A young graduate who was in the employ of Professor Coram of Yoxley Old Place, Kent, when murdered. Following a public school education at Uppingham and a degree from Cambridge, he was employed by Coram as secretary, taking dictation in the mornings and researching in the afternoons.
Circumstances: The maid, Susan Tarlton, heard a cry from the room immediately below hers between 11 A.M. and 12 noon. The cry was

followed by a heavy thud, which "shook the old house." Smith's body lay stretched on the floor of the study, and there was blood pouring from the underside of his neck. A small sealing-wax knife had been sunk into the neck, splitting the carotid artery. The weapon, which had an ivory handle and stiff blade, had been taken from Professor Coram's writing desk. Smith was murdered by an enemy of the Professor, called Anna, who attacked Smith after being seized by him. She had been trying to procure a diary and letters from the Professor's writing desk which would enable her to persuade the Russian government to release her colleague.

Cause of death: Stabbing. The carotid artery is one of the two main arteries which supply the blood to the head. The severing of this artery would cause stupor, leading to coma and death.

STANGERSON, Joseph
Source: STUD
Biographical details: Born 1835. Son of one of the four principal leaders of the Mormon community in Utah. Had four wives and enjoyed a prominent position in the Mormon community. Because he was refused the hand of John Ferrier's daughter, Lucy, Stangerson had him murdered on August 4, 1860. Lucy Ferrier finally married Enoch Drebber, since Drebber had a stronger claim to matrimony than Stangerson. Drebber and Stangerson rebelled against the authority of the elder Mormons and left Utah, travelling to Europe. Stangerson was murdered by Jefferson Hope, who had spent twenty years tracking him down and stabbed him to death in vengeance.

Circumstances: Stangerson's body was discovered at 8 A.M. by Inspector Lestrade of Scotland Yard in a room at Halliday's Private Hotel. The room on the second floor was locked, and, on being forced, Lestrade saw Stangerson's body lying in a nightdress, huddled beside an open window. Since the body was already rigid, Lestrade deduced that the victim had died at around 6 A.M. The word RACHE, meaning vengeance, was written above the body, in letters of blood. Bloodstains were found in the washbasin of the room and on the bedsheets, indicating that the murderer, Jefferson Hope, had washed his hands and wiped the blade of his knife clean before leaving by the window.

Cause of death: A deep knife stab in the left side of the victim, which penetrated the heart.

STONER, Julia
Source. SPEC
Biographical details: 1851-1891. Daughter of Major-General Stoner, an officer of the Bengal Artillery, who died between 1850 and 1853. His widow, Mrs. Stoner, (d. 1875), married Dr. Grimesby Roylott shortly before dying in a railway accident near Crewe. In 1867, Julia and her sister came to live at Stoke Moran, Sussex, Roylott's family home. If married, Julia stood to gain an income of £250 from Mrs. Stoner's total income at death of £1,100. It was because of her impending marriage that Dr. Roylott arranged for her murder.

Circumstances: Julia Stoner was murdered during a storm one night in 1891. Her room lay between that of her stepfather and her sister. Helen Stoner, having heard a low whistle and a clang of metal, rushed into the corridor to witness her sister standing at the door of her room, her body swaying and her face "blanched with terror." She then fell, suffered a series of convulsions, and lapsed into a coma from which she did not recover. Although her body was examined for evidence of poison, none was found.

Cause of death: Probably heart-failure or snake-bite, depending on the length of time the victim took to die. It was Helen Stoner's conviction that her sister died "of pure fright," which would indicate apoplexy (see BASKERVILLE, ARMITAGE, MCPHERSON, BARCLAY). She may possibly have died of the snake venom from the Indian viper, Echis Carinata (see ROYLOTT). The Echis Carinata carries a hemotoxic venom which causes the victim to lapse into coma and then death. The process, however, is a fairly lengthy one.) for a more in depth study of this most ugly and dangerous schemer, see the essay in Volume 2 of this edition.

STRAKER, John
Source: SILV
Biographical details: A retired jockey who rode for five years for Colonel Ross, owner of Silver Blaze, a magnificent race horse. Worked for seven years as a horse trainer with a staff of three boys at King's Pyland,

Dartmoor. A married man, he was reasonably well off and lived in a small villa about two hundred yards from the Colonel's stables. He kept a mistress, of whom his wife was unaware, and ran up considerable bills under the name "William Darbyshire." This problem he endeavoured to solve by fixing a race. Whilst attempting to lame Silver Blaze, he was kicked to death.

Circumstances: Straker was discovered by his wife and two of the boys he employed, the third having been drugged with opium. The body was located about a quarter of a mile from the stables in a bowl-shaped depression of the moor. His head had been shattered by a blow from a horse's hoof, and he was wounded in the thigh, where there was a long cut. In his right hand he held a small knife, covered in blood, and in his left was a red-and-black silk cravat. A local gambler called Fitzroy Simpson was arrested on suspicion but afterwards released when Holmes demonstrated the true cause of Straker's death.

Cause of death: The knife found in Straker's possession was known as a cataract knife. This is used for extremely delicate surgery. Straker's intention was to place a small nick on the tendons of the horse's ham, thus laming it slightly. Since this would be done subcutaneously, Straker hoped it would not be noticed. The horse became frightened and struck Straker on the head, killing him. Holmes observed that "the steel shoe had struck Straker full on the forehead." At first, it had been assumed that the murder had been committed by Fitzroy Simpson, who possessed a bulbous-headed walking stick called a Penang lawyer. It is noted that "The blows... inflicted [produced] terrible injuries." A horseshoe would leave a sharp wedge-like mark, and it is doubtful whether such a blow would actually "shatter the head."

SUTTON: see BLESSINGTON

TARLETON MURDERS (?)
Source: MUSG
Biographical details: As the intrepid Donald. A. Redmond observes (SHJ, Vol. 12, No. 1): "No murders involving a Tarleton as either victim or criminal are recorded in the English or Scottish records from 1865 to 1890."

An identification occurs with the murders of Lord Leitrim and his clerk and driver in April 1875 at Milford in County Donegal.

TOBIN
Source: RESI
Biographical details: Died 1875. Caretaker of the Worthington Bank, murdered by one of the thieves, who got away with £7,000.
Circumstances: Unknown. Cause of death: Unknown.

TREGENNIS, Brenda
Source: DEVI
Biographical details: Died 1897. Member of a Cornish tin-mining family who sold out in the 1890s to a bigger company. After some years of disputation concerning the division of the family estate, her brother Mortimer was estranged. Her lover, Dr. Leon Sterndale, unwittingly gave Mortimer the means of her death, when he demonstrated the hallucinatory powers of the "devil's foot root powder." Miss Tregennis was described as "a very beautiful girl, verging upon middle age. Her dark, clear-cut face was handsome."

Circumstances: Miss Tregennis was found in the sitting-room of the family house at Tredannick Wartha by Dr. Richards and Mortimer Tregennis. Brenda's two brothers had been driven insane by their ordeal and appeared unaware of their sister's death. The victim's face was contorted with terror. Traces of the hallucinatory drug which caused her death were found on the talc-shield of the lamp in Mortimer Tregennis's room, a fact which helped Holmes reach his conclusions.

Cause of death: Probably heart failure or asphyxiation. The identity of "devil's foot root," of Radix pedis diaboli, to give it its Latin name, has long provided speculation among commentators. Exhaustive treatments of the subject have been provided by Verner Anderson (Sherlock Holmes Journal, Vol. 12, No. 2) and Peter Cooper (Sherlock Holmes Journal, Vol. 8, No. 2). The contenders include: (1) reserpine, an African drug related to radix rauwolfiae, (2) lysergic acid diethylamide (LSD), (3) the Calabar bean, (4) strychnon manicon (or datura stramonium), (5) hemp, and (6) mauvi (erythrophleum guineense), an ordeal drug of the Congo region. Of these,

LSD cannot be accepted, simply because the drug was not developed until 1943, in a Swiss laboratory. Reserpine comes from Java and was introduced to the West in 1887. There are two African varieties, and it is the Belgian Congo species which we should consider. Dr. Sterndale says that the drug came from Western Africa (the "Ubanghi country"), so the region is correct. The problem with Rauwolfiae vomitoria is that its hallucinatory effects would not cause extreme facial distortion, The Calabar bean, discovered in 1840 by a West African missionary, comes from the seeds of a plant found in Calabar. The poison of the bean causes muscular paralysis, leading to asphyxiation. The powdered bean appears similar to the "reddish-brown snuff-like powder" of Watson's description. The evidence for physostigmatis venenosum is tempting. Strychnon manicon is a remote possibility since its effects are devilish. The victim laughs, weeps, and talks to himself under its influence. It does not, however, lead to death or insanity. Hemp does not fit, for it has a sweet odour, certainly not "musky" and "nauseous." Mauvi, the ordeal drug, is the most probable choice since it causes immediate convulsions and often leads to insanity.

TREGENNIS, Mortimer
Source: DEVI
Biographical details: Member of a Cornish tin-mining family, described as "a thin, dark, spectacled man, with a stoop which gave the impression of actual physical deformity." Estranged from his brothers and sister, Tregennis lodged with Mr. Roundhay, vicar of Tredannick Wollas. He murdered his sister in 1897 in "an attempt to become the sole guardian of his family's joint property." He was murdered in turn by Dr. Leon Sterndale.

Circumstances: Tregennis was found in his room, sitting in his chair. His limbs were convulsed and his fingers contorted "as if he had died in a very paroxysm of fear." He had died early in the morning, having been awakened by Sterndale, who let him in. Sterndale placed a hallucinatory drug, Radix pedis diaboli, in the talc-shield of the lamp, lit it, and threatened to shoot Tregennis if he moved. Tregennis died within five minutes.

Cause of death: Heart failure or asphyxiation (see TREGENNIS, Brenda).

TREPOFF MURDER (1888? 1889?)

Source: SCAN

Biographical details: "From time to time I heard some vague account of his doings, of his summons to Odessa in the case of the Trepoff murder" (SCAN). (The Dolsky murder [STUD] also happened at Odessa - see DOLSKY). As Chris Redmond noted (SHJ, Vol. 7, No. 4), on January 24, 1878, "General Trepoff, police prefect of St. Petersburg, was shot and wounded by a sixteen year old Nihilist named Vera Lassulic." Clearly, however, there is a problem of chronology.(Note the historical background of this case is dealt with in my essay on Nihilists etc., in Volume 3 of this edition.)

TREVOR Senior: see ARMITAGE, James

VENNUCI, Pietro

Source: SIXN

Biographical details: 1870?-1900. A member of the Mafia, whose sister, Lucretia, had stolen the black pearl of the Borgias. Described as "one of the greatest; cut-throats in London," Vennuci came from Naples. He was murdered by Beppo, another Italian, probably because he was at the time in possession of the Borgia pearl. He was a tall, sunburnt man and powerfully built.

Circumstances: Found murdered on the steps of 131 Pitt Street, Kensington, London, by Horace Harker, of the same address. He was found on his back, with his knees drawn up and his mouth open. His throat had been cut and there was a considerable quantity of blood around the head.

Cause of death: Loss of blood. Throat-cutting is a common form of murder, popularised by Jack the Ripper in the 1880s. The severing of the carotid artery causes a lack of oxygen to the brain, resulting in death within a few minutes.

WATSON, Dr. John H.

Source: 3GAB

Biographical details: Born 1855-? Friend and lifelong companion of Sherlock Holmes. Having spent his early years in Australia, Watson received his education in an English school before taking his medical degree at the University of London. He was employed as a staff surgeon at St. Bartholomew's, London, and played Rugby for Blackheath (as, occasionally did Doyle).. Sometime before 1878, he joined the Army Medical Department and trained as a military surgeon. He went to Afghanistan and was badly wounded in the battle of Maiwand. Returning to England in 1881, he met Sherlock Holmes as the result of a chance meeting with Stamford, his dresser at Bart's. Watson acted as biographer and assistant to the detective for a period of seventeen years.

Circumstances: Watson was shot at twice by "Killer Evans" (q.v.) at a house in Little Ryder Street. "I felt a sudden hot sear as if a red-hot iron had been pressed to my thigh." The wound was described as a "superficial one" by the doctor.

WEST, Arthur Cadogan
Source: BRUC
Biographical details: 1868-1895. A 27-year-old clerk who worked at the Woolwich Arsenal. He was last seen by his fiancée, Miss Violet Westbury, whom he left abruptly in the fog about 7:30 P.M. West had been in Government employ for about ten years and had a reputation of being hot-headed, impetuous, but honest. His daily duties brought him in contact with top-secret plans. He was murdered by Hugo Oberstein after witnessing the theft of the Bruce-Partington plans.

Circumstances: West's body was found by a platelayer named Mason just outside Aldgate Station on the London Underground. The head was badly crushed, indicating that it had fallen from the train roof, having been deposited there elsewhere. This Holmes deduced because of (a) the lack of blood at the scene of the discovery of the body, (b) the fact that the train swayed from side to side where it ran over the points.

Cause of death: West was struck on the head with a life preserver (a Victorian club), which caused severe cranial injuries. He died within five minutes.

INDEX OF MURDERERS

Moriarty, Professor James
Muller, Franz
Murillo, Don Juan
Oberstein, Hugo
Palmer, Dr. William
Parker
Peace, Charles
Peters, "Holy"
Pinner, Arthur
Pritchard, Dr. Edward William
Roylott, Dr. Grimesby
Selden
Singh, Mahomet
Slaney, Abe
Small, Jonathan
Smith, Culverton
Stapleton, Jack
Stark, Colonel Lysander
Staunton, Henry (?)
Sterndale, Dr. Leon
Stevens, Bert
Tonga
Tregennis, Mortimer
Turner, John
Wainwright, Henry

THE MURDERERS' GALLERY

AKBAR, Dost
Source: SIGN
Biographical details: One of three Sikhs and an Englishman called Jonathan Small who murdered an Indian merchant, Achmet, in order to seize the great Agra treasure. Sentenced with his accomplices, Abdullah Khan, Mahomet Singh, and Small to penal servitude for life. (See ACHMET).

AMBERLEY, Josiah
Source: RETI
Biographical details: Born 1835. A retired colour-man from Lewisham who murdered his wife and her lover, Dr. Ray Ernest, in the summer of 1898. His hobby was chess, which Holmes thought was the mark of a scheming mind. He was odd in appearance, having a curved back, huge shoulders and chest, and spindled legs, one of which was artificial. When confronted with his crime, he attempted suicide by taking a cyanide pill.
(See AMBERLEY, ERNEST)

ANDERSON murders
Holmes made reference to these murders, which took place in North Carolina, when comparing them to the death of Sir Charles Baskerville in HOUN.

ANNA
Source; GOLD

Biographical details: Died 1894. The Russian wife of Sergius, who emigrated with her to England and who assumed the alias of Professor Coram. Anna was twenty and her husband fifty and both were Nihilists when they married at a Russian university. Her husband betrayed her over the killing of a policeman, and she was sentenced to a term of imprisonment in Siberia. She murdered Willoughby Smith, her husband's personal secretary, in order to gain access to important papers. (See SMITH, WILLOUGHBY but also see my extended essay on this case in Vol. 2 of this edition.)

BEDDINGTON
Source: STOC
Biographical details: One of two brothers who served five years' penal servitude and, on their release, contrived to plan to rob the firm of Mawson and Williams of £100,000 worth of bonds. Beddington impersonated a young broker called Hall Pycroft in London, in order to execute the robbery. He obtained mouldings of various strongroom locks, overpowered and killed the night watchman, whom he bundled into a safe, and then filled a carpetbag with £100,000's worth of American railway bonds and mine scripts. He was arrested by Constable Pollock and Sergeant Tuson of the City police.

BEDDOES
Source: GLOR
Biographical details: A Norfolk country squire whose real name was Evans. Along with Trevor Senior, he made his wealth in the Australian gold fields before returning with him to England. He disappeared from Norfolk after being blackmailed by the sailor, Hudson, but first sent a coded message to Trevor Senior, which killed him. Although Beddoes cannot be called a murderer, he was inadvertently the cause of Trevor's death. (See ARMITAGE).

BEPPO (second name unknown)

Source: SIXN

Biographical details: A well-known ne'er-do-well among the Italian colony of London. He had once been a skilful sculptor and had earned an honest living, but had taken to evil ways and had been twice imprisoned— once for a petty theft, the other for stabbing another Italian—before he murdered Pietro Vennuci and stole the Black Pearl of the Borgias from him. (See VENNUCI)

BIDDLE
Source: RESI
Biographical details: One of the five known as the Worthington Bank Gang. In 1875, he and his confederates robbed the bank and murdered a caretaker on the premises. Released after serving only part of their sentences, Biddle and two others planned the murder of Blessington (alias Sutton), a member of the gang who had turned informer. This they succeeded in doing. (See BLESSINGTON)

BROWNER, James
Source: CARD
Biographical details: A sailor who plied his trade as a steam-packet steward from Liverpool. He married Mary Cushing, one of three sisters, the others being Sarah and Susan. Sarah introduced Mary to Alec Fairbairn, who became her lover. On discovering this fact, Browner planned to murder both his wife and her lover, and subsequently he did kill them on a rowing-boat half a mile from New Brighton, Liverpool. A package containing a severed ear from each victim was sent to Susan Cushing, mistakenly, and it was this incident which enabled Holmes and the police to identify Browner as the author of the crime. Browner was arrested on board his ship, the S.S. May Day, where he made a full confession.

CALHOUN, Captain James
Source: FIVE
Biographical details: Died 1887. A leading member of the Ku Klux Klan who masterminded the deaths of Elias, John, and Joseph Openshaw of Horsham, Sussex. His ship, the Lone Star, bound for Savannah, U.S.A., foundered at sea, and he was drowned in the Atlantic Ocean.

CARTWRIGHT
Source: RESI
Biographical details: One of a gang of five who in 1875 robbed a bank and murdered the caretaker. On the evidence of Blessington, alias Sutton, Cartwright was hanged.

CROKER, Captain
Source: ABBE
Biographical details. A tall, blue-eyed, fair-haired young man who was first officer of the Rock of Gibraltar. Whilst employed in this capacity, he met Mary Fraser, later to become Lady Brackenstall (see BRACKENSTALL, Sir Eustace). Croker fell in love with her, though this was reciprocated by her only platonically. Later he became captain of the Bass Rock. Through a chance encounter at Sydenham with Lady Brackenstall's maid, Theresa Wright, Croker learned of Sir Eustace's sadistic treatment of his wife and, after a confrontation with him, smashed his skull with a poker.

CUNNINGHAM, Alec
Source: REIG
Biographical details: Son of a Surrey county squire who lived at Reigate. A long-standing feud between Cunningham father and son and the nearby Actons resulted in the Cunninghams' burglary of the Acton household. The Cunninghams' coachman (see KIRWAN), witnessed the burglary, and this inspired his premeditated murder by Alec Cunningham. Holmes also narrowly escaped with his life as a consequence of the Cunninghams' attentions. (See HOLMES)

DOUGLAS, John (alias Birdy Edwards, alias John McMurdo)
Source.VALL
Biographical details: A detective, employed by the famous Pinkerton Detective Agency, to break up the notorious Scowrers, an illegal Irish terrorist organisation operating in Pennsylvania. Under the alias of John McMurdo, he successfully infiltrated the group and managed to destroy them, despite two attempts on his life. His cover blown, he moved to

California where he made considerable money from a successful mining claim at Benito Canyon. His first wife, Ettie Edwards, whom he married in 1875,died of typhoid there. After five years, he emigrated to England, where he rented a moated manor house in Birlstone, Sussex. He met his second wife, Ivy, in London, she being twenty years younger. Douglas, who was described as "about fifty, with a strong jawed, rugged face," soon settled in the local community, where he lived inconspicuously for about five years. An attempt on his life by Ted Baldwin, a Scowrer, failed, resulting in Baldwin's death. Douglas fled and was reported as being lost overboard during a sea voyage two months later. Holmes was of the opinion that he had been assassinated by the Moriarty gang. (See BALDWIN)

DOWSON, Baron
Source: MAZA
Biographical details: Unknown. He was reported as saying, the night before he was hanged, that in Holmes' case the law had gained what the stage had lost.

EVANS, "Killer" (alias Morecroft, alias John Garrideb)
Source: 3GAR
Biographical details: Born 1868. A celebrated American gangster whose real name was James Winter. Aged 44 at the time he came to London, he was a native of Chicago who was known to have shot three men in the States. He escaped from a penitentiary through political influence and travelled to London in 1893. He shot a counterfeiter called Prescott over cards in a night club in the Waterloo Road in January 1895. The man died but Winter was released in 1901 because the victim was the aggressor in this incident. Under the alias John Garrideb, he managed to lure Nathan Garrideb from his rooms at 136 Little Ryder Street, London, and, whilst attempting to extract Prescott's printing outfit from the premises, he was interrupted by Holmes and Watson. The ensuing struggle ended in Watson sustaining a superficial bullet wound.

FERGUSON, Jack
Source: SUSS

Biographical details: The fifteen-year-old son of Robert Ferguson, who attempted to kill his infant step-brother because he was jealous of him. Described as "a remarkable lad, pale-faced and fair-haired, with excitable light blue eyes," he suffered an accident when young which left him with a deformity; He fired a curare-tipped arrow at his one-year-old step-brother.

FOURNAYE, Mme.
Source: SECO
Biographical details: The wife of Henri Fournaye of Paris. Her husband lived a double life, posing as Eduardo Lucas in London. Mme. Fournaye, suspecting that her husband was carrying on an affair with Lady Hilda Trelawney Hope, stabbed her husband in the heart with an Oriental curved dagger. She was later reported as being "insane" at her home in the Rue Austerlitz, where she suffered an amnesiac attack. (See FOURNAYE, Henri)

GRUNER, Baron Adelbert
Source.   I LLU
Biographical details: Born 1860. An Austrian art collector and speculator who specialised in the exploitation of his female victims. He murdered his wife at the Splugen Pass in the Alps and was tried at Prague for the crime, though the case was not proven. A horse fancier and polo player, he lived at Vernon Lodge, near Kingston, where he housed a unique collection of Oriental porcelain. Miss Kitty Winter, one of his cast-offs, was of the opinion that he had murdered two others beside his wife. His infatuation with Miss Violet de Merville led to Holmes's intervention and the subsequent attack on him outside the Cafe Royal (See HOLMES, Sherlock). Gruner was badly mutilated in a vitriol attack at his home..

HAYS, Reuben
Source: PRIO
Biographical details: Landlord of the Fighting Cock Inn and accomplice of James Wilder in the kidnapping of young Lord Saltire. Hays brought Arthur Saltire to his pub after murdering Heidegger, the German schoolteacher (see HEIDEGGER). He shod his horses with shoes which counterfeited the tracks of cows in order to avoid suspicion..

HAYWARD
Source: RESI
Biographical details: Member of the Worthingdon Bank gang, who murdered a caretaker in 1875 and got away with £7,000. Released before serving his full fifteen years' imprisonment, Hayward helped to execute Blessington (alias Sutton), who had turned informer. (See BLESSINGTON)

HOPE, Jefferson
Source: STUD
Biographical details: An American from St. Louis, who avenged the death of John Ferrier, his father's friend, and the forced marriage of his sweetheart Lucy, Ferrier's adopted daughter. Hope spent twenty years tracking Enoch Drebber (see DREBBER) and Joseph Stangerson (see STANGERSON) and succeeded in murdering both of them. After a considerable journey through the Salt Lake Mountains, where he suffered exposure and starvation, Hope emigrated to Britain, where he gained employment as a cab-driver. He traced the murderers of Ferrier to a boarding-house in Camberwell and from there singled them out. Drebber he killed by the forcible administration of poison. Stangerson was stabbed to death at Halliday's Private Hotel. Although arrested for murder, Hope was not brought to justice, since he died of an aortic aneurism.

HOWELLS, Rachel
Source: MUSG
Biographical details: The second housemaid employed by Reginald Musgrave at Hurlstone, Manor, Western Sussex. Described as a woman with "an excitable Welsh temperament," she suffered "brain fever" (mental depression) when her lover Brunton (see H BRUNTON) turned his attentions to Janet Tregellis, daughter of the head gamekeeper. Howells was recruited by Brunton to locate the Musgrave treasure. She was suspected of having entombed him in a cellar at the time of the treasure's discovery and disappeared without trace.

HURET

Source: GOLD

Biographical details: Watson refers in GOLD to "the tracking and arrest of Huret, the Boulevard assassin," an exploit which won for Holmes "an autographed letter of thanks from the French President and the Order of the Legion of Honour." These events probably took place in 1894. It was the late Edgar W. Smith who pointed out (BSJ, Vol. 9, No. 1) that in 1894 the President of France (Marie Francois Sadi Carnot) was assassinated by one Giovanni Santo, a known Nihilist. As Chris Redmond pointed out (SHJ, Vol. 7, No. 4), Santo "insisted that he had no accomplices." Officials were convinced otherwise. Shortly after the assassination, M. Goron, the head of the detective force, was removed from his post because of "financial irregularities." Redmond's contention is that Holmes carried out "an investigation of the whole affair and some reforms... When Holmes was finished with it, he certainly deserved the Legion of Honour..."

KEMP, Wilson
Source: GREE

Biographical details: Described by Watson as a "man of the foulest antecedents," Kemp and his associate Harold Latimer lured Paul Kratides (see KRATIDES) to England, where they kept him prisoner, hoping to force him to sign away his and his sister Sophy's property. Kratides was tortured and finally asphyxiated According to a newspaper report from Buda-Pesth, both Latimer and Kemp were murdered while in the company of Sophy Kratides.

KHAN, Abdullah
Source: SIGN

Biographical details: One of three Sikhs and an Englishman, called Jonathan Small, who murdered an Indian merchant, Achmet, and seized the Agra Treasure from him. He was sentenced, along with his accomplices, to penal servitude for life. (See ACHMET)

LATIMER, Harold
Source: GREE

Biographical details: A criminal, whose affair with a Greek, Sophy Kratides, led to her brother's captivity at a house in Beckenham and his subsequent torture and death. Latimer and his associate Kemp (q.v.) fled to Europe with Sophy Kratides. Both men were stabbed to death by her. (See KRATIDES)

LEONARDO
Source: VEIL
Biographical details: A circus strong-man who, with his lover, Mrs. Eugenia Ronder, planned and executed the death of Ronder, the circus owner (see RONDER). Leonardo, described as having a "clever, scheming brain," made a club with a leaden head, fastened with five long steel nails, so as to give the impression of the mark left by a lion's paw. Although he succeeded in smashing Ronder's skull, the incident ended in tragedy when Ronder's wife was attacked and badly mauled by the circus lion which Render had gone to feed. Leonardo, who escaped justice, was drowned in a bathing incident at Margate.

LUCCA, Gennaro
Source. REDC
Biographical details. An Italian who lived in Naples, where he worked for Augusto Barelli, a lawyer. He eloped with his employer's daughter, Emilia, married her at Bari, and then emigrated with her to New York. Here he saved Tito Castalotte from the attentions of some ruffians and was subsequently offered employment by him, Gennaro settled in Brooklyn, New York, where, by a chance encounter, he met Gorgiano, a member of the Red Circle, a Neapolitan society of criminals Gennaro was impressed into the organisa, tion and expected to help arrange for his employer's assassination, This he failed to do, warning Castalotte instead and fleeing to London with his wife, There Gorgiano hunted him down, an enterprise which led to his own violent death at Lucca's hands. (See GORGIANO).

MOFFAT
Source: RESI

Biographical details: One of the Worthingdon Bank Gang who, in 1875, robbed a bank and murdered a caretaker on the premises. Released after serving part of his sentence, Moffat and two companions executed Blessington (alias Sutton) because he had turned informer. The murder was arranged to look like suicide.

(See BLESSINGTON)

MORAN, Colonel Sebastian

Source, EMPT

Biographical details: Born 1840, Son of Sir Augustus Moran, a former British minister to Persia. Educated at Eton and Oxford, Moran became an officer in the First Bengalore Pioneers and subsequently served in the Jowaki Campaign, the Afghan Campaign, Charasiab (where he was mentioned in dispatches), Sherpur, and Kabul. Described as "the second most dangerous man in London" by Holmes, Moran once showed exceptional daring by crawling down a drain after a wounded man eating tiger. Leaving India, he came to London, where- he was enlisted by Professor James Moriarty and paid a salary of £6,000. Among other crimes, Moran was probably responsible for the death of Mrs. Stewart of Lauder (1897), and he later attempted to kill Holmes at the Reichenbach Falls (see HOLMES). A subsequent attempt in London three years later, which also failed, led to his capture, Moran was arrested in a house in Baker Street and charged with the murder of Ronald Adair (see ADAIR), whom he had shot after an argument over cards. Apparently he escaped the gallows, for he was still alive in 1914. Moran was the author of 'Heavy Game of the Western Himalayas' (1881) and 'Three Months in the jungle (1884) and a member of the Anglo-Indian, Tankerville, and Bagatelle Card Clubs.

MORGAN

Source: EMPT

Biographical details: Unknown. Mentioned by Holmes because he appeared in the commonplace book which Holmes consulted.

MORIARTY, Professor James

Source: FINA, EMPT, VALL

Biographical details: Born 1891. A criminal magnate, who ruled the underworld of London in the late 1880s. A man of good birth and excellent education, he enjoyed a phenomenal mathematical faculty, and, at the age of 21, he wrote a treatise on the Binomial Theorem which won and European vogue. He went on to win the Mathematical chair at one of the smaller universities and later authored 'The Dynamics of an Asteroid'. His involvement with unsavoury matters led to "dark rumours" at the university, and he was compelled to resign the chair. He came to London, where, employed as an Army coach, he began to establish the criminal empire which later attracted the attentions of Holmes. With the assistance of Colonel Sebastian Moran, Moriarty helped organise a series of forgeries, robberies, murders, and other crimes. After several attempts at bringing the Professor to justice, Holmes's life was threatened (see HOLMES). This led to a personal confrontation between the two men at the Reichenbach Falls, Switzerland, which ended in the Professor's death. The Moriarty gang were rounded up, with the exception of Moran, who made a further attempt on Holmes' life. (See MORAN)

Holmes regarded Moriarty as his intellectual equal. He had two brothers, one a station-master in the West of England, and a Colonel James Moriarty, who wrote to the newspapers after his brother's death in an attempt to exonerate the Professor's reputation.

MULLER, Franz
Source: STUD

Biographical details: The case of Franz Muller was mentioned by Holmes on his first meeting with Watson as an important example of the importance of bloodstain identification. Muller was a 25-year-old German tailor who committed Britain's first train murder. On July 9, 1864, Thomas Briggs, a seventy-year-old bank clerk, was found on the Hackney Wick and Bow railway line, beaten to death with his own walking-stick. The motive for the crime was the robbery of Briggs's gold watch and sundry possessions. A silk hat, found in the railway carriage, did not belong to Briggs. Holmesian detective work revealed that the watch had been exchanged for a new one in a Cheapside shop where the jeweller identified a man with a foreign accent. The hat brought forward a man who recognised its owner as Muller. Muller was traced to his lodgings, whence he had already fled, sailing to America on board the S.S. Victoria. Detectives subsequently arrested Muller as he embarked at the New York docks, wearing his victim's hat in a lame attempt at disguise. He was hanged on November 14, 1864.

MURILLO, Don Juan
Source: WIST
Biographical details: A ruthless and despotic dictator of one of the South American countries. He ruled for a decade until a revolution led him to flee the country with his possessions, his two children, and his secretary. Under the alias of Henderson, the ex-ruler travelled to Paris, Rome, Madrid, and Barcelona (1896). Eventually, he moved to England, where he lived quietly in Esher, Surrey, at a large residence called High Gable. Sometime between 1896 and 1902, a revolutionary named Aloysius Garcia (see GARCIA) tracked down Murillo but was lured by Murillo to his house and murdered by him. Under the new name of the Marquess of Montalva, Murillo and his henchman Lopez (alias Lucas) escaped England, only to be murdered at the Hotel Escurial, Madrid.

OBERSTEIN, Hugo
Source: BRUC
Biographical details: A spy who lived at 13 Caulfield Gardens, Kensington, and who was responsible for both the theft of the top-secret Trelawney Hope document and the murder of Arthur Cadogan West (see WEST). Colonel Valentine Walter of the Woolwich Arsenal had made a treasonable pact with Oberstein which uncovered by West. After Oberstein had killed West with a life-preserver, Walter helped him to throw the body onto the roof of an Underground train pausing beneath the window of the house. Three documents were kept by Oberstein because of their technical nature, and the rest stuffed into West's pocket. Oberstein was trapped by a letter written by Walter, under Holmes's supervision, offering him further documents. He was arrested at the Charing Cross Hotel smoking-room and given a fifteen-year prison sentence.

PALMER, Dr. William

Source: SPEC

Biographical details: Holmes mentioned Palmer when commentating on the cunning of Dr. Grimesby Roylott (see ROYLOTT and more detailed treatment in chapter above).

Palmer's trial took place in 1856. He qualified at St. Bartholomew's in 1846 and began practice in Rugeley, Staffordshire. He married, had an affair with his servant, and frequently got into debt. He resolved then to poison his mother-in-law so that her estate would pass to his wife and eventually to hire. Palmer's four children died, then his wife and brother (after they had been insured for very large sums). Palmer was a compulsive gambler and in 1855 attended Shrewsbury Races with a friend, John Cook. Cook won large sums, while Palmer lost. Having collected Cook's winnings for him, Palmer then poisoned his companion. Unfortunately for Palmer, the autopsy showed evidence of antimony. Palmer was subsequently arrested and hanged in 1856. (See also the article re Palmer in the early section of this book.)

PARKER

Source: EMPT

Biographical details: Unknown. (also see appendix material in volume 2 on Parker and the Victorian obsession with and ephemeron of garrotting.). Parker was an employee of Colonel Moran, paid to stand guard outside Baker Street. Holmes regarded him as a "harmless enough fellow" and "a remarkable performer up on the Jew's harp." He was a garrotter by trade, an occupation popular among the criminal classes of London but highly unpopular with the public since it was robbing by strangulation and beating. It is curious, therefore, that Holmes should describe Parker as 'harmless enough.'

PEACE, Charles

(Also see details in volume 2 of this edition).

Source: ILLU

Biographical details: Born in 1832, Peace was perhaps Victorian England's most elusive burglar. Agile, strong, and described as a "monkey of a man," he was an expert in disguise and had a flair for theatricals and music. (The violin case often contained his burgling tools!) Whilst in Manchester, Peace murdered his neighbour, Dyson, after pestering his wife, and was also responsible for the shooting of P.C. Nicholas Cook. Three Irishmen were mistakenly convicted of this later crime. Peace, now with a reward on his head, moved to London. While burgling a house in Blackheath on October 10, 1878, he was arrested by P.C. Edward Robinson, after a struggle, and tried for attempted murder in November. Sentenced to life imprisonment, he made a daring escape attempt by jumping out of a train bound for Sheffield but was immediately recaptured. Whilst awaiting execution for Cook's murder, he made a full confession of his previous crimes. Arthur Griffiths' interview with Peace in his 'Mysteries of Police and Crime' reveals a ruthless but colourful character. Holmes referred to "my old friend Charlie Peace" in ILLU, which suggests that he was on intimate terms with him. This seems surprising because, though wily and possessed of cunning and guile, he was also boastful and merciless.

PETERS, "Holy"
Source: LADY
Biographical details: An unscrupulous con-man from Australia, whose speciality was the beguiling of lonely ladies by playing on their religious feelings. He was badly bitten in a saloon-fight at Adelaide in 1889, and thereafter enlisted the services of an accomplice called Annie Fraser. The two of them gained the confidence of Lady Frances Carfax (see CARFAX), whom they attempted to murder for her jewellery. Peters adopted the identity of Dr. Schlesinger, a South American missionary, in order to effect this crime. His stratagem failed only because Holmes was quick-witted enough to spot the size of the coffin in which Rose Spender was to be buried. It is not made clear if Peters and Fraser were ever brought to justice for this attempted murder.

PINNER, Arthur: see BEDDINGTON

PRITCHARD, Dr Edward William
Source: SPEC.

Biographical details: Holmes, in discussing Dr. Grimesby Roylott, made reference to the celebrated Pritchard. A Glasgow physician who poisoned his wife and mother-in-law with aconite, Pritchard was an egotist of the first order, gave travel lectures about places he had never even visited, became a Freemason, and handed out signed photographs of himself. His motive for murder appears to have been a promise he made to a fifteen year-old servant girl whom he made pregnant, then aborted. Pritchard would never have been caught save for an anonymous letter sent to the Procurator-Fiscal. He was hanged in July 1865. Holmes said Pritchard had been at the head of the medical profession. In fact he purchased his
M.D. in Germany. Holmes's remarks regarding the errant doctor (SPEC) were indeed apt. The Stoke Moran affair took place in April 1883. Only a year before, Dr, George Henry Lamson had poisoned his eighteen-year-old brother-in-law with a little-known vegetable poison, aconitine, contained in a capsule of sugar. He was executed in April 1882. (also see the illuminating account of his trial elsewhere in this edition).

ROYLOTT, Dr Grimesby: see ROYLOT.

SELDEN: see SELDEN.

SINGH, Mahomet
Source: SIGN
Biographical details: One of three Sikhs and an Englishman called Jonathan Small, who murdered an Indian merchant, Achmet, in order to obtain the Agra Treasure. (See KHAN, Akbar; ACHMET)

SLANEY, Abe
Source: DANC
Biographical details: A Chicago gangster who came to England and sought out Elsie Patrick (Hilton Cubitt's wife). Described as "a tall handsome, swarthy fellow" with "a bristling black beard and a great, aggressive, hooked nose," Slaney was one of a gang of seven crooks operating in Chicago, and Elsie Patrick's father was the "boss of the Joint." Patrick's daughter would have nothing to do with her father's dealings and

emigrated to England, although she was engaged to Slaney. Slaney used the "dancing men" cipher to send her messages. These she ignored but finally granted Slaney an interview. Slaney shot Cubitt after he had first fired on him, with fatal results. (See CUBITT)

SMALL, Jonathan
Source: SIGN
Biographical details: Born c. 1838. Born near Pershore, Worcestershire, Small came from a farming community. When he was eighteen, he joined the Third Buffs regiment and was sent to India. He spent five months in a military hospital, recovering from an amputated leg, resulting from an attack by a crocodile. After discharge, Small gained employment as an overseer at a plantation owned by Abel White near the border of the North-West Provinces. White and his wife were killed at the outset of the Indian Mutiny (1857). Small moved to Agra, where he joined three Sikhs and conspired to steal the Agra Treasure, which was being transferred to a place of safety by Achmet (see ACHMET), an Indian businessman. For the theft and murder of Achmet, Small and his associates were sentenced to penal servitude for life on the Andaman Islands. Small arranged for the treasure to be taken by Captain Morstan and brought back to the Islands, after a deal had been struck between Morstan, Major Sholto, and the four prisoners. Since the treasure was not returned and shared out, as had been agreed, Small escaped in 1881 and sailed to England with his native Andaman islander, Tonga, in order to wreak vengeance on Morstan and Sholto. Morstan died before Small could achieve his aim, but he was successful in stealing the Agra Treasure from Sholto at his home in Norwood, although not before Tonga had shot Sholto's son with a poison dart. Small was tracked by Holmes and arrested. (See SHOLTO)

SMITH, Culverton
Source: DYIN
Biographical details: A well-known resident and planter of Sumatra, whose temporary residence was a fine house in Lower Burke Street, Notting Hill. Described as a man with "a great yellow face, coarse-grained and greasy, with heavy double-chin, and two sullen, menacing grey eyes," Smith

appeared to have suffered from rickets in childhood. His study of rare Asiatic diseases such as the black Formose corruption and the Tapanuli fever, led him to arrange his nephew, Victor Savage's, murder. The murder weapon consisted of the bacteria-tipped spring in a small box. Although Smith succeeded in killing Savage, his attempted murder of Holmes, using the same method, was unsuccessful and led to his own arrest. (See SAVAGE, HOLMES)

STAPLETON, Jack
Source: HOUN
Biographical details: Died 1889. Son of Rodger Baskerville, the younger brother of Sir Charles (see BASKERVILLE), who fled with a sinister reputation to South America, where he was said to have died unmarried. Jack "Stapleton" married Beryl Garcia, one of the beauties of Costa Rica, and, having stolen a considerable sum of public money, he changed his name to Vandeleur and fled to England, where he set up a private school in the East of Yorkshire. His reason for attempting this enterprise was that he had struck up an acquaintance with a consumptive tutor on the voyage home. Fraser, the tutor, died, and the school sank into disrepute. "Vandeleur" then changed his name to Stapleton and moved to Dartmoor, where he indulged his taste for entomology (he was an acknowledged expert), and planned the deaths of Sir Charles and Sir Henry Baskerville. Playing on Sir Charles's superstitious fear of the legendary Baskerville hound, he bought a large hound from Ross and Mangles, dealers in the Fulham Road, and starved it into a state of savagery. By this method, he succeeded in killing Sir Charles and would have succeeded in claiming his second victim were it not for the intervention of Holmes. Stapleton fell victim to one of the Dartmoor bogs.

STARK, Colonel Lysander
Source: ENGR
Biographical details: Real name Fritz. A German coiner who operated a hydraulic press in a house at Eyford, Berkshire. With his accomplices, Ferguson and a woman who may have been his wife, Stark manufactured countless fake coins made of tin and nickel. The Colonel was responsible for

the disappearance of Jeremiah Hayling (see HAYLING) and the attempted murder of Victor Hatherley (see HATHERLEY). He and his accomplices escaped justice.

STAUNTON, Henry (?)
Source: MISS
Biographical details: Holmes refers to "Henry Staunton, whom I helped to hang" when referring to his Commonplace Book. This could have been a reference to the Staunton brothers, who in 1877 were charged with the murder of Louis Staunton's 36-year-old wife. It was claimed that they, with the assistance of Patrick Staunton's wife and Louis's mistress, had starved her to death at a house in Penge. They were reprieved from the death sentence, however, because of the unconvincing nature of the evidence against them. Alice Rhodes was released. The others served out prison sentences. Since the Stauntons did not hang, though, we must assume that Henry Staunton was involved in another murder. No doubt the Stauntons found a place in Holmes's index.(Also see details about the case in the early section of this book.)

STERNDALE, Dr. Leon
Source: DEVI
Biographical details: A great African explorer and lion-hunter who fell in love with Brenda Tregennis (see TREGENNIS, Brenda), although he was already married. Dr. Sterndale brought to England Radix pedis diaboli (the "devil's foot"), which he had obtained from the medicine men of Western Africa. This poison fell into the hands of Mortimer Tregennis, Brenda's brother, who killed her in order to gain the family estate. Sterndale took vengeance on Mortimer and forced him to suffer the effects of the ordeal drug at gunpoint. He died as a result of the experience. Holmes took no action against Dr. Sterndale but allowed him to return to Central Africa.

STEVENS, Bert
Source: NORW
Biographical details: Holmes makes a passing reference to this criminal in NORW when he remarks: "You remember that terrible murderer, Bert

Stevens, who wanted us to get him off in'87?" According to Michael Harrison (The World of Sherlock Holmes), Bert Stevens was a cover-name for James Kenneth Stephen, tutor to the Duke of Clarence (Prince Albert, eldest son of King Edward VIII). In 1892, Stephen died in an asylum from a mania which lasted two and a half months. Harrison believes that Stephen was Jack the Ripper and that Holmes, in order to avert a scandal, was called in to investigate on behalf of the aging Queen Victoria. Thus the true identity of the Ripper had to remain a secret.

TONGA
Source: SIGN
Biographical details: Died 1888. A native of the Andaman Islands, who helped Jonathan Small escape from his captivity and who accompanied him to London, where Small sought vengeance against Major Sholto and Captain Morstan. Holmes' gazetteer described the islanders as "fierce, morose and intractable," but the description is quite unfair. (The islands were used from 1858 as a penal settlement by the Indian Government). Tonga assisted Small in the theft of the Agra Treasure and shot Bartholomew Sholto (see SHOLTO) with a poison-tipped dart. Tonga was shot at by Holmes and Watson during a chase down the River Thames and either drowned or died of gunshot wounds.

TREGENNIS, Mortimer: see TREGENNIS, Mortimer and TREGENNIS, Brenda

TURNER, John
Source: BOSC
Biographical details: An Australian bushranger who went by the name of Black Jack of Ballarat in the 1860s. He was part of a gang of six who raided railway stations and held up wagons on the way to diggings during the Gold Rush period. The gang robbed a gold convoy, killing four men, but sparing McCarthy, the wagon- driver (see MCCARTHY). Later, Turner settled in England, where he became a country squire. A chance meeting with McCarthy enabled him to blackmail Turner, but, when asked to put forward his sister's hand in marriage to McCarthy's son, Turner murdered

his old enemy. Holmes did not press charges against Turner, though he kept his confession.

WAINWRIGHT, Henry
Source: ILLU
Biographical details: Mentioned by Holmes when commenting on the fact that all great criminals have complex minds. Holmes claimed that "Wainwright was no mean artist" (ILLU).'

William S. Baring-Gould (Sherlock Holmes: A Biography) mistakenly assumes this to be Thomas Griffiths Wainewright (1794-1852). However, Watson's spelling was correct in this case. Henry Wainwright (executed in 1875) murdered his lover Harriet Lane in September 1874, dismembered her body with the aid of his accomplice, Alice Day, and kept the remains for a year in his warehouse in Vine Court. Lane's relatives had their suspicions aroused when, on visiting Wainwright, he told them that she had deserted him for another man and gone to Brighton to live. Stokes, his assistant, was also suspicious when, a year later, he was asked to load two heavy parcels into a four-wheeler. He looked inside one and discovered a woman's severed head, then gave chase and alerted two constables in the Borough. Wainwright was arrested on leaving the Hen and Chickens public house. An open grave was discovered when the Vine Court premises were subsequently searched, and further proof of murder was provided when it was revealed that Wainwright had purchased quantities of chloride of lime. Wainwright claimed his innocence to the last.

END OF MURDER FILE

THE UBIQUITOUS JACK THE RIPPER; A CONAN DOYLE ENIGMA

Part the first

There is no doubting the sensational effect on the psyches of most Victorians regarding the achievements and reputation of the man (or woman) who, in the sensational press of the time when Holmes was operating in the Metropolis as a forensic crime expert and police consultant. Even few months after the attacks had ceased, an article much like this appeared in 'The Daily Star' for Thursday 15 November 1888, appeared.

'JACK THE RIPPER" MANIA. A SECRET WHEREBY MONEY MIGHT BE MADE.'

'John Avery, aged forty-three, a ticket writer, of Southwick House, Vicarage Road Willesden, was charged at the Clerkenwell Police Court, on Tuesday, with being drunk and disorderly in York Road, the previous night. John Carvell, a private in the 11th Hussars, said that on Monday night he was standing at the corner of York Street, Islington, when the prisoner came up to him caught hold of him, and said, " I'm Jack the Ripper; I will show you how I do all the lot." The witness told him to go away and not to talk nonsense; but Avery, who was intoxicated, followed him and threw his right arm round his neck. A scuffle ensued between them, and the witness's nose was scratched. He soon, however, shook off the prisoner, who said, "Come have a glass of beer, and I will tell you a secret, and you can make some money." They accordingly went into the Duke of York public house, Caledonian Street, and there, in the bar, Avery repeated 2 or 3 times that "he was ' Jack the Ripper.' "

'The witness then thought it best to give the prisoner into custody, and accordingly dragged him outside and gave him in charge of a policeman, who was on duty nearby. It was stated by the police that the prisoner had caused them a deal of trouble, telegraphing and corresponding to find out who and what he was. The name and address he gave were correct, and he was respectably connected. The prisoner, in defence, said he was under the impression that he had only discussed the subject, not admitted he was the criminal. The murder charge was dismissed.'

A similar panic was created in Wales at about the same time as the John Carvell incident. In 'The Star' of Gwent, on Friday 12 October 1888, the following article appeared:

'Jack the Ripper at Cardiff.

YOUNG GIRLS THREATENED.

On Wednesday morning the Mail received the following letter, bearing the London postmark, October 9, and addressed to the Editor, Western Mail, Cardiff, S. Wales:—

'London, October 9h,—Dear Old Bow—What do you think of my little games here— ha! Next Saturday 1 am going to give the St. Mary St. girls a turn. I shall be fairly on their track, you bet. Keep this back until I have done some work. Ha! ha! Shall come down Friday.—Yours, etc., TES (Trade mark).'

'The communication is written, crown, on a half-sheet of plain note paper, and the phraseology is similar to that of the letters sent to the Central News last week.

'Dear Old Bose,' 'ha, ha,' 'give them a turn,' 'their track,' and the broken sentences, all indicate that the letter was written by the same hand, or that the writer has slavishly copied the original missive.

'A CARDIFF LADY THREATENED.

It is reported that a young lady very respectably connected, residing with her parents in Cardiff, has just received a letter, written by a young man with whom she was formerly acquainted; and who has evidently been rendered unsound in mind by reading the accounts of the Whitechapel murders, threatening to do for her the same as "Jack the Ripper" had done for the others. He tells her that he is on the watch…'

I believe that, although Sherlock Holmes never once mentioned the famous Ripper case in any of the 60 chronicles regarding his famous companion, it is surely inconceivable that he would not have been consulted by the team of detectives who were then working on that case.

Similarly, it is quite obvious that if Holmes had been appointed as a consultant to the Ripper case, and succeeded, Watson would have celebrated the fact and flagged it up, in 'The Strand Magazine.'

Certainly Conan Doyle himself showed an unflagging and abiding interest in the Ripper case. Conan Doyle's long association and interest in criminology dated from his early period of development as a writer during his teenage years, when he was much fascinated and influenced by a trip made to the Madame Tussauds in London. His uncle, Richard 'Dickie Doyle,' who he had been staying with in London, had taken him to a performance of the famous Shakespearean play, Hamlet. And he very much enjoyed it. But then they had gone on to another venue, which was in Baker Street, the famous Madame Tussauds. Doyle's use of Baker Street as the famous detective's London address seems therefore most opportune, for he would have recalled it intimately from when he was a young and impressionable man, visiting his elderly relative.

This holiday for young Doyle was, therefore, a golden opportunity for him to familiarise himself with some of the crime and murder stories of Edinburgh displayed at the London waxworks, amongst which, of course, was the famous body snatcher combination of Burke and Hare.

Although Conan Doyle did not write a story involving The Ripper, it was for quite obvious reasons, since this would be unlikely to follow his usual pattern, whereby he invariably nurtured stories from his own imagination, rather than explicitly from the world of criminal fact, and investigation.

Nevertheless Doyle was very familiar with the story of the outrages in Whitechapel, and the appalling deaths of those who had been forced into prostitution in London. He also would have recalled the great publicity surrounding the London performance of the play based upon the novella by his literary acquaintance and fellow Edinburgh resident, Robert Louis

The Coldbath Fields Prison, which was the alternative place of imprisonment to the Newgate prison.

Stevenson, whom Doyle greatly admired. This four-act play had been written by Thomas Russell Sullivan in collaboration with the actor Richard Mansfield, and was initially performed in 1887 in the USA. Significantly, for some 'Ripperologists', however, it opened in London in August 1888, just before the last Jack the Ripper murder.

Doyle was especially interested in the work of Stevenson and in his book 'Through The Magic Door,' he acknowledges Stevenson's powers as a writer and his talent of being able both to entertain and to disturb his readers:

'I can hardly think that healthy boys will ever let Stevenson's books of adventure die, nor do I think that such a short tale as "The Pavilion on the Links" nor so magnificent a parable as "Dr. Jekyll and Mr. Hyde" will ever cease to be esteemed. How well I remember the eagerness, the delight with which I read those early tales in "Cornhill" away back in the late seventies and early eighties.'

Some press reports compared the anonymous Jack the murderer. to the Jekyll-Hyde character, and Mansfield, perhaps because of his utterly convincing performance of the 'divided self' in the adaptation, was suggested as a possible suspect, bizarre though it may seem. Despite significant press coverage, the London production was thought to have been a financial failure.

In the early 1900s, Doyle became aware through his literary connections, of a remarkable club, known as the Crime Club. And in 1905 he was invited to the East End of London to join a small company of people who would look around the sites of the murders in Whitechapel, and then be given some information about the crimes that had been committed there, by police experts, including Dr Frederick Gordon Brown, one of the pathologists who had attended the appalling and visceral savagery of the Ripper's last victim.

Along with Major Arthur Griffiths, fellow member of the Crime Club and author of the much respected 'Mysteries of Police and Crime,' Conan Doyle had his own pet theory about the possible identity of the Ripper. While Griffiths favoured, like several of his contemporaries, the 'mad doctor' version of events, Doyle suspected that the most likely person to have had motive but also opportunity, would also have access to the River Thames, and the murderer's ability to move quickly underground in the sprawling metropolis suggested to him a foreigner, with possible English connections.

In July 1894, only six years after the murder of Mary Kelley, the possible last of the Ripper's victims, an intriguing interview appeared in the 'Yorkshire Evening Post' - a fact which demonstrates how Conan Doyle's fascination with the case had remained undimmed throughout those subsequent years. In the 'Yorkshire Evening Post' for Wednesday 4 July 1894, we read:

"JACK THE RIPPER." HOW SHERLOCK HOLMES WOULD HAVE TRACKED HIM.
'Many people have doubtless wondered what Sherlock Holmes would have done in order to capture "Jack the Ripper." Mr. Conan Doyle in interview with an American journalist has explained this. He says : — "I remember going to the Scotland Yard museum and looking at the letter which was received by the police and which purported to come from the Ripper. It was written in red ink in a clerkly hand. I tried to think how Holmes might have deduced the writer of that letter. The most obvious point was that the letter was written by someone who had been in America. It began, 'Dear Boss,' and contained the phrase, 'fix it up,' and several others which are not usual with the Britishers. Then (I would) have the quality of the paper and the handwriting (examined), which indicates that the letters were not written (without toil? - KJ). It was a good paper, and in a round, easy, clerkly hand. He was therefore a man accustomed to the use of pen. Having determined that much, we cannot avoid the inference that there must be somewhere letters, which this man had written over his own name, documents or accounts that could readily traced him. Oddly enough the police did not, as far as I know, think of that, and so they failed to accomplish anything.

'Holmes' plan would have been to reproduce the letters in facsimile and on each plate indicate briefly the peculiarities of the handwriting. Then publish these facsimiles in the leading newspapers of Great Britain and America, and in connection with them offer a reward to anyone who could show a letter or any specimen of the same handwriting. Such a course would have enlisted millions of people as detectives in the case, or a foreign seaman.'

Conan Doyle continued his fascination with some of the more grotesque and bizarre murder cases which came his way and which appeared in the national newspapers; and the Ripper crimes were certainly very important for him because they represented to him an almost inexplicable puzzle. Yet he had no apparent interest in the solution of the Ripper murders being assigned to his fictional creation.

A speech he delivered in 1898 illustrates and explains his instinctive irritation, with what he judged to be the formulaic Holmes mysteries. His eagerness to be accepted as a main stream writer, provided for him a problem in the world of mass market literature in which he wrote. He was very much concerned that his historical romances, and other works, especially, later, those on Spiritualism, were put into shadow by the Holmes stories, and that they were considerably less worthy than his more serious work. As he remarked to his mother in a letter, prior to his killing of the fictional detective, 'he takes my mind from higher things.'

Nevertheless, Conan Doyle continued his fascination with some of the more grotesque and bizarre murder cases which came his way and which appeared in the national newspapers; and the Ripper crimes were certainly very important for him, because they represented to him, like the Poe stories, an almost inexplicable puzzle.

As a writer of crime fiction, he had created cryptograms in his own short stories, such as the 'Dancing Men', and much later 'The Valley of Fear'. The cryptogram story had been invented by the American writer, Edgar Allan Poe in a magazine he edited. Edgar Allan Poe was a source of inspiration for the young writer. When he began his short stories in the Strand Magazine, Conan Doyle then continued his obsession with cryptograms and secret writing throughout his detective Sherlock Holmes' illustrious career. The most original if somewhat ponderous stories of Poe, which feature a highly cerebral detective with a dutiful companion, were the mainspring for the creation of Conan Doyle's detective. And he made acknowledgement of this debt in his memoirs, 'Memories and Adventures'. Doyle was a highly derivative writer, and this was no less apparent than in his historical romances, which are largely inspired by the historical romance stories of Walter Scott, which the young Conan Doyle read when he was a teenager.

Likewise, several of the Holmes stories are strongly derivative of Poe in their structure, and are usually represented as puzzles, or seemingly unsolvable mysteries. And the mystery element is the part of writing which Doyle most identified with in Poe, the other element of equal importance in Poe being the bizarre or to use Holmes' own phrase, 'outré' nature of the crime committed. While it is true that a proportion of the Holmes stories do not feature violent crime or murder, they are in the main, concerned with bizarre, or often quite inexplicable behaviour of individuals or events, and this as much true of the later as with the very early Holmes stories.

Conan Doyle grew tired of the way that both the critics and the
Reading public seemed to concentrate so much on the Holmes
Stories. Above, the famous caricature of Sir Arthur from 'Punch.'

The speech given by Doyle referred to earlier in this chapter, (to The Author's Club on June 29th, 1889), shows most clearly how the author wished to disassociate himself from the public's perception of his ascetic, obsessed and bohemian, private consulting detective, yet even after he killed Holmes, he was frequently asked by the public to solve for them puzzles and crimes which might well have featured in his Holmes stories, if he had so desired:

> EXCERPT from 'The Queen,'
> Saturday, 4th of July 1896.
> Conan Doyle on How To Write Fiction.

'The chairman has just referred to my killing of Holmes in the Sherlock Holmes stories. I've been much blamed for doing so. I informed someone at the gentleman's desk, that I hold, that it (my killing of Holmes) was not murder but justifiable homicide in self-defence since, if I had not killed him, he would certainly have killed me.

'I possess no particular natural astuteness, and for an author to spend his days in investing problems and building up the chains of inductive reasoning, as his main means of occupation it is better not to rely too much upon the patience of the public. When one has completed 26 stories about one man, one feels it is better this time to put it out of one's power or not to transgress any further.

'What I found annoying about this series of stories, was that the public would insist upon identifying the character with my own character. I have also had enquiries to assist people from the four quarters of the world. From San Francisco to the Philippines, I also have had private communications regarding family mysteries which I was at once required to come and unravel. I refused to take any of them on hand, and I do not suppose that their solution was seriously delayed upon that account.

'And now I have said enough and more than enough about myself. Before I sit down I would like to say a few words about this work of storytelling at which so many of us spend our lives.

'I speak with all diffidence for the subject has many sides to it and when I read some cocksure critic laying down the law about it I always feel, as Sydney Smith said of Macaulay, that I wish I wasn't sure of anything as he was of everything. But one thing I do know, that this art of ours, which has to appeal to the infinite variety of the human mind, should be treated in a very broad and Catholic spirit. The narrow esoteric schools who talk of the writing of the stories as if their own particular formula embraced all virtues, take themselves much too seriously. There is nothing more absurd than the realist who demands merit to the romance writer, unless it be the romance writer who snarls at the realist. A healthy taste should respond to honest words of every kind. The man who does not care for the story is an incomplete man. The man who does not care for the true study of a life is an incomplete man. The man who does not care for anything that has ever been, or can be on God's earth, is an incomplete man.

'There is interest in every view of life, and to interest is the ultimate objective all fiction. That is what every writer and all methods are aiming at, from the old wife telling tales in the nursery to Sir Walter Scott, writing in his study. Kipling seems to me to sum up the whole question with the unerring instinct of genius, when he says there are 5 and 40 ways of writing tribal lays and every blessed one of them is right. Everyone is right if you can interest the tribe. That is the touchstone of our art, And we have a fine tribe to interest. They sit around, the great English-speaking race, a hundred million of them and they say, 'We are very busy folk engaged in every prosaic work, and we should be glad if you could take us out of ourselves sometimes …'

'It doesn't matter what you tell or how you can accomplish that. They don't even care about the bickering of cliques but they welcome all that is good. You may take them back 5000 years with White Melville or on, to the future with Bellamy or H.G. Wells or you may carry them to the moon with Verne or to some other world with Gulliver. Treat of man or woman, or character or incident and you will always get your audience if you put your heart and your soul into your work. If you wish to free yourself of all small dogmatisms about fiction, you have to look at those works which the whole world is now come to look upon as masterpieces: Don Quixote and Madame Bovary… No formula should be considered unapproachable. The writer has attained no higher aim of existence than making the world a little presence in it.'

THE UBIQUITOUS JACK THE RIPPER
Part the Second

"Now, weren't you influenced by Edgar Allan Poe when you wrote Sherlock Holmes?" asked the reporter.

A hush fell in the room. It could be heard as distinctly as the string of a violin had snapped, but Dr. Doyle liked the question and replied to it, at once, impulsively:

"Oh, immensely! His detective is the best detective in fiction." "Except Sherlock Holmes," said somebody.

"I make no exception," said Dr. Doyle, *very earnestly. "Dupin is unrivalled. It was Poe who taught the possibility of making a detective story a work of literature."*

Below: Poe's stories, like Conan Doyle's, often deal with the fear of the unknown. From a Sidney Paget drawing to 'The Hound of the Baskervilles, 'Strand Magazine'. Watson cowers in the stone hut, fearing who the mysterious stranger might be..

- FROM 'The New York Times', 3 October 1894.

By the time that Conan Doyle had obtained a celebrity status for himself as the creator of Sherlock Holmes, (May 1891), he was about to move to a handsome and roomy property in Tennison Road, an expensive quarter of Upper Norwood, which also was, not coincidentally, the setting of his second Sherlock Holmes novel, 'The Sign of Four', a story unlike that of the Jack the Ripper saga, but quite as savage, bizarre and horrific, in many respects in its depiction of brutal murder. The idea of murder as a bizarre concept in human nature, and an example of human perversity, was something Doyle had identified with in the fiction of Poe, to whom he was deeply indebted.

In 1904 the Crime Club, as it was later to be titled, was very much in its infancy and Doyle was invited as a special guest to its first and inaugural proceedings. At the time of his first visit to the club in July of that year he had already published some of the most violent crime stories which he had ever penned, stories in which murder featured, either as the result of rage derived violence or premeditated attack against women.

The first of these stories about women as victims, called 'The Adventure of the Solitary Cyclist', was published in the December of the previous year in The Strand. In this story, concerning predatory males, a female is forced into an illegal marriage but the succeeding stories are much darker and grimmer by comparison. In 'Black Peter' for example, the victim is discovered by the police in a state of putrefaction, having been harpoon to a wall. In the third of the stories, 'The Adventure of Charles Augustus Milverton', a blackmailer is plastered with revolver bullets and Holmes who is hiding in the room at the time of the murder does nothing to prevent it.

'The Adventure of the Abbey Grange' is also a violent story which deals once more with an oppressed woman and an alcoholic husband who exhibits psychopathic tendencies. This in turn reflects the sensational nature of the newspapers which were no less sensational in their reporting of violent crime. It also should come as no surprise that at the turn of the century stories concerning suspects who could have been Jack the Ripper continued to multiply in the press and this was not just confined to Britain, but also these accounts flourished mainly in the big cities of America, where a number of suspects were thought to be the criminal. The notion that Doyle entertained of the killer being of a foreign extraction escaping to America where he would be unnoticed among the teeming millions of the new society was something which he thought was plausible.

In the period prior to his resurrection of the great detective, Doyle had not ceased to be interested in crimes of a sensational nature and in particular, those which involved a psychological twist. Between 1901 and 1903 the author published in 'The Strand Magazine' three accounts of bizarre murder cases. His obsession with the mind of the psychopath is evident in the first of these stories which concerned murder which took place in West Sussex in the 1860s. In an article which he wrote about this crime he remarks,

'The motives and mind of the murderer are of perennial interest to every student of human nature but the vile record of their actual deeds begins to pass away when the ends of justice have once been served by their recital.'

It becomes abundantly apparent that, in this instance, he must have been thinking of the Ripper crimes.

What sort of life had Doyle been living during this period and is there a connection between his activities and interests and that of the Ripper phenomenon?

Let's examine the chronology of the period in question, that is: 1887 - 1905. Here is a summary of the more significant events.

November 1887
Conan Doyle publishes his first Sherlock Holmes story, 'A Study in Scarlet'.

1889
Conan Doyle publishes his first historical novel, 'Micah Clarke'.

7 May 1889
Mr John Beaumont of Bournemouth delivers a scathing attack on spiritualism at the Yorke Rooms, St Paul's Road, Portsmouth. In the Portsmouth Evening News two days later Conan Doyle responds to the challenge, signing himself 'Spiritualist'.

September 30th 1889
Doyle finishes writing his second crime classic, 'The Sign of Four'.

Edgar Allan Poe's horrific crime story, 'The Murders In the Rue Morgue'
shown here and published in 'Graham's Magazine' in 1841. It has been described
as the first modern detective story. Poe referred to it as one of his "tales of ratiocination".

January 1890

Doyle publishes his glowing appraisal of Robert Louis Stevenson in The National Review.

6 April 1891

Conan Doyle sets up as an eye specialist at 2 Devonshire Place, London. He receives few patients.

10 October 1893

Charles Doyle dies in the Crighton Royal Institution, Dumfries. Cause of death is given as epilepsy 'of many years' standing'.

November 1893

Conan Doyle joins the British Society for Psychical Research, just three weeks after the death of his father, Charles. Through the Society he meets such celebrated men as Sir Oliver Lodge, Arthur Balfour, and F.W.H. Myers.

January 1894

Shortly after receiving The Transactions of the Society for Psychical Research, which contains a lengthy address from Balfour on mesmerism, Conan Doyle begins his novella The Parasite, also about mesmerism and sexual obsession.

November 1894

Doyle publishes his novella - length piece, 'The Parasite,' which appears in America in 'Harper's Weekly' in instalments. Thereafter, and even long after Doyle's death, the work is almost universally ignored by critics and biographers.

1906

Conan Doyle's first wife. Louise, dies after suffering from tuberculosis for many years. Unknown to the public at large, Doyle has been carrying on an affair with Jean Leckie for many of these years.

The period embracing 1889 to 1904 marked a period of great creative activity for Doyle. But it also featured a true descent into Doyle's own sealed and impenetrable subconscious, from which his tales merge into darkness in his prose. Work from a section of this period includes not only the historical mediaeval romances, themselves much preoccupied with descriptions of violence, but also a number of short stories, all of which exhibit Gothic references in plot, construction, and tone, thus marking a return in his short fiction to the morbid territory espoused by Edgar Allan Poe to whom the author openly acknowledged his debt as a fiction writer.

Below:

Sherlock Holmes was the first truly forensic investigator of crime
who believed that the detective should concentrate on the evidence
left at a crime scene. This method, involving observation of clues
and the construction of a hypothesis based on their interpretation,
Was first explored by his French predecessor, in Poe's Auguste Dupin
In 'The Murders in the Rue Morgue.' Her he examines blood traces in
VALL.

There is, for example, the grotesque Adventure of Wisteria Lodge where a woman is abducted and drugged, a story which includes ritual slaughter, and an attack on a South American whose is beaten to death.

In 'The Silver Mirror', over which Doyle laboured long and hard, a haunted mirror conveys a dreadful and repeated imagery of violent death to the unwitting onlooker, regarding the details of the death of Richie, the lover of Mary Queen of Scots. Also from this period is a story of 'The Sealed Room', in which a young man comes to learn the truth about his father's mysterious disappearance years earlier. A friend and he find a key and look inside the forbidden room. Still seated at a table is his mummified father, whose mounting debts have forced him to become a victim of a sealed room.

We have here several strands of Gothic's universal obsessive preoccupations, the mountain of debt threatening to engulf Doyle and his family, the madness and subsequent incarceration of his father and the symbol of the sealed room itself, which is a place of concealment and dark family secrets, a Gothic motif used best to its advantage and in fine literary construction, in Poe's 'The Fall of the House of Usher'.

It is regrettable that in most of what has been written about Doyle, very little attempt has been made to demonstrate how, in his short and longer fiction, his preoccupation with the three mainsprings of human behaviour dominates his work: the obsession with death, the obsession with sex and sexual indiscretion, and lastly, the idea of retribution.

As has been pointed out by many Ripperologists, these same factors are most likely to have been part of the obsessive quest of the man or woman known as 'Jack the Ripper' who terrorised London's populace in the 1880s.

In January 1894, shortly after he received the Transactions of the Society for Psychical Research from London, Conan Doyle began work on a novella entitled 'The Parasite'. His fascination with hypnotism had been freshly fired by a lengthy address about mesmerism given by Balfour and reprinted in the Transactions. Although he was extremely dismissive of this short work, The Parasite provides a fascinating insight into the twin areas of sexual obsession and mesmeric control.

The story concerns one Professor Austin Gilroy. An elderly academic who describes himself as a 'highly psychic man', Gilroy conforms precisely to the neurasthenic type of individual who makes his appearance elsewhere in Conan Doyle's fiction: dark eyes, a thin olive face, tapering fingers - in all essentials a dreamer, 'full of impressions and intuitions'.

Gilroy is a rationalist who a departure from reason affects 'like an odd smell or a musical discord'. He scorns the efforts of his colleague, Wilson, a psychic researcher bearing an uncanny resemblance to Myers:

'His whole life and soul and energy works to one end. He drops to sleep collating his results of the past day, and he wakes to plan his research for the coming one... he goes on, uncomplainingly, corresponding with a hundred semi-maniacs in the hope of finding one reliable witness ...collating old books, devouring new ones, experimenting, lecturing, trying to light up in others the fiery interest which is consuming him ...'

Despite his scepticism, Gilroy accepts an invitation from Wilson to attend a private demonstration of mesmerism at his house. There he and his fiancée, Agatha, are introduced to a clairvoyant, Miss Penelosa, a crippled woman of West Indian origin with penetrating grey-green eyes. Agatha allows herself to be hypnotized and later appears at Gilroy's house and announces that their engagement is at an end. Perplexed and dismayed, Gilroy discovers that Agatha, who has retained no conscious knowledge of the refusal, carried out the action whilst under post-hypnotic suggestion. Following this convincing demonstration, Gilroy becomes convinced of the power of hypnotism and is willing to concede that the human soul possesses its own individual identity. Previously his materialistic interpretation of the universe had led him to assume that consciousness was a mere by-product of the body's functions. At this point in the novella, Gilroy's views closely resemble those of the young Conan Doyle:

'The brain, I thought, secreted the mind, as the liver does the bile. But how can this be when I see mind working from a distance, and playing upon matter as a musician might upon a violin. The body does not give rise to the soul then, but is rather the rough instrument by which the spirit manifests itself. The windmill does not give rise to the wind, but only indicates it .. .'

Eager to learn more about the powers of Miss Penelosa, Gilroy submits to hypnotic treatment. Conscious of her eyes (grey-green, deep, inscrutable) boring into his, Gilroy soon loses consciousness and afterwards realizes that he is a perfect subject for such mesmeric experiments.

Although he is warned by his colleague Charles Sadler (a young anatomist) about the baleful influence exercised by Miss Penelosa, Gilroy ascribes this to professional envy and continues to participate in the experiments. Slowly, his personality begins to change:

'Agatha says that I am thinner, and darker under the eyes. I am conscious of a nervous irritability which I had not observed in myself before. The least noise, for example, makes me start, and the stupidity of a student causes me exasperation instead of amusement.'

Added to this complication is the unacceptable fact that Miss Penelosa has developed a strong attraction for the professor and, try as he may, he cannot now resist her summons. Gilroy, now conceiving her as 'a monstrous parasite' and himself as a puppet dancing to her every command, locks himself in his room. However, his feelings of success at this attempt to defend his free will are dashed when he discovers that the clairvoyant has fallen ill and has thus experienced a diminution of her powerful will.

Once Miss Penelosa has recovered, Gilroy breaks out his room and finds himself in her boudoir. A scene of implied sexual perversity follows in which Miss Penelosa passes her hand over Gilroy's hair 'as one caresses a dog'. Gilroy thrills to her touch ('I was her slave, body and soul, and for the moment I rejoiced in my slavery'). A few minutes later, as her power fades, Gilroy's revulsion comes flooding back and he abuses the clairvoyant in a blind fury.

Now a vendetta is launched against Gilroy by Miss Penelosa. His concentration lapses during lectures and his mind slowly deteriorates to such an extent that he is suspended by the university authorities. The picture looks even blacker when, following a reported raid on a branch of the Bank of England, Gilroy discovers his own coat, impregnated with the same green paint which had appeared on the bank window.

Gilroy decides to act. He confronts Miss Penelosa and threatens to murder her if she does not desist. The clairvoyant treats him with utter contempt, warning him that when his *fiancé* returns from holiday with her parents she will be the next object of her machinations.

Returning to his lodgings, Gilroy falls into a deep sleep. When he awakes, he finds himself in Agatha's boudoir, clutching a small phial of sulphuric acid. He realizes that he has been the intended perpetrator of a vitriol throwing but is unable to comprehend why Agatha has escaped her fate. Recognition dawns when, on hurrying to his home, he is given the news of her death that very afternoon.

This theme of sexual obsession, leading to death or rejection is something that was at the heart of Edgar Allan Poe's prose and poetry and it continued to fascinate Doyle right the way through his literary career. It is also one that emerges countless times in the Holmes saga.

The theme of a strong sexual obsession, or passion, is also exploited in several of the short stories in the Holmes series. The most obvious that come to mind are those of the 'Adventure of The Cardboard Box,' where the adulterous wife and her lover are both drowned at sea, having had one of their ears removed. The topic also arises in 'A Study In Scarlet'. 'The Valley of Fear' is a notable example, as is 'The Adventure of the Sussex Vampire' 'The Adventure of The Devil's Foot,' as also is the case with the much later examples of 'The Adventure of the Creeping Man' and 'The Veiled Lodger'. Both 'Thor Bridge' and 'Lady Frances Carfax' feature sexual passion and perversity. These are to name only a few.

In his memorable book about writers who deeply influenced and fascinated him, Conan Doyle, in 'Through The Magic Door', makes this significant comment about Edgar Allan Poe, the progenitor of the vast and fertile genre of fiction we now ascribe the label to as 'Crime':

'Poe is to my mind, the original short story writer of all time. His brain was like a seed-pod full of seeds which flew carelessly around, and from which have sprung nearly all our modern types of story. Just think of what he did in his offhand, prodigal fashion, seldom troubling to repeat a success, but pushing on to some new achievement. To him must be ascribed the monstrous progeny of writers on the detection of crime--"quorum pars parva fui!" Each may find some little development of his own, but his main art must trace back to those admirable stories of Monsieur Dupin, so wonderful in their masterful force, their reticence, their quick dramatic point. After all, mental acuteness is the one quality which can be ascribed to the ideal detective, and when that has once been admirably done, succeeding writers must necessarily be content for all time to follow in the same main track. But not only is Poe the originator of the detective story; all treasure-hunting, cryptogram-solving yarns trace back to his "Gold Bug," just as all pseudo-scientific Verne-and-Wells stories have their prototypes in the "Voyage to the Moon," and the "Case of Monsieur Valdemar." If every man who receives a cheque for a story which owes its springs to Poe were to pay tithe to a monument for the master, he would have a pyramid as big as that of Cheops.'

By early summer, 1889, Conan Doyle had been operating as a well-established and busy GP, and was living in Southsea, a suburb of Portsmouth, with his wife, Louise, who had recently given birth to a daughter called Mary. At that time in his life, he was happily married to Louise, heavily involved in local sporting events and had had a book published, a Gothic novel, entitled 'The Mystery of Cloomber'. Sadly, for the aspiring author, it had enjoyed limited success. He was still sending his short stories to magazines, some of which had expressed an interest in his work. But at that time, 'The Strand Magazine' had only just been conceived. Later on, he would find it a most useful magazine to contribute to.

We know that Doyle had a considerable interest in the newspaper reporting of the Ripper crimes. He was, like Holmes, a self-confessed 'omnivorous reader,' and read widely in the local newspapers, one of which was a well-established newspaper called the 'Portsmouth Evening News'. Throughout the year of 1889 and beyond, into the next decade and century, 'The Portsmouth Evening News' reported widely on many examples of violent crime, which they thought might be applicable to the identity of the Ripper. This 'shock/false horror' event would most certainly have caught his attention:

PORTSMOUTH EVENING NEWS
11 JAN 1889
'"JACK THE RIPPER." EXTRAORDINARY IMPOSTURE BY A GIRL.
    The Watch Committee of the Manchester Corporation have issued a report on a remarkable imposture, which they think may probably suggest an explanation of other cases in which "Jack the Ripper" letters have been

received. The Chief Constable (Mr. C. Wood) reported to the Committee that on November 21st last a young woman about 19 years age (whose name is suppressed), informed the police that she had received a threatening letter signed "Jack the Ripper," and couched in the usual language. Letters continued to arrive, some post and others being put under the door. Nineteen letters in all were received, threatening to take the girl's life and that of a companion. Some of the letters were stained with blood, and others had coffins rudely drawn upon them.

'Whilst the police were trying to discover the sender of the missives some young women who work with the girl pointed out a man having followed them, and accused him of being the writer of the letters. The man was spoken to the police, but turned out to be quite innocent of the affair. Next day, however, the girl received a letter by post purporting to come from Jack the Ripper and saying that she has got him "pinched," but that he bad squared the police, and again threatening to kill her. A companion of the complainant's also received two similar letters. The matter became more serious later on, for on the 21st December the girl reported that she had been stabbed. She stated that she went into the backyard home with a jug to empty, and saw a man on the wall with a knife in his hand. He at once struck at her, and in order to save her face, she put up her left arm, and received a cut near the wrist. She then screamed, and her father ran out, but could see no one. She was taken to a surgery, when it was found that her arm was severely cut, and had to be stitched.

'The matter created great alarm and excitement in the neighbourhood, and at the Roman Catholic chapel, where the complainant and the other girl who had received letters attended, special prayers were offered for their safety, and that the man might soon brought to justice ; and the clergy paid frequent visits to both families. After the report of the stabbing, the police set a close watch on the two houses, and from something recently discovered, the district superintendent of police sent for the complainant and questioned her, and she ultimately confessed that she had written all the letters herself. As to the alleged attack in the back yard, she stated that she never went into the yard, and never saw any man. She herself cut her arm with a knife in scullery, and then set up a scream. The only explanation of conduct that the girl could give, was of being " unhappy at home."

Over the years that followed this case there were to be other cases of the kind based on delusion, sadomasochistic fantasy or just plain mischief. Doyle, who somewhat demeaned his forensic skills, claiming he was only a 'Mr Average' when it came to real crime, would have regarded these claims as an example of female, uterine-originated hysteria.

However, a little later that same year, the doctor with a fascination for criminology and horror, was to read of a second piece connected to the Ripper in his 'Portsmouth Evening News':

6 April 1889
'"JACK THE RIPPER." THE LIVERPOOL POLICE RECEIVE A LETTER.
The Head Constable of Liverpool has received a letter signed "Jack the Ripper," and addressing Captain Nott-Bower as "Dear Boss." In this missive, the chief of the police is informed that the writer was going to operate in Liverpool after the Whitechapel manner, and that the special neighbourhood has chosen a street not far from the sailors' home. Of course, the letter may be a stupid practical joke on the part of somebody who might easily be much better employed, and it may be hoped that this is really the case. But the Head Constable resolved to take adequate precautions, and he has consequently put the whole police force on their guard, the letter of the so-called "Jack the Ripper" being read to the men on the setting of the night and other watches at the various divisional stations. A little over six months have elapsed since the ghastly-looking letter and postcard bearing the above signature reached the head of the Metropolitan police, after four women had been murdered and horribly mutilated; and after some months' quietude, it was hoped that the last had been heard of "Jack the Ripper."'

Was this, perhaps, the foundation of Doyle's cherished theory that the Ripper was a seaman or some kind of commercial traveller and probably not English? Certainly this letter and its contents would have suggested as much to him.

Later that same year, Conan Doyle's evening newspaper had this to tell him.

29th OCTOBER 1889
THE FATE OF JACK THE RIPPER.

There is a West of England member who privately (writes the London correspondent of the Nottingham Guardian) declares that he has solved the mystery of Jack the Ripper. His theory, and he repeats with so much emphasis that it might almost be called his doctrine, is that Jack the Ripper committed suicide on the night of his last murder. He cannot give details, but the story is so circumstantial that a good many people believe it. He states that a man with blood-stained clothes committed suicide on the night of the last murder, and he asserts that the man was the son of a father who suffered from homicidal mania. I do not know what the police think of the story, but believe that before long a clean breast will made, and that the accusation will be sifted thoroughly.'

Was this a mere attention - grabbing headline or was it actually based on fact as opposed to supposition. And who was that member of Parliament, and was the information obtained second hand from, perhaps, a senior-ranking police officer? Was that senior police officer none other than Sir Melvile Macnaghten? This man was the Assistant Chief Constable of Scotland Yard.

Macnaghten was promoted to the job of the Assistant Chief Constable of Scotland Yard from June 1889, to December 1890 and after this, was promoted to Chief Commisioner, a position he held until 1903, when he then became the Assistant Commissioner of the London Met. After he retired in 1913 he produced a memoir about his experiences. He expressed his feelings about the Ripper's motives and later told the Daily Mail newspaper how it was his regret that he had not joined the force, until some six months after the last of the Ripper crimes. He went on to express his opinion about the case and that he was frustrated about identifying in public, the man whom he is suspected of being the perpetrator. He told reporters that he thought the body of a man subsequently found in the River Thames was a sexual maniac but that he would never reveal his own secrets about the criminal. He told them that he had destroyed all his documents, and that there was no further possibility of any information being revealed from the records. When he came to write his biography, 'Days of My Years', published in 1914, he dismissed the possibility of two of the murder victims of Emma Smith and Martha Chamberlain, as having been the victims of the Ripper, a man who had been seen chatting to them, and expressed the opinion that the first real Whitechapel murder took place in August 31 when Mary Nichols was found with her throat cut. He also believed that the last of the Ripper's murder victims, Mary Kelley who was founded in ninth of November 1888, was the very last. And he then said, 'It will have been noticed that the fury of the murderer, as evinced in his method of mutilation, increased on every occasion, and his appetite appears to become sharpened by indulgence.' He thought that in the room at Miller's Court where the last murder took place, 'the moment you found scope for the opportunities you've been seeking, and that 'After all, his is brain gave way,' and this encouraged him to commit suicide. He thought the man was a sexual maniac. But he also had the view that sexual matters are the most difficult for police to bring home to their perpetrators, for they do not appear to be direct motives. He believed that the murderer had a diseased body and that this was a kind of revenge killing. But one of Macnaghten's most important statements on the notice was written in 1894, and is now referred to as the Norton memoranda. This was a written account explaining how he did not agree with the current theories about the crimes. The claims being made in a newspaper   that Thomas Cutbush, who was at that time being confined to an asylum were in his opinion, insubstantial. In a much later discovered memorandum, which was not intended for public use, he named three individuals, any one of whom could have been more likely than Cutbush to have committed the murders. The three men were Mr. M. J. Druid, a schoolmaster from Blackheath, Kozminski, and Michael Armstrong. He did not say that any of one of the three was the murderer, but that they were more likely than Cutbush to have carried out the crimes.

In recent times much has been made of the possibility that the murders were done by Druitt.

The schoolmaster, who lived at Blackheath, and may have been the murderer, would have been someone Doyle was interested in. Doyle knew the area of Blackheath intimately, for it was there that Holmes' old friend Charles Peace was arrested. I personally know that Doyle would have been familiar with the location since, in a letter to me from Jean Bromet, the youngest daughter of Sir Arthur, she stated her father had 'known the Leckie family' for some years' prior to his meeting with the daughter, Jean

Leckie in 1896 - this being much earlier than previous biographers had assumed. Also we know that Conan Doyle played a cricket match in the grounds of a sumptuous villa in Blackheath, known as The Cedars, close to where the Leckie family were themselves living a couple of roads down from here in what was then called Lee, and that the match took place on August 1st, 1891 when Doyle knocked out two wickets of his opponents' team. (mentioned in Brian Pugh's comprehensive 'Chronology of the Life of Sir Arthur Conan Doyle'.)

Certainly, it appears that Macnaghten had a considerable expertise as a detective. In an appreciation published about him in the Sunday Post, for the 15th of May 1921, the reporter commented that 'the study of crime was his hobby, and a keen judgement of character enabled him to select the best men for the elucidation of crime to work in conjunction with the most famous officers in London speak of him in terms of great admiration'. And that 'there was nothing of the detective of fiction about him. He was better than that. He had all the scientific methods of crime detection at his finger ends. And combined with this was a wonderful mathematical brain which could work out problems which few men would be capable of solving crimes.'

Yet how far would Conan Doyle have accepted Macnaghten's theory about the Ripper? In his real life as an amateur detective, in the case of George Edalji and of Oscar Slater, the writer used methods of forensic examination and witness evidence to prove that the perpetrators of these crime were completely innocent. Is the truth that in the case of the Ripper, he also found their methods rather clumsy and ill thought out? It would be unlike him if he did not. Wasn't it Sherlock Holmes who once said that he did not wished to be 'confused with the official police force?'

What are we to make of this? We do not know whether or not Macnaghten was a member of the famous Crime Club. But this does not rule out the possibility that he may well have gone to one of the many early meetings and might have explained to other club members about his theories. And perhaps they disagreed on the solution that both men might have put forward. What do we know about the enigmatic Mr J Druitt and what were the circumstances surrounding his death and the discovery of his body in the Thames at Christmas time, 1888?

Jean Leckie, in later years, when she was accompanying Conan Doyle as his second wife on their world wide spiritualist tours. She met Conan Doyle at Blackheath, where also worked one of the Ripper suspects, Montague Druitt. Photo c. www. arthur-conan-doyle.com.

Druitt worked as a barrister and supplemented his income at the bar by working as an assistant schoolmaster at a boarding school in Blackheath, now south east London, that was run by Mr. George Valentine.

Macnaghten maintained that Druitt had been a doctor of about 41 years of age and of fairly good family, who disappeared at the time of the Miller's Court murder, and whose body was found floating in the Thames on 31st December a gap of 7 weeks after the said murder. This time lapse may be significant in suggesting he was not the Ripper. Macnaghten also got his age wrong. At the time he died he was ten years younger than the detective had suggested. In itself this may not prove to be significant. However, what it does show is that Macnaghten was not always accurate, despite the glowing account given to him by some of his former colleagues.

In fact, as I have discovered from my analysis of contemporary news reports about this suspect, Druitt, on 5th January 1889, the 'Acton, Chiswick, and Turnham Green Gazette' reported on the inquest into Druitt's death, and reported at some length on the facts about him by his brother, William. William Druitt told the coroner's court that Druitt said he lived at Bournemouth, and that he was an actually by training and occupation, a solicitor, not a humble schoolmaster. And his brother was 31 last birthday. He was a barrister-at-law, and an assistant master in a boarding school in Blackheath. The brother went on to say that a friend told him that on the 11th of December, Druitt had not been heard of at his chambers for more than seven days and that he then went to London to make inquiries about his brother and at Blackheath he found that his brother had got into serious trouble at the school, and had been summarily dismissed. This was on the December the 30th. Notably, however, no one at the school was prepared to state what was the nature of and reason for his dismissal.

Although such a significant reason may not be immediately obvious to modern readers we should recall that this was a mere three years after Oscar Wilde had been convicted of gross indecency and received a sentence of hard labour for his offence. Thus, the very mention of an adult male having 'feelings' for the boys for whom he had pastoral responsibility would have had a severe effect on the young Mr Druitt. And such dalliances were not unheard of in the English public school of that period. In a letter he wrote to his brother he said: - "Since Friday I felt I was going to be like mother, and the best thing for me was to die." Witness, continuing, said deceased had never made any attempt on his life before. His mother became insane in July last. If it were the case with Druitt that he had committed an assault on a boy, it would make sense of why he was so abruptly got rid of and it also makes sense of the brother's comment that Druitt had said something to him in a letter which was to the effect that he felt he might be going mad.

It was most usual for so-called 'normal' heterosexual males to look upon homosexuality among men as an 'illness', as is evident, for example in the classic psychological studies conducted at about that time in Germany by Krafft - Ebing. Indeed, in a remark Doyle himself made of Wilde, whom he had met many years back, when he shared a literary luncheon in London at the behest of an American publisher, Lippincotts, outside of the heterosexual norm, only 'hateful and unnatural vices were to be found.'

After the inquest had been concluded, the jury returned a verdict of suicide by drowning "whilst of unsound mind" and Druitt's body was returned to his family for burial.

What circumstantial or other evidence did Macnaghten have by which he might have tried to convince Doyle and the other members of the Crime Club that Druitt was real the killer of the Whitechapel women? It is true that his death coincided with, what was then perceived to be, the last of the murderer's victims, Mary Kelley. But that might just be a coincidence. It is also true that he might have got into and out of Whitechapel on his way to or from Backheath, using the very popular Brighton railway line which had more regular trains running, than those of the much older South Eastern Railway Company. Moreover, it would have been comparatively easy for Druitt to have avoided the scrutiny of pedestrians in and upon Blackheath and its adjoining village since, as I pointed out many years ago in my monograph, 'Sherlock Holmes and The South Eastern,' Blackheath Station was supplied with then its own cab rank, run by the enterprising Mr Tilling, who operated his rank immediately opposite the station along with '15 other cabs.'

But this is all circumstantial, and, as Holmes once remarked to Watson 'circumstantial evidence can be a pretty tricky thing.' Equally tricky is the claim by Macnaghten that Druitt's family thought he was the real Ripper -

an assertion which more recent biographical accounts have proved quite erroneous. Of course, Macnaghten did not say in the public domain that Druitt was the Ripper, only that the police had 'suspicions' that *he might have been*. To quote his own words:-

'...from private information I have little doubt that his family believed him to be the Ripper..."

So what exactly was his private information? We shall probably never know at this distance of time. Could it have been something that Doyle himself was privy to?

Then there is the case of whom I shall refer to as Macnaghten's 'partner in crime' regarding the theory or theories regarding the elusive Jack The Ripper. This gentleman was most decidedly a member of Conan Doyle's much loved 'Crime Club' and was on friendly terms with Conan Doyle.

His name was Arthur Griffiths. Griffiths' importance to the search for the Ripper is that not only was he a friend of Robert Anderson and Melville Macnaghten, but he was the first to describe in public and with certainty, the three suspects for the Whitechapel murders which were then named in Macnaghten's report of 23rd February, 1894; Kosminski, Ostrog, and Druitt, but without naming them. However, he did so in his book, 'Mysteries of Police and Crime', Cassell & Co., 1898, 2 vols.

As Griffiths explained in his introduction to Volume One of his huge work (and we can be certain there was a copy of it on the shelves in Doyle's home):

'The outside public may think that the identity of that later miscreant, "Jack the Ripper," was never revealed. So far as actual knowledge goes, this is undoubtedly true. But the police, after the last murder, had brought their investigations to the point of strongly suspecting several persons, all of them known to be homicidal lunatics, and against three of these they held very plausible and reasonable grounds of suspicion. Concerning two of them the case was weak, although it was based on certain colourable facts. One was a Polish Jew, a known lunatic, who was at large in the district of Whitechapel at the time of the murder, and who, having afterwards developed homicidal tendencies, was confined in an asylum. This man was said to resemble the murderer by the one person who got a glimpse of him— the police-constable in Mitre Court.

The second was a Russian doctor, also insane, who had been a convict both in England and Siberia. This man was in the habit of carrying about surgical knives and instruments in his pockets; his antecedents were of the very worst, and at the time of the Whitechapel murders he was in hiding, or, at least, his whereabouts were never exactly known. The third person was of the same type, but the suspicion in his case was stronger, and there was every reason to believe that his own friends entertained grave doubts about him. He also was a doctor in the prime of life, was believed to be insane or on the borderland of insanity, and he disappeared immediately after the last murder, that in Miller's Court, on the 9th of November, 1888. On the last day of that year, seven weeks later, his body was found floating in the Thames, and was said to have been in the water a month. The theory in this case was that after his last exploit, which was the most fiendish of all, his brain entirely gave way, and he became furiously insane and committed suicide.

'It is at least a strong presumption that "Jack the Ripper" died or was put under restraint after the Miller's Court affair, which ended this series of crimes. It would be interesting to know whether in this third case the man was left-handed or ambidextrous, for both suggestions having been advanced by medical experts after viewing the victims. Certainly other doctors disagreed on this point, which may be said to add another to the many instances in which medical evidence has been conflicting, or to say confusing.

'Yet the incontestable fact remains, unsatisfactory and disquieting, that many murder mysteries have baffled all inquiry, and that the long list of undiscovered crimes continually receives many mysterious additions. An erroneous impression, however, prevails that such failures are more common in Great Britain than elsewhere. No doubt the British police are greatly handicapped by the law's limitations, which in England act always in protecting the accused. But with all their advantages, the power to make arrests on suspicion, to interrogate the accused parties and force on self-incrimination — the Continental police meet with many rebuffs.'

Were Griffiths and Macnaghten right then, to assume that they had, between them, narrowed down the identity of the killer to just these few? And was Druitt the man who committed those crimes, this 'evidence' in particular, being based on what was thought to be the last murder at

Miller's Court? I have reason to think they were mistaken and I believe that Conan Doyle disputed this too. And if it been left to the most famous of all detectives, Sherlock Holmes, I think he would have gone a long way to solving this most famous and ghastly of all Victorian crimes, as I shall demonstrate in the next chapter relating to Conan Doyle and Jack The Ripper.

APPENDICES

I. A NIGHT IN AN OPIUM DEN
By the author of 'A DEAD MAN'S DIARY,'
From 'The Strand Magazine, January to June,1891, volume1.

Yes, I have smoked opium in Ratcliffe Highway and through the pipe which had the honour of making that distinguished novelist sick.

"And did you have lovely dreams? And what were they like ? " asks a fair reader.

Yes, I had lovely dreams, and I have no doubt that by the aid of imagination, and a skilful manipulation of De Quincey, l could concoct a fancy picture of opium smoking and its effects, which might pass for a faithful picture of what really occurred. But, "My Lord and jury "- to quote the historic words of Mrs, Cluppins, when cross-examined by Serjeant Buzzfuzz," My Lord and jury, I will not deceive you ": what those dreams were, I could not for the life of me now describe, for they were too aerial and unsubstantial to be caught and fixed, like hard facts, in words, by any other pen than that of a Coleridge, or a De Quincey. I might as well attempt to convey to you, by means of a clay model, an idea of the prism-fires and rainbow-hues that circle, and change, and chase each other round the pictured sides of that floating fairy sphere which we call a soap- bubble, an attempt, unassisted, to describe my dreams in words.

Hence it is that in this narrative, I have confined myself strictly to the facts of my experiences. The proprietor of the den which I visited was a Chinaman named Chang, who positively grinned at me over from head to foot - not only what made sense to him by the friend who had piloted me to the establishment, but as long as I remained within grinning range. An uninformed onlooker might not unnaturally have concluded that I was stone-deaf and dumb, and that our host was endeavouring to express, by his features, the cordiality he was unable to convey in words. In reply to every casual remark made by my companion, the Chinaman would glance up for a moment at his face, and then turn round to grimace again at me, as though I, and only, were the subject of their conversation, and he was half afraid I might think he did not take a becoming interest in it. ln the few words which I exchanged with him, I found him exceedingly civil, and he took great pains to explain to me that his wearing no pigtail was attributable, not to his own act and deed, but to the fact that that ornament had been cut off by some person or persons unknown, when he was either drunk or asleep - I could not quite make out which. The deadliest insult which can be offered a Chinaman (so I understood him) is to cut off his pigtail, and it was only when referring to this incident, and to his desire to wreak a terrible vengeance upon the perpetrators, that there was any cessation of his embarrassing smile. The thought of the insult to which he had been subjected, and of his consequent degradation in the eyes of his countrymen, brought so evil a look upon his parchment-coloured features, and caused his small and cunning eyes to twist and turn so horribly, that I was glad to turn the conversation to pleasanter topics, even though it necessitated my being once more fixed by that bland and penetrating smile so peculiarly his own. The smile became more rigid than ever, when I informed him that I was anxious to smoke a pipe of opium. The way in which he turned his face upon me (including the smile, which enveloped and illumined me in its rays) was, for all the world, like the turning-on by a policeman of a bull`s-eye lantern.

With a final grin which threatened to distort permanently his features, he bade us follow him and led the way up the most villainous, treacherous staircase which it had ever been my lot to ascend.

"Den" was an appropriate name for the reeking hole to which he conducted us. It was dirty and dark, being lit only by a smoking lamp on the mantel-shelf, and was not much larger than a full-sized cupboard.

The walls, which were of a dingy yellow (not unlike the "whites" of the smokers' eyes) were quite bare, with the exception of the one facing the door, on which, incongruously enough, was plastered a coarsely - coloured and hideous print of the crucifixion. The furniture consisted of three raised mattresses, with small tables on which were placed pipes, lamps, and opium.

Huddled, or curled upon these mattresses lay two wretched smokers - one of them with the whites, or, I should say, "yellows," of his eyes turned up to the ceiling, and another, whose slumbers we had apparently disturbed, staring about him with a dazed and stupefied air. Something in the look of these men-either the ghastly pallor of their complexion, or the list- lessness of their bearing, reminded me not a little of the "white lepers" of Norway. I have seen patients in the hospitals there whose general aspect greatly resembled that of these men, although the skin of the white leper has more or a milky appearance - as if it had been bleached, in fact than that of the opium-smoker, which is dirtier and more yellow.

The remaining occupants of the room, two of whom were Chinamen, were wide awake. The third was a partly naked Malay with a decidedly evil aspect, who shrank back on my entrance and coiled himself up in a dark corner, whence he lay watching me. very much in the manner in which the prisoned pythons in a serpent-house watch the visitors who come to tap at the glass of their cages.

The Chinaman, however, seemed pleased to see me; and, after l had handed my cigar case to the nearest, begging that he and his friend would help themselves, they became quite companionable. One of them, to my surprise, relinquished the drug which immediately he had been smoking and began to suck with evident relish at the cigar.

The other, after pocketing the weed, lay down on his back with his arms behind his head, and with his legs drawn up to his body, in which singularly graceful and easy attitude, he carried on a conversation with a friend, watching me narrowly all the time, through the chin between his knees. At this point of my visit, and before I could take any further stock of the surroundings, l was not a little surprised by the entrance of a young, and by no means ill-looking English woman, to whom I gave a civil " good evening," receiving, however, only a suspicious and surly nod in reply. She occupied herself at first by tickling one of the Chinamen under the armpits, evidently enjoying no little amusement in the fits of wild, unearthly, and uncontrollable laughter into which he broke, but growing weary of this, she seated herself on the raised mattress where I was located, and proceeded to take stock of her visitor. Beginning at my boots, and travelling up by way of my trousers and waistcoat, up to my collar and face, she examined me so critically and searchingly from head to foot that I fancied once or twice I could see the row of figures she was inwardly casting up, and could hear her saying to herself, "Boots and trousers, say, sixty bob; and watch and chain, a couple of flimsies each; which, with coat and waistcoat, would bring it up to thirty shiners; which, with a couple of guineas for links, loose cash and studs make about forty quid. That's your figure, young man, as far as I can reckon it."

While this was going on, my host, Mr Chang, was busily making preparations for my initiatory opium smoke, by putting small pellets of the opium, (a brownish, glue-like substance) upon a pin, and rolling and re-rolling them against the pipe, which is about the size of a small flute, and has a big open bowl with a tiny aperture at the base. Into this aperture the drug-smeared pin is slipped, and the pipe is then held over a lamp, and the fumes of the burning opium inhaled. The occupation is by no means a luxurious one; for, as surely as I removed the pipe from my lips to indulge in a furtive cough (and it did make me cough a bit at first), it inevitably went out. By means of repeated applications to the lamp, however, I managed to get through the allotted number of pipes, and sank slowly and insensibly into the deep waters of slumber, until at last they closed over my head, and I was swept and borne unresisting away upon the vast, seaward, setting tide of sleep.

Of my dreams, as I have already said, I have but the haziest of recollections. I can just recall a sensation of sailing, as on a cloud, amid region of blue and buoyant ether; of seeing, through vistas of purple and gold, a scene of sunny seas and shining shores, where, it seemed to me, I beheld the fabled "Blessed Isles," stretching league beyond league from afar; and of peeps of paradisal landscapes that swam up to me as through a world of waters, and then softened and sank away into a blending of beauteous colours, and into a vision of white warm arms and wooing bosoms.

And so we slept on, I and my wretched companions, until, to quote Rossetti :-

Sleep sunk them lower than the tide of dreams,
And their dreams watched them sink, and slide away.
Slowly their souls swam up again, through gleams
Of lowered light, and dull, drowned weeds of day ;
'Til, from some wonder of new woods and streams,
He awoke and wondered more.

Yes, awoke to wonder where I was, and where were my boots, my hat, and my umbrella; woke to find the faithless friend, who had promised to guard my slumbers, sleeping peacefully at his post; and woke with a taste in my mouth which can only be likened to a cross between onions and bad tobacco. And this taste, in conjunction with a splitting headache and a general lowness of spirits, served, for the next day or two, to keep me constantly in remembrance of my visit to the Opium Den in the Ratcliffe Highway.

A NOTE ABOUT HANDCUFFS

In the business of the arrest of suspects concerning Scotland Yard detectives and constables and their charges was the means of their safe transport, once apprehended, and their confinement.

What was not always easy, as is clearly visible in the Sherlock Holmes saga, for example, in the arrest of the hoodlum and killer, Abe Slaney, in 'The Dancing Men', and the most difficult arrest of the perpetrator in 'A Study in Scarlet', was the methodology used. These are but two examples of how difficult it was to physically arrest criminals. Among methods which were at hand was the use of handcuffs. However, in Victorian times, cuffs, or bracelets as they were known popularly at The Yard, were not always easy to apply. A most curious article about the use of police handcuffs occurs in the 'Strand Magazine' in the January to June edition, in volume seven of that wonderful magazine, which launched the Holmes Stories ,in an article, written by a former Inspector Morris Moser, who was once leader of the Criminal Investigation Department at Great Scotland Yard.

The author remarks that, until 1850, there were two kinds of these handcuffs in existence in the UK. One, which went under the name of 'the figure of eight', allowed the prisoner not even a small amount of liberty and was really used only for suspects who showed extreme violence, keeping the hands in a fixed position on the back of the body. But the pain inflicted made it by nature of a punishment rather than a preventive against resistance or attack. It was universally dreaded, the author goes on to say, by prisoners of war crimes, for it caused a great deal of unbearable pain.

The most popular type of handcuff, and certainly that's the one I would imagine the police detectives in Holmes stories used, was known as the 'flexible', which in fact resembled the type of handcuffs used, even 30 years ago, by detectives in the UK although the Victorian version was very much heavier than that used in the USA, since it contained a greater amount of iron. These were often referred to as the 'darbies,' an American term for handcuffs. The English version was much larger, was extremely unwieldy, and under most circumstances, extremely difficult to apply. It weighed over a pound, and would have to have been unlocked with a key rather like the operation of winding up an eight day clock.

This lengthy and disagreeable operation at a time when a prisoner was struggling and fighting, was almost unbearable for the detective or the arresting officer.

These British handcuffs (above) were at least less vicious than the notorious and cruel 'nippers' used principally in S America in the '80's. (Below).

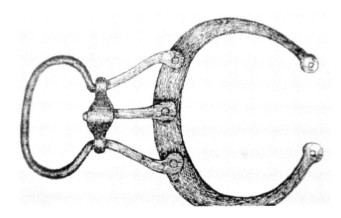

In order to apply the bracelets, as for example in The Red Headed League' when the arrest was made on a notorious safe breaker John Clay, the prisoner had to be virtually overpowered or made to submit before the cuffs were applied. Even when the handcuffs were actually attached, a very muscular person could certainly still reach for a cudgel or similar weapon and inflict blows upon his arresting officer.

Equally problematic was the fact that those sorts of handcuffs, did not fit all types of wrist. One can imagine the problem of a detective, trying to apply a pair of handcuffs which were either too small or too large. The American version, which appeared around 1880, only just prior to the Holmes period, was much lighter and made of a thinner steel. It also had a much smaller key and was therefore very popular in usage.

When he had to go and arrest one of a group of Russian rouble - note forgers, he discovered the prisoner had a stick which he tried to hit people with, and adds that he then had given himself several sized pairs of handcuffs of the British type. However, it was not until he'd obtained assistance that he was able to find a suitable size for the man's wrists. The police officers managed to force this man into a four wheeler in order to take him to the police station but he once again renewed his efforts and attacked them.

The detective writing this article explained how he sustained several blows from the man's handcuffed wrists when the prisoner brought them down heavily on his head, completely crushing his bowler hat.

The Scotland Yard ex-detective finishes his fascinating article by explaining that, in France, the use of handcuffs by police at that time was entirely forbidden, and prisoners were only handcuffed on being brought together before the judge or when crossing from court to court. He also remarks that women were never handcuffed in England. However, on the continent, it was a not uncommon occurrence.

He concludes by saying that in most criminals, once they had been arrested, they offered no resistance to the application of the handcuffs. However, certain expert thieves had been known to open handcuffs without a key, by means of knocking the part containing the spring on a stone, or a hard substance. And he says that it will be remembered that when the notorious criminal Charlie Peace was being taken to London by train, he contrived, although still handcuffed, to make an escape through the carriage window, which he was able to do, because he was so small. When finally he was captured, it was noticed that he had freed himself from one of the handcuffs.

These observations throw a great deal of light on the incidents of arrest which are described in several of the Holmes stories.

More handcuffing, as American gangster, Abe Slaney submits to the 'bracelets,' in DANC.

Portrait of Conan Doyle in his successful years. By now he was the owner of one of the largest libraries devoted to the subject of crime, criminals and forensic science. Sadly, after his death in 1930 this collection was auctioned. Portrait c. of www.arthur-conan-doyle.com

A CRIMINAL WORLD DICTIONARY

Being a dictionary of the more obscure names and phrases relating to the criminal investigations of Mr Sherlock Holmes, as mentioned in the accounts of his many cases recorded about him, by his friend and chronicler, Dr John Watson.:

My reasons for inclusion of a word or phrase in this dictionary are based largely on these criteria: a) the word or phrase must have a direct or oblique connection to the case, which may be unfamiliar to the modern reader, 2) the word would also require inclusion if it were related to a serious criminal case studied by, or would have certainly been known about by Holmes and now is unfamiliar or obscure, c) if a word which was obscure was related to the use of weapons in the cases Holmes encountered, and finally d) words or phrases the average reader would be unfamiliar with, including medical terms, if that word or phrase were likely to be obscure to a modern reader. Naturally, I accept that on the question of the *precise* function or meaning of any word, there can never be a consensus of opinion, and this is often made evident in many murder cases of our own period.

ACETONES (Ger. keton) The simplest of those organic compounds consisting of a carbonyl group united to two like or unlike alkyl radicals. Holmes did some research into their properties. Possibly he may have been interested in ketosis, an excessive formation in the body of acetone bodies, due to incomplete oxidation of fats - a condition which occurs in diabetes.
Source: COPP.
ACUSHLA (Irish: loved one: dearest) Dear: beloved. The Pinkerton agent, 'McMurdo' refers to Ettie Shafter as his 'acushla'. 'Follow your heart, acushla.'
Source: VALL, Pt.2, Ch.2.

A.D.P. BRIAR-ROOT PIPE A briar-root pipe manufactured by the firm of Alfred Dunhill. (A.D.P.: Alfred Dunhill Pipe) Part of the effects of John Straker. See also brier-pipe.

Source: SILV.

AGONY COLUMNS Personal columns of a newspaper. Holmes frequently had recourse to them in the course of his investigations.

Source: 3GAR; REDC; VALL, Ch.1.

AIR-GUN A gun that discharges missiles by means of compressed air. The air is usually released by a valve and the air contained in a reservoir situated either in the stock of the gun or outside it. Some air guns use a trigger-released spring which compresses the air behind the missile. Colonel Sebastian Moran used an ingenious air gun to kill the Hon.. Ronald Adair.

Source: EMPT

ALBERT CHAIN A watch-chain with stout links, popularised by Prince Albert Edward, (d.1861), the consort of Queen Victoria. Enoch J. Drebber possessed a gold Albert chain (STUD), Jabez Wilson and Hosmer Angel also wore one.

Source: STUD, CH.3; REDH; IDEN.

ALIENIST A specialist in the study of mental disorders: a psychiatrist. Watson uses the term when referring to Professor Presbury. 'Speaking as a medical man,' said I, 'it appears to be a case for an alienist." The O.E.D. quotes Romanes' In Nature, XXV, 193 (1881): 'All alienists are agreed as to the greater frequency of mental alienation in the summer season.' The term *alienation* still enjoys current usage, whilst alienist is obsolete.

Source: CREE

ALKALOID (Arabic: algaliy: the calcined ashes). A body resembling an alkali in properties (O.E.D.). Vegetable alkaloids are very bitter to taste and act powerfully on the CNS of mammals. They feature predominantly in the Canon and Holmes conducted considerable research into their properties (see, for instance, STUD and SIGN).

Source: STUD, Ch.l.; SIGN, Ch.6; SUSS.

ALPENSTOCK (L. Alpes: the Alps - perhaps a Celtic term) A staff with an iron point used for mountain climbing. Holmes used one in Switzerland. 'There was Holmes's alpenstock still leaning against the rock by which I had left him.' The O.E.D. quotes (1829) C. Latrobe's 'The Alpenstock; Or Sketches of Swiss Scenery'.

Source: FINA.

AMALGAM (L. L. amalgama) A combination of mercury and solid metal. Holmes assumed that the coiners at Eyford (ENGR) had used an amalgam to take the place of silver, but since nickel and tin were discovered in the outhouse this seems unlikely.

Source: ENGR.

AMBER A yellowish fossil resin used in the manufacture of pipe stems. Holmes possessed a pipe with an amber stem. '[Holmes] began to smoke over (the map), and occasionally to point out objects of interest with the reeking amber of his pipe.' The O.E.D. derives amber from ambergris. Its earliest English usage occurs in Howard: Household Books, as 'Imber-gres'. (Cf. O.Fr.: armaire, aumaire.) Source: PRIO.

AMERICAN RAILWAY BONDS Bonds for investment in North American railways. The criminals who raided Mawson & Williams' premises stole 'Nearly a hundred thousand pounds' worth of American railway bonds...' Source: STOC.

AMETHYST (Gr. amethystos) A precious stone of clear purple or bluish violet colour consisting of quartz coloured by manganese. Holmes received a present of a gold snuff box with an inlaid amethyst after the Irene Adler affair (SCAN).

Source: IDEN.

ANARCHISM (Gr. anarchia: leaderlessness). The teaching of the anarchists; that group of 19th century idealists whose ideal of society was one without government of any kind; also, one who seeks to advance such a system by acts of terrorism. The anarchist sect emerged circa 1872 and suffered considerably from a reactionary press in Europe. Much of the romanticism attached to their movement can be attributed to the popular writers of the later 19th century (Chesterton, Conrad, etc.). Morse Hudson commented (typically) that nobody but an Anarchist would go around smashing busts of Napoleon.

Source: SIXN.

ANEURISM, AORTIC (Otherwise: aneurysm: Gr. aneurysm). A condition of the heart in which the aorta (the great trunk of the arterial system) swells out. Often caused by syphilis. Jefferson Hope (STUD) died as a result of this condition.

Source: STUD, Pt.2, Ch.6.

APACHE A lawless ruffian or hooligan from Paris or elsewhere (Fr. a-pash). Le Brun was crippled by apaches when he opposed Baron Von Gruner.

Source: (1) NOBL, (2) ILLU.

APOPLEXY (Gr. apoplexia: apo - completeness: plexia - to strike) A sudden loss of sensation and motion, generally the result of thrombosis or a haemorrhaging in the brain. Victor Trevor reported to Holmes that his father had suffered an apoplectic fit. James Barclay died of apoplexy. The O.E.D. quotes Chaucer's Nun's Prologue: 'Napoplexie, ne poplexie ne shente nat hir head.' Source: GLOR; CR00.

AQUA TOFANA (L.) A poison used by Sicilian secret societies, alluded to in The Daily Telegraph article about the murder of Enoch Drebber. At the end of the 1600's a woman called Tofana admitted to the murder of six hundred people by the administration of this poison.

Source: STUD, Ch.6.

ARAB, STREET Homeless or slum boy, a child of the street. The Baker Street Irregulars, Holmes' band of street urchins, were referred to as 'street arabs'. The O.E.D. has the original as 'Arab of the City' or 'City Arab', and quotes (1848) Guthrie, Plea for the Ragged School: 'The Arab of the City.' A speech made in Parliament by Lord Shaftsbury 16 June 1848 refers to 'City Arabs.. .are like tribes of lawless freebooters, bound by no obligations, and utterly ignorant or utterly regardless of social duties'.

Source: STUD, Ch.6; CR00

ARCADIA MIXTURE   (Arcadia: a rustic or rural place) A blend of tobacco, popular in Victorian times. Watson smoked it. 'Hum! you still smoke the Arcadia mixture of your bachelor days, then! There's no mistaking that fluffy ash upon your coat.'

Source: CR00.

ARC AND COMPASS BREASTPIN A tie pin bearing this masonic device and worn by Jabez Wilson. The symbol is an open pair of compasses pointed down to meet an upturned are and represents the unity of Masons and the unity of mankind.

Source: REDH.

ATAVISM (L. atavus, a great-great-great-grandfather: ancestor) The appearance of ancestral, but not parental characteristics; a reversion to an ancestral type. Holmes discussed the subject with Watson and showed an interest in the subject in HOUN and FINA.

Source: GREE; HOUN, Ch.1.

BANG (Hind. bhag: Pers. bang: Sans. bhanga) Or 'bhang': Indian hemp, marijuana. In the city of Agra, the rebels were 'drunk with opium and with bang' - Jonathan Small, SIGN.

Source: SIGN.

BARITSU-WRESTLING   Bartitsu, a system of self-defence named after E.W. Barton-Wright who introduced the system into England in 1899.

Holmes claims to have been familiar with it in

Baritsu- an anachronism. Correct spelling: bartitsu. The word should have been 'ju-jitsu, a form of self-defence using arms, legs and a considerable amount of balance and pre-emptive movement; all reasons why Holmes survived Reichenbach, but Moriarty did not.

1891 – an anachronism. He was probably referring to jujitsu, a method of fighting involving techniques of hitting, kicking, immobilizing holds, etc. which arose from the feudal warrior clans in 17th century Japan. It was his knowledge of Bartitsu (misspelt by Watson) which enabled Holmes to defeat Professor Moriarty.

Source: EMPT.

BARNEY (sl.) An argument, a quarrel. Also a prize-fight (its original meaning). From the late 1850's, the word refers to Barney, a noisy Irishman, and was, according to Partridge, common usage in the late 19th century. (It can be found much earlier in 'Sessions', July 1877.) Holmes' client, Mr James Dodd, refers to having 'a bit of a barney' with Colonel Emsworth on his visit to Tuxbury Old Park.

Source: BLAN.

BARYTA (Gr. barys, heavy) Barium monoxide. Holmes claimed to have been analysing a sample of bisulphate of baryta, a substance which doesnot exist. More probably he was experimenting with baryta paper, a paper coated on one side with an emulsion of barium sulphate and gelatine. This substance is used for photographic printing paper.

Source: IDEN.

B DIVISION A section of the Metropolitan Police Force responsible for sections of Chelsea, Victoria, Knightsbridge and Westminster. Inspector Bradstreet of B Division gave evidence against John Horner after the theft of the blue carbuncle.

Source: BLUE.

BELLADONNA (Atropa belladonna) Otherwise deadly nightshade. The plant's leaves and roots are used to produce atropine, but also assist in the manufacture of cosmetics; hence Holmes use of the substance in DYIN. Belladonna is so-called because Italian women discovered that the pupils of their eyes became greatly expanded if a drop of the juice of this herb were applied.

Source: DYIN.

BELL-PULL A bell-handle, common in nineteenth century houses, linked to bell wires communicating with the kitchens and servants' quarters. Irene Adler had one which was situated above a sliding recess containing the much coveted photograph of her and the King of Bohemia.

Source: SCAN.

BELL-ROPE A rope attached to a series of wires, which then rang in servants' quarters and the kitchens of a large house. A dummy bell rope provided a clue for Holmes in SPEC and a bell-rope was supposed to have been used to tie up Lady Brackenstall (ABBE).

Source: SPEC; ABBE.

BILLET (sl.) 1. Job. Duncan Ross used the term while referring to Jabez Wilson's new task. Partridge notes the word as c.1880: e.g. 'get a billet' - 'get a soft job in prison'. See also Source: REDH; STOC; MUSG and also crib. 2. A small log of wood used as fuel. The cellar at Musgrave was strewn with 'billets'.

Sources: as above.

BILLYCOCK A bowler hat said to be from the name of 'William Coke', nephew of Thomas William Coke, the Earl of Leicester (1752-1842)1. It was Henry Baker's billycock which formed the basis for an analysis in BLUE.

Source: BLUE.

BIRD'S-EYE A manufactured English pipe tobacco, in which the ribs of the leaves are cut along with the fibre - thus giving the spotted appearance, suggesting the name.

Source: SIGN.

BISULPHATE OF BARYTA Barium hydrogen sulphate, an obscure chemical compound. Holmes had been asked to identify this compound at the conclusion of the Mary Sutherland affair (IDEN). See also *baryta*.

Source: IDEN.

BLACKTHORN A dark-coloured thorn bearing sloes: a stick made from its stem, extremely hard and robust. Often used as a means of attack or prevention from footpads.

Source: ABBE.

BLUDGEON A short stick, weighted at one end. (See also life preserver) The word's origin is unknown and does not occur before the 18th century. In early 18th century usage it is spelt as 'Bailey, Bludgeon', and defined as an 'oaken stick or club'. Holmes was once attacked by a 'rough with a bludgeon'.

Sources: GREE; FINA.

BODKIN (Of unknown origin. The O.E.D. has the original form as 'boydekin') A long pin, originally used for piercing holes in cloth and later used by women for fastening their hair (O.E.D.). Holmes pricked his finger with a bodkin whilst demonstrating a blood test.

Source: STUD, Ch.1.

BOODLE (Amer. sl.) Money; property. Holmes demanded his 'boodle' from the spy, Von Bork.

Source: LAST.

BOXER CARTRIDGES Centre-fire cartridges named after their inventor, Edward Mourner Boxer (1822-98). Holmes used a supply of 'a hundred Boxer cartridges' to help adorn a wall of the Baker Street sitting-room with 'a patriotic V.R. done in bullet-pocks'.

Source: MUSG.

BRAIN FEVER A loose, popular term which includes congestion of the brain and its membranes, delirium tremens and inflammation of the brain substance itself. Percy Phelps was presumed to have suffered from the condition. However, it is more likely he suffered a nervous breakdown.

Source: NAVA.

BREECH-BLOCK A metal cover which closes the breech of a gun once the cartridges have been loaded. Colonel Moran 'snapped' the breech-block on his powerful air rifle before firing.

Source: EMPT.

BRIER PIPE A pipe made from the root of a bush called the White Heath, (Erica arborea), from Southern Europe.(Also briar) Holmes smoked an 'old brier pipe'. The O.E.D. has brier, briar and brere as variants, but notes that briar is much later. Cf. Introd. England, 1859; 'brier-wooder: smoker of brier pipe'. The reference to Holmes' use of the briar pipe first occurs in SIGN. Afterwards, reference is ONLY made to him smoking his 'pipe' save for TWIS where it is mentioned as a 'brier.'

Source: TWIS. SIGN.

BULL'S-EYE A lantern with a hemispherical lens. The boss of glass was formed from a sheet of blown glass (O.E.D., 1832). 'Lend me your bull's-eye, sergeant', Holmes, SIGN.

Source: SIGN, Ch.7.

CABLE An American term meaning a telegram. The OED quotes Schele De Vere, Americanisms 1872 and The Times, 14 Apr. 1882, 5/3. (See cable form and telegram).
Source: SOLI.
CABLE FORM A form on which a telegram message is written. Holmes used one to contact Hilton Cubitt.
Source: DANC.
CABLEGRAM See 'cable form'.
Source: DANC.
CANNULA (L.) A small surgical tube designed to drain fluids from the body or to help a patient's breathing. Trevor Bennett discovered Professor Presbury's secret whilst searching for a cannula. The O.E.D. has it as a diminutive of canna, a reed or pipe, and quotes Foster (1876), Phys. ii, iv, p.378: 'When a weter is divided.. .and a cannula inserted.'
Source: CREE.
CARBOLIC or RECTIFIED SPIRITS
1. Carbolic acid (a disinfectant).
2. Purified alcohol spirit. Both substances were used to preserve medical specimens. Holmes refers to these substances when discussing the severed ears in CARD.
Source: CARD.
CARBOLIZED BANDAGES Bandages impregnated with carbolic acid, a strong antiseptic. Watson applied these to Victor Hatherley's wound (ENGR), a method which today would be frowned upon because of their effect upon the surface of the skin.
Source: ENGR.
CARBONARI (It.: literally, charcoal burners) Members of a secret political association formed in the Kingdom of Naples in the early 19th Century, whose aim was to introduce a republican government. Alluded to in The Daily Telegraph article about the murder of Enoch Drebber.
Source: STUD, Ch.6.
CARBUNCLES (L. *carbunculus,* dim. of carbo, a coal) Red precious stones (garnets) cut into a boss shape. The Agra treasure comprised carbuncles, among other stones. The blue carbuncle was unique because of its colour.

Source: SIGN, Ch.12; BLUE.

CARD-CASE A small case, usually of leather, in which visiting cards were stored. A card-case was found among the effects of Miss Hatty Doran. The Army And Navy Catalogue for 1901 has a variety of folding card-cases on offer and they were clearly a useful asset to the Victorian gentleman or lady.

Source: NOBL; SECO; BLAN; MAZA; LION.

CARDSHARPER (Fr. carte, sharper, a cheat: Sl.) A cheat at cards. Moriarty stood at the head of a criminal chain which ended with 'the minor criminal such as the cardsharper'.

Source: VALL.

CAROTID (Gr. karotides, pl. - karos, sleep, the ancients supposing that deep sleep was caused by the compression of the artery(ies)). One of the two large arteries which carries blood to the head and brain. Young Willoughby Smith's carotid artery had been severed.

Source: GOLD; CREE.

CAST PADRE (0.N. kasta, to throw) An unfrocked clergyman. Carruthers referred to the priest in SOLI by this term. The O.E.D. has no less than 83 variants of the word 'cast'. Its basic meaning is 'that which is thrown off or out'.

Source: SOLI.

CATALEPSY (Gr.katalepsis, seizure) A state of more or less complete insensibility, with bodily rigidity. The presumed Russian patient who came to see Percy Trevelyan was supposed to be suffering from this condition. Catalepsy is a rare condition but was a popular subject among nineteenth century fiction-writers, particularly, Poe..

Source: RESI.

CATARACT   (L. cataracta: Gr. kataraktes, portcullis) An opaque condition of the lens of the eye, unaccompanied by inflammation. Ronald Adair's mother suffered from this condition. Cf. Bourde, Brev. Health (1547), lxvi, 28b: 'A Catharact, the which doth let a man to se perfytly.'

Source: EMPT.

CATARACT KNIFE (L. cataracta: Gr. kataraktes, portcullis) A small, delicate knife which is common in the removal of the lens of the eye in cataract surgery. A knife of this type was found among the personal effects of John Straker.

Source: SILV.

CAVENDISH See long-cut Cavendish.

CHLOROFORM (Gr. *chloros*, pale green) A limpid, mobile, colourless, volatile liquid (CHCL3) with a characteristic odour and sweetish taste, used to induce insensibility. Lady Carfax was a victim of chloroform, as was Mrs Maberley.

Source: 3GAB; LADY; LAST.

CHOKEY Gaol. (Victorian sl. Originally Anglo-Indian; from the Hindi hauki, shed, adopted in England c.1850. From 1880 the word meant 'imprisonment') Jonathan Small spoke of being 'stowed in chokey'. 'The Queen's Chokey was a prison diet of bread and water (1884).

Source: SIGN, Ch.12

CHUBB'S KEY A key to a Chubb lock (invented by Charles Chubb, b. 1845). Mrs Marker the servant at Professor Coram's residence, refers to the buro having a 'Chubb's key'.

Source: GOLD

CIPHER (O.Fr. cyfre: Ar. cifr: zero, empty).

A secret form of writing. Holmes made it his business to know several forms of cipher and claimed to have authored a 'trifling monograph upon the subject, in which (he) analyse(d) one hundred and sixty separate ciphers'. The source for these codes is Poe. See his collected American edition, Harpers, 1869, volume 7.

Source: DANC; VALL, Ch.l.

CIPHER TELEGRAM A telegram in cipher. (See telegram and cipher) The cipher telegram was used by the Foreign office in SECO.

Source: SECO.

CLUB FOOT (O.N. and Sw. clubba; and O.E. fot). A deformed foot; a congenital condition apparent at birth. Ricoletti had a club foot but Watson has left no details of this case.

Source: MUSG.

COAL-TAR DERIVATIVES By-products of coal-tar, including ammonia, creosote, benzine, etc. obtained from the distillation of coal-tar. These were first identified in the mid nineteenth century. Holmes conducted research into their properties whilst at Montpellier.

Source: EMPT.

COCAINE (Sp. Quechua: coca) An alkaloid obtained from the leaves of the coca plant, a Peruvian shrub (erythroxylon coca) of a family akin to flax. Cocaine is a powerful narcotic and stimulant which in Holmes' day was a relative newcomer to the West. (Sigmund Freud pioneered its use as an anaesethetic, although he later had misgivings about it.) Holmes was for many years a user of the drug with which he injected himself subcutaneously in a 7% solution. Source: FIVE; SCAN; SIGN; TWIS; YELL.

COINER (L. cuneus, a wedge). Coining (or the manufacture of forged coins) was a large industry among the criminal fraternity of Victorian England. Colonel Lysander Stark was guilty of the offence of coining. Cf. Dickens, Nicholas Nickleby, Ch.X.: 'The longest-headed, queerest-tempered old coiner of gold and silver ever was.'

Source: ENGR; SHOS.

COLLEEN The Gaelic has 'cailin' (girl, a diminutive of caile, a country woman). 'Well, it's the colleen inside of (these girls) that must settle the question, for its outside the jurisdiction of a body-master, and the Lord be praised for that.' (McGinty)

Source: VALL, Pt.2, Ch.2.

COMISSIONAIRE (L.L. commissarus) A uniformed messenger or light porter, common in Victorian times. The corps of commissionaires was an association of pensioned soldiers started in London in 1859 who were organised to act as porters and messengers. It was a commissionaire who brought a letter to Holmes in STUD and Peterson the commissionaire whose wife cooked the goose (BLUE).

Source: STUD, Ch.2; BLUE; NAVA; MAZA.

COMMONPLACE BOOK A note or memorandum book (from commonplace, v.t., to make notes of; to put into a commonplace book) Holmes possessed a number of commonplace books which needed an index. In addition he maintained a number of scrapbooks and an index of biographies. He also appears to have filed the agony columns (q.v.) of the daily newspapers. The terms 'index', 'index of biographies' and 'commonplace book' often seem to be interchangeable.

Sources: BRUC; 3STU; FIVE; MUSG; REDC; ENGR; HOUN; SUSS; VEIL; IDEN; SCAN; PRIO; EMPT; MISS; SPEC; CREE.

COMPOUND OF THE BUSY BEE AND EXCELSIOR Holmes described Watson's remark 'we can but try' as a compound of the Busy Bee and Excelsior - i.e., a mixture of industriousness and a desire to achieve a higher standard. (Excelsior, higher still, after Longfellow: L. excellere- ex, out, up; celsus, high)

Source: CREE

CONDYLE (Gr. kondylos, knuckle) The protuberance at one end of a bone which forms a joint with another. Watson refers to the 'upper condyle of a human femur' - an impossibility since the femur has a condyle only at the lower (knee) end.

Source: SHOS.

CONSUMPTION (L. consumere, to destroy)Tuberculosis. Godfrey Staunton's wife died of this disease, as did Victor Trevor's sister. The O.E.D. has the word from 1398 onwards. Cf. Florence Nightingale's Nursing (1861), p. 26: 'That consumption is induced by the foul air of houses...is certain.'

Source: MISS; GLOR.

COOEE (Native word; otherwise 'kooee!') An Australian signal-call, given to attract attention by the aboriginals and adopted by white settlers. The recognition of this cry provided a major clue in 'The Boscombe Valley Mystery'.

Source: BOSC.

COOLIE (Probably from Koli, a tribe of W. India; or Tamil, kuli; hire) An Indian or Chinese labourer who has emigrated under contract to a foreign land; also a derogative, racist term for a hired native labourer in India. (In S. African usage, an offensive, racist term for an Indian.) Holmes told Watson he was suffering from a Sumatran coolie disease (DYIN). Abel White employed Jonathan Small as a supervisor of his plantation coolies (SIGN).

Source: DYIN; SIGN.

COP To arrest, to capture. Sam Merton described his arrest by Holmes as a 'fair cop'.
Source: MAZA.

COPTIC PATRIARCHS (Gr. Aigyptios, Egyptian) The Coptics were a sect of Christians, supposed to have been descended from the ancient Egyptians, although there is little historical evidence for this assumption.. Professor Coram (GOLD) had conducted research into documents from the coptic monasteries of Egypt and Syria and maintained that his conclusions 'cut deep at the very foundations of revealed religion'. Holmes also dealt with the case of the two Coptic Patriarchs although the full details of this were never revealed.
Source: GOLD; RETI.

CORN-CHANDLER (Fr. L.L. chadelarius - orig. a candle-maker.) A dealer in corn and other grain. Cf. Stubbes, Anatomy of Melancholy, 1583.
Reuben Hayes, proprietor of The Fighting Cock Inn was sacked 'on the word of a lying corn-chandler'.
Source: PRIO .

COSTER (Orig. costard, perhaps from L. costa, a rib) A costermonger or street trader who sells fruit and vegetables from a barrow. In REDH: 'Pope's court looked like a coster's orange barrow.' Cf. Mayhew, London Labour, 1. 26/1: 'The costers never steal from one another.'
Source: REDH.

COVE (S1.) A man, a companion; fellow rogue. Partridge has this originating c.1560 and says that it is probably cognate with the Romany: cova, cova; 'that man'. Sam Merton, the prize-fighter, used the term.
Source: MAZA.

COVERT FOR PUTTING UP A BIRD (Fr. couvrir). A covert is a bush used for cover by birds (such as pheasants). Holmes uses this sporting term to refer to his use of the agony columns (q.v.).
Source: 3GAR.

CRACKSMAN (S1., O.E. cracian, to crack). A burglar, especially a cracker of safes. Beddington (STOC) was a 'famous forger and cracksman' as was John Clay (REDH). Partridge has the originate as housebreaker (c.1810). The word is current in Lytton, Barham and Dickens.

Source: STOC.

CRANIOLOGY (L.L. cranium, Gr. kranion, skull). The study of skulls. Dr Mortimer was interested in this subject.

Source: HOUN, Ch.10.

CREAM-LAID PAPER (O.Fr. cresme, creme) Paper of a cream colour or white, with a laid water-mark and expensive to produce and buy. The note to Aloysius Garcia was written on cream-laid paper (WIST). J. Davenport wrote to Mycroft Holmes on royal cream paper, (GREE) measuring 24" x 19" (q.v.).

Source: WIST; GREE

CRIB   (Sl. O.E. crib: Ger. krippe) A job. Jabez Wilson referred to 'a nice little crib all ready for me to step into' (REDH)(See also billet and berth).

Athelney Jones referred to Jonathan Clay's capacity to 'crack a crib'(also in REDH), here referring to a burglary. Partridge has crib as 'to break open, burgle' from c.1720.Cf. Dickens, Oliver Twist: 'There's one part we can crack, safe and softly.'

Source: REDH; STOC

CRIPES! (Sl. Euphemism for Christ (By) Christ!) Kitty Winter uses the term. Partridge describes it as low, late c .19th-20th century.

Source: ILLU.

CROAKER   (Amer., sl.) Pessimist; or a dying person; or a corpse. Partridge maintains that it is possibly cognate with the dialect   word, croke, dross, core of fruit. 'Brother Morris', said (McGinty), 'you were always a croaker. So long as the members of the Lodge stand together there is no power in this United States that can touch them.'

Source: VALL, Pt.2, Ch. 3.

DARBIES See derbies.

Source: CARD

DARK LANTERN First mentioned as early as 1650, this is a lantern possessing a sliding panel which enables it to provide partial illumination. Holmes often carried one (e.g. during the all-night vigil in REDH). Made of tin or brass, they were fuelled by signal or railroad oil. Designed and used at first solely in Britain they eventually found their way to the USA. The fluted chimney of the lantern enables the smoke to escape while the bull's eye lens concentrates the light.

Source: REDH; STUD; SIGN; GREE; WIST; EMPT; REDO; SHOS; SPEC; MILV; SIXN; BRUC; CHAS.

DEAL-TOPPED (M.L.G. dele: cf. O.E. thel, thille). An old word for pine wood of a standard size. Holmes possessed an 'acid-stained deal-topped' table for his chemical experiments. One would have thought oak to be more suitable.

Source: EMPT; VALL, Pt.2, Ch.7

DEBONNAIRE (Fr.) Genial, relaxed. Holmes is described as 'debonair' at one point in VALL.

Source: VALL, Ch.6.

DECANTER (Fr. decanter: L. de, from cantnus, beak of a vessel) . An ornamental, stoppered bottle used for holding wine or spirits. Lord Brackenstall threw a decanter at his maid, Teresa Wright.

Source: ABBE.

DE JURE INTER GENTES' On International Law'. The title of a book which Holmes picked up at a London street stall, published at Liege in the lowlands in the year 1642, and printed by Philippe de Croy.

Source: STUD, Ch.5.

DIGGINGS (Coll: orig. U.S.) Lodgings or quarters (O.E.D., 1838). The term is used by Stamford (STUD): 'My friend here wants to take diggings...'

Source: STUD, Ch.1; STOC.

DIME NOVEL

(Amer. sl.: Fr. orig, disme: from L. decima (pars), a tenth part). A cheap novel. Originally the word meant a tenth part and was a tithe paid to the Church or to a temporal ruler. 'When I reached this place (Vermissa Valley) I learnt that I was wrong and that it wasn't a dime novel after all' - McMurdo, at the climax of VALL.

Source: VALL, Pt.2, Ch.7.

DINTED (M.E. - O.N. dynta, dent - O.E.D.) Struck or knocked. The use of the word is rare, Holmes observed (SIGN, Ch.l) that Watson's brother's watch was 'dinted in two places'. Partridge has the word as c.1910 (?) and describes its use as a 'facetious colloquialism'.

Source: SIGN, Ch.1

DIO MIO! (It.) 'My God!'

Source: REDC

DISPATCH-BOX A box for carrying valuable papers used by cabinet Ministers and army officers on campaign. Trelawney Hope referred to his 'dispatch-box'. Webster (1864) has: 'Dispatch box; a box for papers and other conveniences of a gentleman when travelling'. Source: SECO; THOR.

DISJECTA MEMBRA (L.) Scattered parts. Alteration of Horace's disjecta membra potae: 'limbs of a dismembered poet'.
Source: BLUE

DISTRICT MESSENGER An employee of the District Messenger Service Company which used an express delivery service throughout London and the suburbs. The rates charged were twice as expensive as those of the General Post Office. Holmes used the services of a district messenger to communicate with Baron Gruner. He also visited the district messenger offices in HOUN.
Source: ILLU; HOUN, Ch.4.

DOCTORS' COMMONS A legal body whose premises stood between Knightrider Street and Queen Victoria Street, London. One department on these premises dealt with wills but in 1874 this Registry was moved to Somerset House. Holmes visited Doctors' Commons to examine the terms of Mrs Stoner's will.
Source: SPEC.

DO DOWN (sl.) To cheat; to get the better of. Sam Merton said of Holmes that he would 'do him down a thick 'un'. See thick 'un.
Source: MAZA.

DOG-CART (So named because of the small box designed to accommodate a dog situated at the rear of the cart.) A two-wheeled trap with seats situated back-to-back. The back seat was made so as to accommodate a box for carrying a dog. (See trap) Holmes and Watson travelled in a dogcart to The Cedars, Lee.
Source: TWIS; GLOR; MUSG; SOLI; HOUN, Ch.10; VALL, Ch 1.

DOG-GRATE A detachable fire-grate which stands in a fireplace on supports known as dogs.
Source: WIST.

DOLICHOCEPHALIC (Gr. dolichos, long) Long headed. Holmes had a 'dolichocephalic' skull, according to Dr Mortimer.
Source: HOUN, Ch.1

DOSS-HOUSE (sl. Perhaps from doss, a dial. English name for a hassock; or perhaps dorse - from dorsal, pertaining to the back) A very cheap lodging-house.

Source: ILLU.

DE NOVO (L.) Anew. '...had we approached the case de novo and had no cut-and-dried story to warp my mind, would I not have then found something more definite to go upon?' (Holmes).

Source: ABBE.

DERBIES (sl.) Handcuffs. '...hold out while I fix the derbies' -Athelney Jones to John Clay, REDH. (See also bracelets and darbies.) The O.E.D. has the word as handcuffs from c.1660 onwards. Cf. Marryat in Japhet: "We may as well put on the darbies", continued he, producing a pair of handcuffs'. The word originates from a rigid form of usurer's bond called 'Father Dierby's'.

Source: REDH.

DRAGHOUNDS Hounds trained to pursue an artificial scent instead of that of a wild animal. Pompey was the 'pride of the local drag hounds'. Cf. The Times, 4 February 8/2 (1884): '… heading the Household Brigade Drag Hounds...'

Source: MISS.

DRAGS Drag nets; an apparatus of nets drawn over the bottom of lakes, rivers, etc. for dredging. Reginald Musgrave used drags to discover the whereabouts of Brunton, his butler. (The O.E.D. mentions Doyle's use of the word.)

Source: MUSG.

DRAW A COVER (Originally to draw a covert. Hunting term) To send the hounds into a cover to frighten out a fox. Holmes said he would 'draw the larger cover' of the Adelaide-Southampton line (ABBE) and once resembled a foxhound 'drawing a cover' as he rushed about the vicarage at Tredannick Wollas.

Sources: ABBE and DEVI.

DROPSY A disease characterised by an accumulation of watery fluid in the cavities of the patient's body. Lord Norberton's sister died of this disease. The O.E.D. has the word as early as c.1290, regarding it as an aphetic form of the M.E. 'ydropsy'. (Otherwise hydropsy).

Source: SHOS.

DUMB-BELLS A pair of short bars of wood or iron weighted at each end and held in the hands for exercise. A missing dumbbell formed a clue in VALL. Dumbbells were formerly an apparatus like that for swinging a church-bell but without the bell itself, thus making no noise (O.E.D.). Cf. Wesley, Works, 1784, XI, 520: 'If you cannot ride or walk abroad, use, within, a dumb bell or wooden horse'.

Source: VALL, Ch. 4.

DYSPNOEA (Gr. dyspnoia: des - ill; pnoea - breathing) Difficulty in breathing, caused by a weak heart. Sir Charles Baskerville suffered from this condition. Cf. The Lancet 27 Sept, 1890, 663/2: 'Obesity develops... so that the least exertion will produce dyspnoea'.

Source: HOUN, Ch.2.

EARFLAPPED TRAVELLING CAP A cap (usually comprised of woollen segments) designed to cover the ears. The flaps could be tied under the chin. Sherlock Holmes wore one in SILV. It is commonly assumed Holmes wore a deerstalker, (1881 O.E.D.) but several ear-flapped caps possessed, for instance, just one peak and had not the low crown exhibited by the deerstalker.

Source: SILV.

ELEPHANT GUN A large-bore shotgun employed in the hunting of elephants. Godfrey Emsworth was hit by a bullet from an elephant gun.

Source: BLAN.

ELEY'S NO.2 A Webley's No.2; a small pocket pistol which took Eley .320 cartridges. Holmes suggested Watson take his 'Eley's No.2' with him to Stoke Moran.

Source: SPEC.

EPITHELIAL SCALES (Mod.L.: Gr. - upon; thele - nipple). Scales of the outer tissue of the skin, often pertaining to the mucous membranes of animals. In this case, flakes of dandruff. Holmes examined these through a low power microscope at the beginning of SHOS. Cf. Mivart's Elementary Anatomy (1872) p.237.

Source: SHOS.

ERYSIPELAS (Of doubtful etymology. Commonly regarded as EPVOI-S. An inflammatory disease, the face, reddening) generally of marked by a bright redness of the skin and often named 'St Anthony's Fire'. Holmes was rumoured to have suffered this condition after his attack by Baron Gruner's thugs.

Source: ILLU.

ETHER (Injected) (L. aether: Gr. aither, the heavens). An anaesthetic given to Lady Frances Carfax to help her condition. Now frowned on by the medical profession in cases such as this.

Source: LADY.

EXPANDED REVOLVER BULLET Otherwise known as a 'dum-dum' bullet, (older references don't use the hyphen), so named because it was first made at Dum Dum, near Calcutta. The soft-nosed bullet mushrooms out when it makes impact, thus causing extensive wounding. Ronald Adair fell victim to a dumdum bullet fired from Colonel Sebastien Moran's air-gun.

Source: EMPT.

EXTRAVASATED (L. extra - outside; vas - vessel) Split, disseminated. An examination of McPherson's body revealed a number of dots showing 'extravasated blood'. Cf. MacCormac, Antiseptic Surgery, (1880) p.103: 'Blood is extravasated into the tissues'.

Source: LION.

FELONY (O.Fr: L.L. fello-onis, a traitor), A crime (including burglary and murder) more serious than a misdemeanour but less serious than treason. The distinction between a felony and a misdemeanour no longer exists. Holmes used the term in referring to James Ryder.

Source: BLUE; 3GAB; BRUC.

FENCE (sl. Aphetic, from defence). A receiver of stolen property. Shinwell Johnson uses the term.

Source: ILLU.

FIRM (THE) Holmes' reference to his own consulting practice.
Source: CREE.

FLY PAPER Brown paper, impregnated with arsenic and used as a method by which to kill flies (popular in Victorian times and also sometimes used as a method of murder). The message which struck Victor Trevor's father dead made reference to supplies of fly paper.

Source: GLOR.

FORMOSA CORRUPTION (BLACK) An invented disease, referred to by Holmes in DYIN. Formosa is an island off the south-east coast of China.
Source: DYIN.

FOWLING-PIECE Shotgun (so named because these guns were used to shoot wild fowl). The murder weapon in VALL was a fowling-piece. Cf, G. Bird, Nat. Phil, p130 (1839): '...the well-known double report of a fowling-piece, fired at a distance'.
Source: VALL, Ch.7.

FULLER'S EARTH (As early as 1523, O.Fr. fuler and O.E. fullere, fuller). A sandy clay used for industrial and medical purposes. The earthy, hydrous aluminium silicate, of which it is composed, is ideal for the absorption of grease. Colonel Lysander Stark claimed it to be mining fullers earth at Eyford.
Source: ENGR.

GARROTTER (From garotte, a Spanish method of putting criminals to death.) A criminal who strangles his victims with a piece of knotted cord prior to robbing them. This was a popular method in Victorian London. Parker who watched Holmes' apartments in Baker Street, was a garrotter. Cf. Law Times (1885), 14 Mar, 348/1: "Lord Bramwell...sentenced many a garrotter to his death'. Source: EMPT.

GILA (In full, gila, monster) The only known poisonous lizard named after the Gila River in Arizona, U.S.A., where it is found. Holmes had an entry about this reptile in his index volume.
Source: SUSS.

GRAPPLING-HOOK (Cf. O.Fr. *grappil* -grape, a hook) An instrument consisting of a hook fixed to the end of a long pole, designed for the retrieval of objects (e.g. the revolver with which Mrs Neil Gibson shot herself).
Source: THOR.

GUAIACUM TEST, THE OLD An old and 'unreliable' (Holmes' word) blood test which used to be carried out by criminologists, involving resin from the guaiacum tree. A stain would turn blue if blood were present. The Guaiacum tree is native to the West Indies and South America.
Source: STUD, Ch.l.

HAIR-TRIGGER   (From 1830 onwards).

A secondary trigger which releases the main trigger by slight pressure. Holmes possessed a revolver with a hair trigger. Cf. T. Hook, G. Gurney 2, 192: 'My pistol, which had the hair-trigger set, went off'. Also cf. the official catalogue of The Great Exhibition, p 353: 'Double rifle, with single hair-trigger'.

Source: MUSG.

HALF-PENNY A coin worth half a penny (a penny being a coin, originally silver, later copper, bronze from 1860 and later worth 1/12 of a shilling, or 1/240 of a pound). The halfpenny no longer exists as British currency. Neville St. Clair's coat was stuffed with half- pennies when it was discovered in the River Thames.

Source: TWIS.

HANSOM CAB Named after its inventor, Joseph Aloysius Hansom (1802-82). These were the popular two-wheeled cabs which dominated London's transport in the '80's and '90's. There was room inside for two passengers and the driver's seat was exposed. Holmes and Watson were inveterate users of the hansom and frequently travelled to scenes of crime in a hansom cab.

Sources: REDH; EMPT; NAVA; DANC; CHAS; ILLU; CREE; VEIL; DYIN; LADY;

HOUN, Ch.4.

HEAVY-GAME SHOT   A hunter of big game - tigers, elephants, etc. Colonel Moran was one.

Source: EMPT.

HEELED (Amer. sl.) Armed. Abe Slaney, the Chicago gangster, used the term.

Source: DANC.

HONEYDEW TOBACCO (As early as 1857 - O.E.D.) Tobacco sweetened with molasses or sugar syrup. The box which contained the human ears was a 'half-pound box of honeydew tobacco'. Cf. The Daily News, 12 Mar. 1894, 6/2: 'I took up a paper containing 2oz of sun flaked honeydew'.

Source: CARD

HOOKAH   (Urdu-Arab hukkah, casket, vase, cup, O.E.D.) Λ pipe, of Eastern origin, having a long tube which draws the smoke through a vase containing scented rosewater. The cool smoke which results from this method is especially popular among opium and cannabis users. Thaddeus Sholto possessed a 'huge hookah'.

Source: SIGN, (Ch. 4).

HOOLIGAN A street rough; a young violent person, said to be the name of a leader of a gang, possibly Hooley's gang, a family resident in the mid 1890's in Islington (W. Ware). The alternative theory is that the word derives from the Houlihans, an Irish family resident in the Borough (London). Is there a link though with the Hindi Hoolee, hoili - that great festival held at the vernal equinox.

Source: REDC.

HORSE FAKER A person who conceals the identity of a horse by dyeing its coat and mane. Holmes suspected Silas Brown of being one. Partridge has: horse dealer - low (1887). Cf. Baumann: horse- capper.

Source: SILV.

HOTTENTOT (A Dutch imitative word approximating to the S.W. Africa khoi-khoin - men of men). One of a dwindling, nomadic, pastoral, pale-brown-skinned race of S.W. Africa resembling the Bushmen and the Bantu: also, a barbarian or a coloured person (derogatory). The Hottentots were all but exterminated by the Boer settlers. Dr Mortimer and Sir Charles Baskerville spent 'many a charming evening' discussing the comparative anatomy of the Hottentot and the Bushman, a discussion which one commentator has suggested might have centred upon their pronounced buttocks, a condition classified as steatopygia. (modified L. from STEARIN (fat) and Gk. puge, rump) The excessive development of fat on the buttocks of the Hottentot and Bushman drew considerable comment from Victorian ethnographers, who considered their easy means of sexual intercourse to be abnormal, frequent and vigorous. (HOUN).

HYDROCARBONS (Coined by Cavendish (1766) from Gr. hydor, water). A compound of hydrogen and carbon with nothing else, occurring chiefly in oil, natural gas and coal. The analysis of carbon compounds from the mid 1860's onwards led to a number of commercial applications at the turn of the century. Holmes succeeded in 'dissolving' a hydrocarbon (SIGN) and later continued research into coal-tar derivatives at Montpellier.

Source: SIGN

HYPODERMIC SYRINGE (Gr. hypo - under; dermis - skin). A syringe equipped with a fine hollow needle. Holmes possessed one.

Source: CREE; SIGN, Ch.l.

ICHNEUMON (Gr. ichneumon, lit. tracker). Any animal of the mongoose genus (Herpestes) of the civet family, esp. the Egyptian species that destroys crocodiles' eggs. Henry Wood used the term when referring to his pet mongoose.

Source: CROO

ICTHYOSIS (Gr. ichthys, fish). Sometimes called 'fish-skin disease'. A condition in which the sufferer's skin takes on a whitened, sealy aspect. Similar to leprosy but without the long term effects. Godfrey Emsworth suffered from the disease.

Source: BLAN

IDEE FIXE (Fr.). A fixed idea; a monomania. See monomania.

Source: SIXN.

IODOFORM (Gr. ioeides, violet-coloured, eidos, form).   A compound of iodine, used as an antiseptic and analogous to chloroform, Watson smelled of iodoform when he walked into Holmes' rooms.

Source: SCAN

HOUN, Ch.6

JACK-IN-OFFICE (from c.1660 - O.E.D.; Coll. till 19th Century; possibly from Jackin, dim. of John). A self-important, or imperious, official. Jonathan Small refers to his being the butt of every petty 'jack-in-office'.
Dr Grimesby Roylott accused Holmes of being a 'jack-in-office' (SPEC). Cf. 'Jack in the pulpit': a pretender.

Source: SIGN, Ch.12; SPEC

JACK-KNIFE (Of U.S. origin: Cf. jackleg-knife). A large clasp knife. Holmes kept his unanswered correspondence transfixed to the wooden mantlepiece of his Baker Street sitting room by means of this. Cf. Smyth's Word Book (1867): 'Jack Knife - a horn handled clasp-knife with a lanyard, worn by seamen'.

Source: MUSG.

JAY (O.Fr., jay. Coll. until 1889. Ware dates this as 1880. American Sl.).
A fool, a simpleton. Abe Slaney, the Chicago gangster, used the term. Cf.

Punch, Feb. 22, 1890:   'She must be a fair as a mater'. 'J' is probably an abbreviation of juggins, a U.S. term meaning a fool.

Source: DANC.

JEMMY (Partridge has this as 1811. By 1870 the term was colloquial. (A common variant is jimmy) A crowbar used by burglars.

Sources: NAVA; CHAS; SHOS; 3GAR; BRUC.

JEW'S HARP (O.Fr. Jueu; L. Judaeus). A musical instrument consisting of a flexible metal prong set in a pear-shaped metal frame. Sound is produced by pressing the frame against the teeth and twanging the metal prong at one end. The shape of the mouth determines the pitch. Parker, a garrotter (q.v.), who watched Holmes' apartments in Baker Street, was 'a remarkable performer upon the Jew's harp'.

Source: EMPT.

LAG (sl. From c.1823) To arrest, e.g. 'He can lag us over this stone'. (Sam Merton, MAZA). Originally the word meant to transport, or send to penal servitude.

Source: MAZA

LAGGED (sl.) Sent to prison. From 'lag' a person doing time. Origin unknown (O.E.D.). 'It's cursed hard that I should be lagged over this young Sholto...' - Jonathan Small, SIGN.

Source: SIGN, Ch.11.

LAUDANUM (Coined by Paracelsus: perhaps laudanum, transferred to a different drug) An alcoholic preparation of opium in liquid form, commonly administered as a pain reliever in Victorian times. S.T.Coleridge and De Quincey became addicted to it, among others.   Isa Whitney 'drenched his tobacco' with laudanum having been inspired by De Quincey's 'Confessions of An English Opium Eater'.

Source: TWIS

LEADER The leading editorial article of a newspaper which gives a distinct opinion on social and political issues. Holmes expressed the opinion that the typeface of a Times leader was extremely distinctive (HOUN). The leaders of several London newspapers carried columns on 'the Brixton Mystery' (STUD).

Source: STUD, HOUN.

LE MAUVAIS GOUT MENE AU CRIME. 'Bad taste leads to crime' A phrase used by Stendhal and quoted by Thaddeus Sholto.

Source: SIGN, Ch.4.

LENS (L. lens, lentil, from the similarity in form) Magnifying glass. Holmes preferred the word 'lens', probably because of its more scientific connotation. The word has a scientific usage: see E. Halley (1693): Phil. Trans.

Source: RESI; GOLD; THOR; SHOS; LION; BRUC; DEVI; VALL, Ch.4.

L'HOMME C'EST RIEN - L'OEUVRE C'EST TOUT (Fr.) 'The man is nothing - the work is everything'. The correct wording is 'L'homme nest rien, l'oeuvre tout'. Holmes from Flanbert's letter quoted as a comment on his involvement in The Red-Headed League.

Source: REDH.

LIFE-PRESERVER   (From c.1837).

A stick or bludgeon, loaded with lead at one end, intended for self-defence. Sir George Burnwell threatened Holmes with one at his house in Streatham. Cf. Arm. Reg 11, 'The prisoner was given in charge to the police a life-preserver having been found upon him'; also from The Illustrated Catalogue of The Great Exhibition, p.1056: 'Life-preservers, of whale-bone and cane, covered with leather'.

Source: NOBL; GREE; BRUC.

LOAFER (Sl. Orig. 1835 - U.S. but anglicized c.1850, although Dickens uses the term in his American Notes) Idler. Loafers were a common feature in the Victorian age, often to be seen collecting on street corners and outside public houses. The wall to Lauriston Gardens was adorned with a 'small knot of loafers'. The word is probably ex. Low German from land/laufer - a landloper.

Source: SCAN.

LONG-CUT CAVENDISH Tobacco (O.E.D. 1839) softened and pressed into solid quadrangular cakes, and often sweetened with syrup or molasses. A pouch containing half an ounce of this tobacco was found among John Straker's personal effects.

Source: SILV.

LUMBER-ROOM (Perhaps from lumber: arch. sl.; to pawn) A room for storing things not in use, usually to be found (but not always) at the top of a house. Holmes used one of the Baker Street lumber- rooms to store back copies of daily newspapers (SIXN), the bureau of Alexander Holder was opened in the lumber-room (BERY) whilst Elias Openshaw kept his American mementoes in his (FIVE).

Source: FIVE; BERY; SIXN

LUNKAH A thin cigar, open at both ends. In SIGN Holmes discussed the possibility of a criminal depositing the ash of a lunkah at the scene of the crime. (The O.E.D. quotes Doyle's use of the word.) Orig. use of Hindi: lanka, a local term for the islands of the Godavery Delta in which the tobacco is grown - see Yule: Hobson- Johnson, 1886.)

Source: SIGN, Ch.1.

LURCHER (Connected with lurk: one who lurches: a glutton). A dog with a distinct cross of greyhound, especially a cross of greyhound and collie. Toby, whom Holmes used to trace the whereabouts of Jonathan Small and his assistant Tonga, was said to be half spaniel and half lurcher.

Source: SIGN.

MACINTOSH (or mackintosh) The name of Charles Mackintosh (1766-1843), attributed to garments made of the waterproof material patented by him. This consisted of layers of cloth cemented to India-rubber. The original mackintosh was a very heavy affair. The unfortunate Straker (SILV) wore one on the night of his death.

Source: SILV

MAGNIFIQUE (Fr.) Magnificent. Holmes' monographs were judged to be 'magnifique' by a representative of the French Surete.

Source: SIGN, Ch.l .

MAGNUM OPUS (L.) Great work. Holmes claimed to be preparing a magnum opus which was to be the last word on the subject of criminal investigation. Its projected title was: 'The Whole Art Of Detection'.

Source: GOLD; LAST.

MARTINI BULLET An Army rifle bullet, devised by Frederic Martini (18321897). Cf. Holmes: 'I would sooner face a Martini bullet myself. Are you game for a six-mile trudge, Watson?' - SIGN.

Source: SIGN, Ch.7.

MENDICANTS (L. mendicare, to beg). Beggars. Holmes investigated the affair of the 'Amateur Mendicants'. Neville St. Clair of Lee also posed as a mendicant. The Order of Mendicant Friars was famous in medieval England.

Source: FIVE; ILLU.

MITRAL VALVE (Gr. mitra, fillet) The valve in the heart which prevents blood in the left ventricle from returning to the left auricle. Thaddeus Sholto had 'grave doubts' as to his 'mitral valve' and asked Watson to examine him.

Source: SIGN, Ch.4.

MONOGRAPH A short work on a single (usually specialised) subject. Holmes claimed to have been 'guilty' of several of these. Originally the word applied to a separate treatise in Natural History, e.g. on a single species, a genus or larger group of plants, animals or minerals. By 1880 the Athenaeum has (12 June, 762): 'Monographs on Poe, Hawthorne, etc.'

Source: THOR; DANC; SIGN; BRUC; HOUN, Ch.2

MONOMANIA An obsession of the mind by one idea or interest (from the French: monomanie). The concept of monomania was popular among certain French alienists at the turn of the century. Victor Hatherley imagined that Colonel Stark's female companion might have been a monomania.

Source: ENGR; CHAS

MORNING POST A newspaper popular among the servant classes of Victorian England which followed the doings of royalty. Founded in 1874, it was later merged into The Daily Telegraph. Watson quotes from this paper in NOBL when referring to the marriage of Lord St. Simon (NOBL).

Source: NOBL.

MOROCCO A thin leather made from goatskin and tanned with sumac, first brought from Morocco. Holmes kept his hypodermic syringe in a 'neat morocco case'. Cf. Chambers Cyclopaedia (1727-52): 'We have Morocco-shiny brought from the Levant, Barbary, Spain, Flanders and France'.

Source: SIGN, Ch.l.

MORPHIA (Gr. Morpheus, God of Dreams). An opiate, designed to relieve pain. An injection of morphia was administered to Baron Gruner, following the vitriol attack made on him by Kitty Winter. Holmes took morphine on one occasion and Ian Murdoch shouted for morphine after his attack by Cyanea Capillata.

Source: ILLU; CREE; SIGN; LION.

MULATTO (Sp. mulato, dim of mulo, mule; Fr. mulatre) The offspring of a Negro and arson of European stock. Cf. Drake's Voyages (1595): 'By means of a Mulatow and an Indian we had, this night, forty bundles of dried beife'.

Source: WIST.

MULTIPLEX KNIVES (L. multiplex-plicare, to fold) A knife with several blades. Holmes claimed that the killer of Lord Brackenstall had one in his possession.

Source: ABBE.

NAPOLEONS Twenty-franc gold pieces issued by Napoleon, 1769-1821, Emperor of the French. They were worth less than sovereigns (q.v.). There were 2,000 Napoleons in Merryweather's bank vaults (REDH).

Source: REDH.

NARK (Si. Romany nak, nose) An informer: a police spy, as copper's nark: one who curries favour, a pick-thank.

Source: ILLU

NERVOUS LESIONS (Fr. lesion - L. laesio-onis-laedere, laesum, to hurt) Damage to the brain or central nervous system caused by disease or injury. Percy Trevelyan had written a monograph on the subject and Watson had read it.

Source: RESI.

NIGHT-GLASS A spy glass with a concentrating lens for use at night. Source: SIGN.

OCCIPITAL BONE (L. occiput: ob - over against; caput - head) The bone that forms the back of the skull. James McCarthy 's father's occipital bone was shattered (BOSC).

Source: BOSC.

OMNE IGNOTUM PRO MAGNIFICO (Latin) 'Anything incomprehensible is mistaken for something marvellous' - a quotation from Tacitus' Agricola, used by Holmes when regretting his explanation of his deductive methods.

Source: REDH.

OPIUM(L. opium: Gr. opion, dim. from opus, sap). The dried narcotic juice of the whole poppy. It was Britain's commercial interests which led to the Chinese Opium Wars and which later led to apowerful lobby among M.P's to ban the import of opium into Britain. Opium was widely used in several medicinal preparations during the 19ᵗʰ Century, including paregoric (q.v.), laudanum (q.v.) and morphine (q.v.). Holmes himself injected himself with the latter (SIGN). The tragedy of opium and morphine addiction among 19thCentury users (including Coleridge and De Quincey) was that they simply did not appreciate its addictive qualities. Dr Alexander Wood, the American who perfected the hypodermic syringe in 1853, lost his own wife when she died from an overdose of morphine. Yetmorphine was widely used as an anesthetic. Watson regarded Holmes as being 'well-up in opium and other poisons (STUD, Ch.1); Isa Whitney became addicted to opium smoking; the sepoy mutineers were drunk with opium (SIGN); Ned Hunter was drugged by opium (SILV)whilstIan Murdoch cried out for it after his attack by Cyanea Capillata. (LION).
Source: LION; WIST; SILV; TWIS; STUD.

OUTRE   (Fr.) Extraordinary, shocking. Holmes claimed that many human motivations led to outre results (REDH).
Source: REDH; SIGN, Ch.9; STOC; HOUN, Ch.15

OUVRIER   (Fr.) Workman. Holmes appeared as an ouvrier in LADY.
Source: LADY.

PAREGORIC (L. paregoricus) Paregoric elixir. A solution of opium, benzoic acid, camphor and oil of anise in alcohol, used as a pain killer. Holmes recommends the use of a paregoric (somewhat unkindly) as a cure for the maid Susan's wheezing. Cf. British Pharmacoepia, Nov. 1888: 'any medicine that assuages pain, an anodyne'.
Source: 3GAB.

PARIETAL BONE (L. parietalis, paries, parietis, a wall) One of two bones situated at the side and back of the skull. James McCarthy's father had the posterior third of the left parietal bone shattered (BOSC). Dr Mortimer (HOUN) asked Holmes if he would have any objection to his running his finger along his (Holmes') parietal fissure.
Source: BOSC; HOUN, Ch.l.

PEA JACKET (Probably from the Du. pijjakker: O.E.D.) A sailor's double breasted overcoat of coarse woollen cloth. Holmes donned a pea-jacket as part of his disguise in SIGN. He also wore a pea-jacket during the all-night vigil in REDH.

Source: SIGN, Ch.9; REDH; VALL, Pt.2, Ch.2.

PENAL SERVITUDE (L. poenalis, poena: Gr. poine, punishment). A type of imprisonment. The minimum allowable sentence was three years which was reducible by a quarter for good behaviour. Penal servitude usually involved hard labour in convict gangs. The term is derived from the original notion which involved the confiscation of the criminal's property and his reduction of status to that of a slave. Holmes suggested that the thief who appropriated the blue carbuncle would get 'seven years' penal servitude.

Source: BLUE; STOC; DANC.

PENANG LAWYER (Licuala acutifolia - Griffith) A walking stick with a large round head, imported from Penang, an island off the west coast of Malaya and made from the stem of a dwarf palm. Fitzroy Simpson, the suspected murderer of John Straker, possessed one which he had weighted with lead. So also did Dr. Mortimer. The term is often misapplied in England to the Malacca cane. It was originally applied with jocular reference to the use of the weapon settling disputes at Penang. It has been suggested that the name is a corruption of the Malay pinang liyaar, wild areca, or Pinang layor, fire dried areca. Cf. P. Cunningham, N.S. Wales (1828), ed. 3.11.64: 'With a Penang Lawyer hugged close under his right arm'. Doyle is quoted in relation to this term in the O.E.D.

Source: SILV; HOUN, Ch.1

PENNY (O.E. penig: cf. Ger. Pfennig: Du. penning) A coin, originally of silver, later, copper; bronze from 1860, formerly worth 1/12th of a shilling.

Source: VALL, Ch.7.

PHIAL (L. phiala: Gr. phiale, a broad shallow bowl) A small tube in which a chemical is stored. Holmes had a supply of these at his rooms in Baker Street.

Source: LION and CREE.

PIN FIRE REVOLVER A revolver fitted with a pin enabling the hammer to strike the powder in the cartridge. A revolver of this type was found in Wisteria Lodge, following the death of Charles Milverton (CHAS).
Source: WIST.

PINNA (L. pinna, a feather, dim. pinnuta) The broad part of the upper, external ear. Holmes uses the term in referring to Sarah Cushing's amputated ear.
Source: CARD

PIPETTE (Fr, dim. of pipe, pipe) A tube for transferring and measuring fluids and gases. Holmes used one at his chemical corner in Baker Street.
Source: STUD, Ch.1; NAVA.

PLASTER ROSE Piece of decorative plaster work shaped in the form of a rose, from which candelabra, etc. hung. The gas pipe that killed Mrs Amberley ended in the plaster rose.
Source: RETI.

PLETHORIC (Gr. plethora, fullness.) Plethora, an excess of red corpuscles in the blood. Athelney Jones' face was described as 'plethoric'.
Source: SIGN, Ch.6

PLUG (App. Du. plug, a bung, a peg. Cf. Sw. plugg) Chewing tobacco; or something worthless. (See plugs and dottles)
Source: CARD

PLUGS AND DOTTLES Pieces of tobacco pressed into a hard section and unburnt, or semi-burnt pieces, retrieved from a half smoked pipe. Holmes was in the habit of collecting these, drying them on his mantlepiece, then re-smoking them the following day: a revolting practice, resulting in a nauseous taste and disgusting stench. (Believe me - I've tried it!). Cf. Swift (1728) and Dickens, Martin Chuzzlewit, XXI: 'Cutting a quid or plug from his, cake of tobacco'.
Source: ENGR

PLUMBER'S SMOKE ROCKET A device fired by a percussion cap used to test for leaks in drains and pipes. Watson threw one into Irene Adler's house to create a diversion.
Source: SCAN.

POCKET LANTERN A lantern of the same design as a dark lantern (q.v.) but compact enough to be concealed about the person. Holmes owned a pocket lantern and made notes by its light whilst on his way to the Lyceum Theatre (SIGN). He also examined footprints outside Wisteria Lodge using a pocket lantern (WIST).

Source: SIGN; WIST.

POLE-AXED Struck down with a pole-axe (a butcher's axe with a hammer- faced back).

Source: MISS; RED.

PRUSSIC ACID Hydrocyanic acid, a colourless, deadly liquid with a distinctive almond smell. So-called because it was first obtained from Prussian blue, ferric ferrocyanide, a colour pigment, discovered in Berlin. Mrs Merrilow had considered taking prussic acid.

Source: VEIL.

PSEUDO-LEPROSY See icthyosis.

QUEER STREET (Sl.) In debt: in trouble. Inspector Lestrade uses the term in SECO (c.1840-1890.) Cf. Dickens: 'You are in the wrong box - planted in Queer Street, as we say in London'.

Source: SECO

QUID (sl. Origin obscure) Pound, e.g.: 'Give up a hundred thousand quid?' Cf. Dickens (1857): '"Take yer two quid to one" adds the speaker, picking out a stout farmer'.

Source: MAZA.

RECHERCHE (Fr.) Far-fetched; particularly rare or exotic. Holmes referred to the affair of the Musgrave Ritual as *recherche.*

Source: MUSG

RECTIFIED SPIRITS (Fr. rectifier: L.L. rectificare, to make). Purified or distilled alcohol. Referring to a severed ear, Holmes observed that a medical mind would have preserved the trophy in 'carbolic' or 'rectified spirits'.

Source: CARD

RED REPUBLICAN (L. respublica, commonwealth) A revolutionary or radical advocate of republicanism, i.e. that form of government which rejects monarchy and in which supreme power is vested in the people and their elected representatives. Morse Hudson commented that his bust of Napoleon may have been destroyed by red republicans.

Source: SIXN.

RIGOR MORTIS (L. rigor-rigere, to be stiff). Stiffening of the body after death, by the muscles. In SIGN Holmes observed that Bartholomew Sholto's muscular contraction was more pronounced than that usually attributable to rigor mortis.

Source: SIGN.

RISUS SARDONICUS (L.) A sardonic grin, caused by tie drawing back of the corners of the mouth by an involuntary spasm of the muscles. The condition is often caused by tetanus. In SIGN, Bartholomew Sholto displayed this feature after his death from some 'curare-like substance'.

Source: SIGN, Ch.6.

ROYAL CREAM PAPER Heavy, ribbed, cream-coloured writing paper measuring 19" by 24". The letter writer, J. Davenport, wrote to Mycroft Holmes on paper of this description.

Source: GREE.

SAFETY LANTERN A miner's lamp, with the flame concealed, and which will therefore not readily cause a fire. The most famous example of a miner's safety lantern is the Davy Lamp, named after the Cornishman, Humphrey Davy, who invented it.

Source: VALL, Pt.2, Ch.1

ST. VITUS' DANCE Otherwise, chorea, a nervous disorder in which the muscles of the face twitch spasmodically or it's sometimes used as a reference to what is now called Parkinson's Disease. Old Mr Farquhar, from whom Watson purchased his practice in Paddington, suffered from this complaint.

Source: EMPT.

SCORBUTIC (L.L. scorbuticus, poss. from M.L.G. schorbuk) Of the nature of, or affected with, scurvy, a disease marked by bleeding and sponginess of the gums, due to a lack of fresh vegetables and consequently of Vitamin C. Watson remarked that Shinwell Johnson, Holmes' contact in the underworld, was scorbutic.

Source: ILLU; STOC.

SCOWRERS (sl. 17th C., 18th C.) A band of wild and boisterous men who roamed the streets, terrorising people. The Molly Maguires were so-named. The word originates from stover, scowre, to decamp or run away. The v.i. is 'to roam noisily about at night, smashing windows, waylaying and beating wayfarers, attacking the watch' (Shadwell, Prior).

Source: VALL, Pt.2

SCREW (Sl. c.1859. Earlier scrue; app. O.Fr. *escrone,* of obscure origin) Payment, as with 'to turn the screw', or to exact payment. Hall Pycroft refers to 'the screw' being 'a pound a week rise'.

Source: STOC.

SHAG (From the O.E. sceacga and Norse skegg-beard). A course, strong, cheap, finely-cut pipe tobacco, popular among Victorian artisans. Holmes smoked shag and in SCAN received 'two fills of shag tobacco' for rubbing down horses.

Source: SCAN; CREE; HOUN, Ch.3.

SHEENY (sl. Orig. unknown. 1824 - O.E.D.: occasionally Sheeny-nie or Sheney. From c.1890 sometimes as an adjective.) A pejorative term for a Jew. Hall Pycroft referred to Arthur Pinner's nose as having 'the touch of Sheeny about (it)'. Cf. Thackeray, 1847: 'Sheeney and Moses are… smoking their pipes before their lazy shutters in Seven Dials'.

Source: STOC .

SHIP'S (O.E. scip: Goth. skip: O.N. skip) A strong, rough-cut Dutch tobacco popular among sailors in the Victorian era. The proper name was Schippers Tabak Special. Patrick Cairns smoked it, as did John Watson.

Source: STUD, Ch.l; BLAC.

SHORT ODDS Odds (in gambling) which are in the better's favour. Short odds would vary from four to one, to evens. Holmes uses the term in referring to the horse "Silver Blaze".

Source: SILV

SHOVE THE QUEER (Amer. sl. orig. Mid. 19th C.) To pass or circulate counterfeit money.

Source: VALL Pt.2, Ch.2.

SINGLE-STICK A heavy wooden stick approximately three feet long with a protected handle at one end. Originally designed for sabre-training, it became, in the late Victorian period, a weapon in its own right. Single-stick combat was a popular sport in Victorian gymnasiums. Holmes professed to being a 'bit of a single-stick expert'.

Source: ILLU; STUD, Ch.2.

SINGULAR (L. singularis, as early as 1684, O.E.D.) Strange: odd. The word is often applied in the Holmes Chronicles.

Source: SIXN; GOLD; HOUN, Ch.2.

SKELETON KEYS Simple keys with their serrated edges or the shaped part of their bits filed down, used to open a range of locks. Holmes possessed a set of these.

Source: CHAS.

SLUGGING (Northern and U.S. Orig. Ger. slugfest, a festival; later a match characterised by heavy blows) Hitting, coshing, e.g. If slugging is no use, then it's up to you' (Sam Merton). Cf. C.C. Robinson, Dialect of Leeds, (1862) p.413: 'Give him a good slugging lad'.

Source: MAZA

SMASHER (sl. Imit; cf. Sw. dial. smaske, to smack) One who passes bad or counterfeit money.

Source: REDH.

SNACKLED (Si. Cf. snabbled or snaffled: to arrest, to capture - etymology dubious. Cf. Du. snavel: Ger. schnabel, beak, mouth) Jefferson Hope said that he was 'neatly snackled' by Holmes. Source: STUD

SNIB (Cf. L.G. snibbe, bleak) To fasten with a snib; i.e. a catch for a window-sash. The window of Bartholomew Sholto's chamber was 'snibbed' on the inside (SIGN).

Source: SIGN

SNORTER (sl.) Literally, anything exceptional, esp. in size or strength. A tricky one. Used by White Mason, VALL.

Source: VALL, Ch.2.

SOVEREIGN (O.Fr. sovrain: lt. sovrans) A gold coin from Henry VII to Charles I worth 22s. 6d. to 10s., from 1817 a pound. Irene Adler gave Holmes a sovereign which he vowed he would wear on his watch chain in memory of her.

Source: SCAN; REDH; GREE; HOUN, Ch.5.

SPECIAL (L. specialis; species) A railway train privately hired and usually for a special event. In Holmes' day specials could be hired from the private railway companies on limited notice. Moriarty hired a special from Charing Cross Station in order to pursue Holmes through Kent.

Source: FINA.

SPINAL MENINGITIS (Gr. meninx-ingos, a membrane) An infectious disease which inflames the membranes of the spinal cord. It was supposed that Bob Ferguson's pet spaniel was suffering from this condition.

Source: SUSS.

SPIRIT LAMP A small lamp used for heating or boiling and powered by methylated spirits. Holmes possessed one which he used for his chemical experiments.

Source: NAV.

SPIT (sl. from the phrase: 'as like him as if he had spit him out of his mouth') Image: exact likeness. Sam Merton described Tavernier's bust of Holmes as 'the living spit of him'.

Source: MAZA.

SPLIT (sl. Du. splitten, related to s li ten: Ger. spleissen) To inform on accomplices. John McMurdo killed Jonas Pinto because he threatened to split, while Ikey Sanders did split on Count Sylvius and Sam Merton. Source: 3GAR.

SPRING LOCK A lock fastened by means of a spring action (similar to a Yale lock).

Source: MAZA; VALL.

STOOL PIGEON (orig. U.S. slang. Anglicized by 1916) A decoy: a police informer. (Shortened form: stoolie) Used by Holmes as part of his Irish American slang (LAST).

STREET ARAB See *Arab, street*.

Source: STUD. Ch.6 CROO

STRYCHNINE (Gr. strychnos, nightshade). A highly poisonous alkaloid ($C_2H_{22}N_2O_2$) obtained from flux vomica seeds. Strychnine stimulates the vaso-nator centre and causes a contraction of the blood vessels and an increase in blood pressure. Death results either from asphyxia or exhaustion of the nerve centre. Enoch J. Drebber (STUD) died of strychnine poisoning (in this author's opinion) as did Bartholomew Sholto (SIGN).

Source: STUD; SIGN

STUDENT LAMP A small, portable lamp on a vertical standard which can be raised or lowered.

Source: CHAS.

SUBCLAVIAN (ARTERY) (Prefix: sub - under; clavicle - collar-bone) A large artery situated at the base of the neck. The jezail bullet which wounded Watson at the fatal battle of Maiwand "grazed" his subclavian artery.

Source: STUD, Ch.1.

SUBCUTANEOUSLY (L. sub - under; cutis - the skin) Under the skin. John Straker nicked a horse's tendons in this manner and Holmes administered cocaine to himself in this way.

Source: SILV; SIGN.

SUPRA-ORBITAL (L. supra - above; orbis - the eye) The area above the eye-sockets. Dr Mortimer observed that Holmes had 'well-marked supra-orbital development'.

Source: HOUN, Ch.1

SWAG (sl. Related to sway: prob. Scand.) Booty, plunder, e.g: 'But he'll let us slip if we only tell him where the swag is'. By 1890 the word implied any unlawful gains, e.g. Dickens, 1838: '"It's all arranged about bringing off the swag is it?" asked the Jew. Sikes nodded'. (Oliver Twist)

Source: MAZA; BOSC

SWAMP ADDER According to Holmes, an Indian swamp adder killed Julia Stoner and Dr Grimesby Roylott. There is, however, no snake known to science as a 'speckled band'. Several vipers could be considered. However, Holmes states that Roylott died 'within ten seconds' of being bitten. In fact there is no snake venom that would kill a man or woman in that time. Both types of Indian viper - the Elapidae and the Viperidae kill by hemotoxic venom which acts on the blood; but Watson does not describe the familiar symptoms of viper poisoning in his account. The identity of the swamp adder' therefore remains something of a mystery.

Source: SPEC.

SUPRA-ORBITAL (L. supra - above; orbis - the eye) The area above the eye-sockets. Dr Mortimer observed that Holmes had 'well-marked supra-orbital development'.

Source: HOUN, Ch.1.

SWAG (sl. Related to sway: prob. Scand.) Booty, plunder, e.g: 'But he'll let us slip if we only tell him where the swag is'. By 1890 the word implied any unlawful gains, e.g. Dickens, 1838: '"It's all arranged about bringing off the swag is it?" asked the Jew. Sikes nodded'. (Oliver Twist).

Source: MAZA; BOSC.

Source: SPEC.

TANNER (sl) A sixpence. Holmes gave each of his Baker Street irregulars 'a tanner' for assisting him.

SOURCE: SIGN.

TELEGRAM The Telegraph system was first developed in the 1830's as a means of communication between railway stations. Morse code enabled the system of telegraphy to spread more widely. A telegram is a message sent by telegraph. Holmes frequently contacted other individuals by means of this method.

Source: DANC; STUD; 3GAB; RETI.

TETANUS (L.: Gr.: Tetanos, tenein, to stretch) A disease due to bacillus, marked by painful tonic spasms of the muscles of the jaw and other parts. Bartholomew Sholto showed symptoms of tetanus (SIGN).

Source: SIGN

TINKER (M.E. tinken, to tink) A mender of pans, kettles, etc., a butcher or bungler. Also (Scot) tinkler: a vagrant or gypsy. Nowadays a term of abuse for Roma people.

Tinkers were legion in the 19th Century.

Source: ILLU; TWIS.

TOFF (Sl. Perhaps from tuft. Originally a gold tassel worn on a nobleman's cap in English universities; hence a person of social consequence) A person of the upper classes: a Swell. John Clayton described his passenger as a 'toff'.

Source: HOUN

'TO PUT HIS HEAD INTO A HALTER' To commit a murder and be hung for it. Holmes uses the term in relation to Jonathan Small.

Source: SIGN, Ch.7

TOR A rocky hilltop. These abound on Dartmoor. The word occurs as an element in topography and is probably cognate with the Gaelic 'torr'-hill. It was on a Dartmoor tor that the convict Selden slipped and fell to his death but more likely was pushed off, Stapleton mistaking him for Sir Henry Baskerville.

Source: HOUN, Ch.6.

TOFF (S1. Perhaps from tuft. Originally a gold tassel worn on a nobleman's cap in English universities; hence a person of social consequence) A person of the upper classes: a Swell. John Clayton described his passenger as a 'toff'.

Source: HOUN

'TO PUT HIS HEAD INTO A HALTER' To commit a murder and be hung for it. Holmes uses the term in relation to Jonathan Small.

Source: SIGN, Ch.7

TRANSPORTATION The removal of offenders beyond seas to a penal colony. Transportation was common in England even for minor offences until it was finally abolished in 1868. Victr Trevor was transported to Australia in 1855 (GLOR).

TRICHINOPOLY CIGAR A cigar made from dark tobacco grown near Tiruchirapali in southern India. Enoch Drebber's killer smoked a Trichinopoly cigar. Holmes was acquainted with the ash of a Trichinopoly (RESI): 'To the trained eye there is much difference between the black ash of a Trichinopoly and the white fluff of bird's eye as there is between a cabbage and a potato" (SIGN).

Source: STUD, Ch.3; SIGN, CH.1; RESI.

UN SOT TROUVE TOUJOURS UN PLUS SOT QUI L'ADMIRE 'A fool can always find a greater fool to admire him'. A quote from Nicolas Boileau's poem, 'L'Art Betique, 1674, cited by Holmes as a jibe against Scotland Yard.

Source: STUD, Ch.6.

VALETUDINARIAN (L. valetudinarius - valetuds, state of health - valere, to be strong)   A person who suffers from ill-health, a weakly, sick person, one who worries about his or her health.   Thaddeus   Sholto claimed he was compelled to be a valetudinarian.

Source: SIGN.

VESTA   (Orig. the Roman goddess of the hearth and household). A wax-stemmed match, a short match with a wooden stem. Vestas were produced in vast quantities in England in the 19th Century, mainly by sweated labour; they were often sold on street corners in the poorer parts of London by vagrants, etc.

VOODOO (W. African vodu, a spirit) Superstitions, beliefs and practices of African origin found also among the Negroes of the West Indies and southern United States, formerly including serpent-worship, human sacrifice and cannibalism, but now confined to sorcery. The mulatto (q.v.) cook practised voodoo, whilst Holmes consulted Eckermann's 'Voodooism'.

Source: WIST.

WALKING-STICK A stick used as a support for walking. These were popular among all classes in Victorian England, partly for defensive reasons and partly for reasons of fashion. Holmes owned both an alpenstock (q.v.) and a walking cane (SPEC; THOR) and Watson also carried a cane (SHOS). Dr Mortimer (HOUN) and Fitzroy Simpson (SILV) carried Penang lawyers (q.v.)

Source: GLOR; NOUN; SHOS; SPEC; THOR; FINA; EMPT; SILV; CARD; ABBE; SCAN; NORW; BLUE; STUD; REDH; GOLD.

WAND (O.N. vondr, a shoot of a tree) A thick stick set in the ground as a marker. Stapleton used these to help guide his way to the hound's lair.

Source: HOUN, Ch.14.

WARD A part of a lock of a special configuration to prevent its being turned by any except a particular key, or the part of the key to corresponding configuration. Holmes noted scratches on the ward on the inside of Blessington's strong box.

Source: RESI.

WARM (S1. O.E. wearm; cf. Ger. warm) Amorous: indelicate. According to the landlord of the country pub Holmes visited, Williamson's weekend visitors were 'a warm lot'.

Source: SOLI.

WET (Sl. From c.1592). A drinking bout. Watson refers (in SIGN) to 'rough-looking men...emerging, rubbing their sleeves across their beards after their morning wet'. At this period many London pubs opened in the early morning for the benefit of market and warehouse workers. Cf. Thackeray: 'a wet night' and Hindley, Cheap Jack, 1876, (268): 'I shall be back again shortly when we will wet the deal'.

Source: SIGN, Ch.7

WELTED (Origin obscure). Flogged. 'I welted the little devil [Tonga] with the slack end of the rope...' Jonathan Small, SIGN.

Source: SIGN.

LIST OF TEXT ILLUSTRATIONS IN 'THE CRIMINAL WORLD OF SHERLOCK HOLMES, VOLUME ONE'

Page 195
Conan Doyle, the student of criminology
Page 196
Holmes grapples with Moriarty but wins, using bartitsu.
Page 201
A ruminative Holmes in 3GAB.
Page 249

Illustrations between pages 79 and 100
Cesare Lombroso, criminologist.
Page 78
A distinctly American looking William Gillette.
Page 79
Alphonse Bertillon, distinguished inventor of the Bertillonage system.
Page 80
A letter from ''Jack the Ripper.'
Page 81
Jim Browner, murderer in 'The Carboard Box' is restrained by the wearing of the 'derbies.'
Page 82
Two contrasting drawings: in the first, a mob attack police in Whitechapel, 1888. In the second, the Cold Bath Lane riot, 1836. But in both, police use truncheons.
Pages 83-84
The River Thames, a convenient escape route for The Ripper. From Griffiths.
Page 85
Another prostitute killed in Whitechapel. Punch Magazine.
Page 86
A young Conan Doyle on an early literary trip to America.
Page 87
Set of housebreaking tools, attributed to Charlie Peace.
Page 88
'Sign of Four' murder scene with daring Tonga escaping.
Page 89
Inspector Abberline, senior Met detective who led the hunt for The

Ripper.
Page 90
George Lusk, Chairman of the Whitechapel Vigilance Committee, who, like Susan Cushing in CARD, received a severed human part (a kidney) in The Criminal World of Sherlock Holmes, Volume One the post.
Page 91
Charles Peace, master burglar and Holmes' 'good friend.'
Page 92
The hideous boat murder of the lovers in CARD, portrayed by Sidney Paget.
Page 93
Holmes with Toby the dog, pursue a creosote trail in SIGN.
Page 94
Sherlock Holmes conducts a chemical investigation in Baker Street in NAVA. Drawing by Paget.
Page 95
Victorian opium den, from 'The Strand.'
Page 96
Jack Prendergast, preparing for transportation in GLOR. Paget drawing.
Page 97
Francis Galton, the man who revolutionised fngerprint identification techniques, but not adopted by the British until 1903.
Page 98
The ubiquitous Hugh Boone, businessman and beggar in TWIS. Paget drawing.
Page 99
The Cedars, Lee, where Boone lived and where Doyle almost certainly played cricket, unknowingly, with a Ripper suspect.
Page 100

THE CRIMINAL WORLD OF SHERLOCK HOLMES INDEX

Holmes, Sherlock:

"Look out of this window Watson, See how figures loom up, or are dimly seen, and then bend once more into the cloud-bank...'

Strand , 'The Adventure of The Three Garridebs,' drawing by Howard Elcock.

Lightning Source UK Ltd.
Milton Keynes UK
UKHW030733031221
394904UK00005B/109